RESEARCH IN
THE HISTORY OF
ECONOMIC THOUGHT
AND METHODOLOGY

Archival Supplement 3 • *1992*

RESEARCH IN THE HISTORY OF ECONOMIC THOUGHT AND METHODOLOGY

Editor: WARREN J. SAMUELS
Department of Economics
Michigan State University

ARCHIVAL SUPPLEMENT 3 • 1992

 JAI PRESS INC.

Greenwich, Connecticut

London, England

CONTENTS

EDWIN R. A. SELIGMAN'S LECTURES ON THE HISTORY OF ECONOMICS: INTRODUCTION

Warren J. Samuels

THE LECTURER AND THE NOTES

There have been several magisterial and duly celebrated lecture courses given in the United States in the history of economic thought. Those given by Wesley C. Mitchell at Columbia, Jacob Viner at Chicago and Princeton, and Joseph A. Schumpeter at Harvard are perhaps among the best known. Another was that given by Edwin R. A. Seligman at Columbia University, the source of the notes from his lectures published in this supplementary volume.

Edwin Robert Anderson Seligman (1861-1939) was, with Frank William Taussig, Richard T. Ely, John Bates Clark, Irving Fisher, Francis A. Walker, and others, one of the leading economists in the United States during the period when the field became a professional academic discipline. Seligman was one of the founders of the American Economic Association and its president from 1902-1903. From 1885 to 1931 he was on the faculty of Columbia University, from which he had received four degrees, including a Ph.D. and LL.B. He also was a founder of the American Association of University Professors, the

Research in the History of Economic Thought and Methodology,
Archival Supplement 3, pages 1-6.
Copyright © 1992 by JAI Press Inc.
All rights of reproduction in any form reserved.
ISBN: 1-55938-503-0

first chair of its Committee on Academic Freedom and Academic Tenure, and its president from 1919-1920. Seligman was editor-in-chief of the *Encyclopedia of the Social Sciences* (New York: Macmillan, 1930). His principal area of specialization was public finance, in which he concentrated on progressive taxation based on ability to pay, the incidence of taxation, and the effects of taxation on production. Seligman was also interested in larger conceptual and historical questions, one result of which was his *The Economic Interpretation of History* (New York: Columbia University Press) published in 1902. He was also noted for his impressive professional library, including a wide collection in the history of economic thought, which he left to Columbia University.

The notes presented in this supplementary volume were taken by P. S. Allen in Economics 203-204, during 1927-1928. The notes and course outline are published with permission from the collection of the Joseph Dorfman Papers, Rare Book and Manuscript Library, Butler Library, Columbia University, which owns the original documents. Another copy of the notes, with syllabus and, unfortunately, only the second half of the reading list, resides in the Bass Collection in Business History at the University of Oklahoma, which has also given permission for publication. That copy was item 396 in Catalogue 29 (19-89) of Robert H. Rubin Books.

The title page of the notes indicates that they were taken stenographically by Allen and the prefatory note indicates that they were taken in shorthand and that "they have not been revised or corrected by Prof. Seligman." Either the stenography or the transcription, or both, were awkward: Both the syntax of the text and the clarity of the discussion often leave much to be desired. The original documents are in mimeographed form in which portions of the text along the right margin of many pages faded; in some cases the typing at the right end of the line was not complete, perhaps due to either fading or failure to use the margin release; and the last few pages are in a partially tattered condition with portions of the text torn off. Although numerous typographical errors have been corrected, and certain name spellings have been corrected and/or modernized, no effort has been made to polish the text, although a few corrections and other amendments have been inserted by the editor in square brackets. The several ellipses are in the original; nothing has been deleted. Also no effort has been made to provide accurate quotations from sources which Seligman is reported to have either directly quoted or paraphrased and which the notes sometimes place within quotation marks; and little effort has been made to correct apparent errors of fact and none of putative errors, or disagreements, of interpretation.

I am indebted to various members of the staff of the Rare Book and Manuscript Library, especially Kenneth A. Lohf and Bernard R. Crystal, to Donald Dewey, Lawrence Shute, and Robert H. Rubin, and to Daniel A. Wren and Sydona Baroff (Librarian of the Bass Collection) of the University of Oklahoma.

SUBSTANTIVE CONTENT OF THE NOTES, IN RETROSPECT

The view of the history of economic thought reflected in the course syllabus and the notes was one scholar's perspective, or definition of disciplinary past and then-current reality as of 1927-1928. Several matters may be noted.

    1. The syllabus presents a more elaborate array of figures than does the lectures, at least as reflected in the notes, which must be presumed to be complete and accurate. Either Seligman could not cover them all (and certainly he could not in any depth) or he wanted to present the student with a wider array, as a matter of perspective, than he covered in class.

    2. A considerable sense of the diversity of past and, especially, then-contemporary economic thought is given in both the syllabus and the notes. There is very little filtration effectuated through concentration on the principal doctrinal themes of mainstream schools as we understand them today. Examination of the material covered in Book VI, in both syllabus and notes, readily reveals the wide diversity of thought during the period of the classical school. This is also true in Book IV with regard to the Physiocratic period and in various sections of Book VII regarding the panorama of economics, even and perhaps especially within the mainstream, during the early decades of the twentieth century. Some of the sections in Book VII—those dealing with the historical and socialist schools—revert to the middle of the nineteenth century and others—dealing with what we would now call the early period of the neoclassical movement, including the Austrian school. But both the sections dealing with the late nineteenth century and those dealing with the early twentieth century display the wide-ranging varieties of economics, including varieties within what now appears as the neoclassical mainstream and within American economic thought in particular (*vide* sections 55-59).

    An historian's perceptions of the past may be a function of his or her perceptions of the present, from which the past is viewed, but the perceptions of the present may themselves be a function of perceptions of the past, from which the present is viewed. Whatever the case with Seligman, he clearly felt that there had been and still continued to be considerable diversity within economics.

    3. Considerable attention is called, though not given in detail, to a variety of Italian writers and thereby to the types of economics practiced by them.

    4. Not surprisingly, Seligman often singled out developments in his specialty, public finance. However, he also singles out work in such other specialized fields as money and banking, agricultural economics, and labor.

    5. Interestingly, there is no mention or even hint of a so-called revolution of 1870, implying that the perception of such a revolution (which may or may not have occurred and may or may not, if it did in fact occur, have involved

a paradigm shift in the sense of Thomas Kuhn) is a product of subsequent developments, for example, the rise to predominance of neoclassical microeconomics, the greater formalization of economic theory coupled with the use of utility-maximization models of analysis, and efforts to differentiate and legitimize both of the foregoing developments. Moreover, the paradigmatic importance for the twentieth-century microeconomics of Marshall and Walras, which now seems so great, is conspicuous by its absence (this is true also, of course, of the textbooks of the period and for some time thereafter).

6. Seligman apparently had no serious, or at least no conclusive, reservations or hesitation about discussing, however generally, relatively recent work. This position is in contrast with that of his successor in the field, Joseph Dorfman (who apparently made use of Seligman's materials in his own work), who strongly felt that historians of economic thought did not have sufficient perspective to satisfactorily summarize and interpret recent work even several decades past. Still, there is relatively little specific work from the 1920s presented in the notes; for example, neither the early work on risk and profit by Frank H. Knight nor the developments in monetary theory (which presaged later developments in what became, with John Maynard Keynes, macroeconomics), though mention is made of the Cambridge School in the syllabus (Section 55(d)). Notwithstanding these omissions, however, the works of Schumpeter (who had been by 1927 already professionally active for over two decades), Jacob Viner, and Paul Douglas are cited.

7. Their are several interesting and, from the perspective of the present-day view of the history of the discipline, striking treatments. Several examples will suffice: (1) Section 59(d) lumps together such diverse figures as Ely, Hadley, Taussig, Hollander, and Veblen, as "the eclectics." (2) There is no treatment of Adam Smith's *Theory of Moral Sentiments*. (3) Several writers are identified for their mathematical methods but not for the specific substantive content of their analyses, notably, Cournot, Dupuit, Gossen, Walras, Pareto, Barone, Fisher, and Moore. (4) At several points the notes record Seligman as saying "grooves" rather than "curves" in regard to developments in the conduct of economic theory. Whether this is what Seligman actually said or a mistranscription from shorthand is not known.

8. Some comparison of earlier ideas with then-current theories is occasionally made, but such presentism does not unequivocally extend, at least in the notes, to an assertion of the superiority of the then-present way of looking at things.

9. Seligman does not explicitly deny the role of relatively autonomous theoretical speculation but he does emphasize that ideas, on the one hand, and institutions and circumstances, on the other, mutually interact, to such a degree that he would now be considered a relativist or externalist with regard to the origins of economic thought. He stresses the system- and institution-dependence of economic ideas and theories; economic law, or its explication,

changes with the times, with the implication that they should be held tentatively and used carefully. In the concluding paragraph of the notes, Seligman is reported to have lectured that "The only thing I hope that I have in the first place impressed upon you [is] that all theories are relative and they are bound up with particular institutions of the time and place." This echoes the statements reported in the introductory paragraphs: "In dealing with laws of economics every man is more or less influenced by conditions in the environment that he lives in and above all by the institutions of his own age and his own country which differs from place to place and from time to time. Therefore all ideas of social life are dependent upon this change in time. We can say therefore that there is a mutual interaction, action and reaction between the institutions and the ideas. The subtle influence of one's thinking by the spirit of the times necessarily influences the laws, principles and interpretations in the science. It is impossible to divert our gaze from the institutions in studying the historical growth of doctrines. There is an interaction of the facts upon the ideas of a time, and vice versa." The notes go on to say, therefore, that "What we have today in the last century is explanations of our age, capitalism, factory system, etc." Moreover, "While institutions have modified theory, there are on the other hand examples of theories modifying the institutions;... This is a question of interaction and a question of mutual influence." The clear implication is that while economics has an object of study, that object of study is itself in part dependent upon economic thought and the uses made of that thought in the social (re)construction of economic reality.

It may also be pointed out that the notes indicated that Seligman occasionally relates economic thought and its development to social structure and to changes in social structure. Equally important and more frequently, Seligman is shown to have given considerable attention to writers and writings that do not unequivocally accept as given the status quo economic and property system. On the one hand, the question of the relation of economic thought to the status quo is raised; and on the other, the ideas of both defenders and critics of the status quo are reported (and of course for Seligman the status quo is something which itself changes, in part because of changes in economic ideas). For Seligman, it seems clear, the history of economics very much included what today would be called heterodox and radical ideas, or what to him were exercises in criticism. While it is also true, apparently, that Seligman did not identify institutional economics as a body of critical thought, this may well be because he did not identify a hard and fast neoclassical mainstream: diversity reigned, not a rigid orthodoxy calling forth a derivative reaction—again, as evidenced, for example, in Section 59. Seligman, in that section, identifies "the orthodox school" with Sumner, Perry, Newcomb, Wells, and Dunbar; it may well be that he was missing the contemporary formation of the successor version of orthodoxy—but that is another matter. For whatever reason, Seligman apparently did not think in terms of a very few grandiose contemporary schools. For him there was one group of designated "eclectic" (the syllabus at Section 59(d) actually reads "electic," but, there being no such word, one must treat it as "eclectic"), but economics as a whole seemed so diverse as to be fundamentally eclectic.

10.   Seligman also made clear what he considers the reasons for studying the history of economic thought. The notes of the Introductory section have him arguing that the study of the history of economics, first, makes one "more critical towards ideas. It puts you in a critical attitude to evaluate literature which appears upon a subject in economics." Second, it conveys a "more tolerant and more sane attitude towards economic laws and principles," this because of the relativity or mutability over time of institutions, laws, and even explanations themselves. "[T]he laws which have been advanced at one time and place are not the same as those which have been advanced at others." Moreover, "The study of this development [of ideas, etc.] prevents one from being too conservative or too radical. It has been said," the notes read, "that with every progress in science the history of that science becomes shorter. This is one attitude. We must distinguish, however, between the old and the antiquated.... between the erroneous and the antiquated." And, again adverting to the concluding paragraph of the notes, if the first intended lesson concerned the relativity of economic doctrines, because of the relativity of institutions, the second was "that all scientists in social problems must recognize the importance of the predecessors, and it is a very foolish idea to think that we can afford to neglect the past thinkers because in some respects their analysis does not carry our views.... If we can learn from this course sympathy and appreciation and tolerance then my object will be complete."

11.   So far as the notes indicate what Seligman had to say about the substance of the economic thought of various writers and schools, much of the presentation (again assuming that the notes accurately present the lectures, which there is no reason to doubt) is fairly conventional. Individual readers will be differentially alert or sensitive to variations between Seligman's apparently chosen configuration of topics and those of the reader and/or contemporary textbooks, such as those by Mark Blaug, Ray Canterbery, Robert Ekelund and Robert Hebert, E. K. Hunt, and Henry Spiegel, among others, as well as the works of Joseph Schumpeter and Jacob Viner, and also the vast body of more specialized interpretive literature.

OUTLINE OF LECTURES

COLUMBIA UNIVERSITY
IN THE CITY OF NEW YORK

ECONOMICS 203-204

OUTLINE OF LECTURES
on the
HISTORY OF ECONOMICS

By Edwin R. A. Seligman

Sec. 1.   Introduction:
Explanation of course, utility and methods.

Sec. 2.   Literature.

PART I.   PRIOR TO ADAM SMITH

BOOK I.   ANTIQUITY

Sec. 3.   Oriental Nations:
Egypt, India, Persia, The Jews, China.

Sec. 4.   Greece:
Economic conditions. Xenophon, Plato, Aristotle.

Research in the History of Economic Thought and Methodology,
Archival Supplement 3, pages 7-14.
Copyright © 1992 by JAI Press Inc.
All rights of reproduction in any form reserved.
ISBN: 1-55938-503-0

Sec. 5.   Rome:
Economic conditions. Early writers: Cicero, Seneca, Pliny;
Scriptore de re rustica: Cato, Varro, Columella,
Economic Doctrines of the Roman Code.

BOOK II.   THE MIDDLE AGES

Sec. 6.   The Church Fathers:
Economic influence of Christianity.
Attitude to private property.

Sec. 7.   The Literature of the Thirteenth to the Sixteen Century:
The Theologians. The Canonists. The Legists.

Sec. 8.   Thomas Aquinas:
His predecessors and successors.

Sec. 9.   Mediaeval Doctrines of Value:
Economics and ethics.

Sec. 10.   Mediaeval Doctrine of Usury:
The four stages in the theory. Influence on legislation and trade.
Application of the theory to the doctrines of Interesse,
Census, Societas and Montes. Development to the views of
Calvin, Dumoulin and Saumaise.

Sec. 11.   Mediaeval Doctrine of Reasonable Price:
The transition from the Roman doctrine. Connection with the
theory of usury. Intrinsic value and natural price.

Sec. 12.   Mediaeval Doctrine of Money:
Theories of Buridan and Oresme. Alteration of money. Bimetallism.

Sec. 13.   Connection between Mediaeval Doctrines and Economic
Institutions:
Theory of the guild system. Markets and fairs. Mediaeval banking.
Trade and speculation. Custom versus competition.

BOOK III.   THE MERCANTILISTS

Sec. 14.   The Transition in the Sixteenth Century:
Growth of capital. Development of the national economy. The
Humanists, the Reformers, the Radicals, the Utopians.

Sec. 15.   The Leading Principles:
     a. The balance of power.
     b. Money and wealth.
     c. The balance of trade.
     d. Population and labor.

Sec. 16.   The Revolution of Prices in the Sixteenth Century:
Bodin and Hales.

Sec. 17.   The English Controversy on Monopolies:
Milles, Wheeler, Digges, the report of 1604.

Sec. 18.   Balance of Bargain vs. Balance of Trade:
Malynes and Misselden.

Sec. 19.   The Founders:
     a. England: Mun.
     b. Italy: Serra.
     c. France: Laffemas and Montchretien.

Sec. 20.   Development in England:
     a. Petty, Child, North, Barbon, Locke.
     b. Davenant and Gee.
     c. Writers on socialism, money, trade and agriculture.

Sec. 21.   Development in France:
     a. Agrarian protection: Boisguillebert.
     b. Fiscal reform: Vauban and Saint Pierre.
     c. Money and credit: John Law and Freres Paris.
     d. General theory: Melon, Dutot, Forbonnais.

Sec. 22.   Development in Italy, Germany and Spain:
     a. Italy: Galiani and Genovesi.
     b. Germany: The Cameralists.
     c. Spain: Ulloa and Ustaritz.

Sec. 23.   Criticism:
Relation of Mercantilism to agriculture, industry and commerce.
Balance of trade and equilibrium of commerce.

BOOK IV.   THE PHYSIOCRATS

Sec. 24.   The Transition to Physiocracy:
The economic conditions of France.
The later Mercantilists: Gournay.
The economic radicals: d'Argenson.

Sec. 25.   The Founder:
Quesnay.

Sec. 26.   The Cardinal Principles:
a. Laissez faire or absolute liberty.
b. Produit net or agriculture as the sole source of wealth.
c. Impot unique or the single tax.

Sec. 27.   The Followers:
Mirabeau, De la Riviere, Baudeau, Letrosne, Dupont de Nemours.

Sec. 28.   Turgot:
His theories. His practice. The six edicts. Relation of his doctrines
to the economic condition of France.

Sec. 29.   The Opposition:
Voltaire, Mably, Galiani; Condillac.

Sec. 30.   Development in other Countries:
England: Asgill, Cantillon, Spence.
Germany: Charles, Frederick, Mauvillon.
Italy: Bandini, Filangieri, Verri, Ortes.

Sec. 31.   Influence of Physiocracy:
The ethical factor.
Positive views on production.
Opposition to Mercantilism.

PART II.   SINCE ADAM SMITH

BOOK V.   ADAM SMITH AND HIS IMMEDIATE PRECURSORS

Sec. 32.   The Precursors:
The philosophers: Mandeville, Hutcheson.
The economists: Berkeley, Vanderlint, Massi, Hume, Tucker,
Steuart.

BOOK VI. THE CLASSICAL SCHOOL

Sec. 45.   Ricardian School:
a. Individual utilitarianism: Bentham.
b. The orthodox writers: Mill, McCulloch, Whateley, Senior.
c. The independents:
Torrens, Craig, Ravenstone; the writers on value.
Read, Ramsay, Longfield, Scrope.
d. The philanthropists: Chalmers.
e. Currency and banking: Overstone, Norman, Fullarton, Newmarch.
f. The Manchester school: Cobden and Bright.
g. The social standpoint: John Stuart Mill.

Sec. 46.   Opposition to the Orthodox School:
a. The historians and psychologists: Jones, Banfield, Jennings.
b. The socialists: Owen; the Ricardian socialists; the Chartists.
c. The humanitarians: Carlyle.
d. The sentimentalists: Ruskin and Lalor.
e. The Christian socialists: Maurice and Kingsley.
f. The reformers: Oastler, Ashley.

Sec. 47.   Development in France:
a. The founder: J. B. Say.
b. The eclectics: Garnier, Rossi, Chevalier.
c. The reaction: Sismondi, Perquer.
d. The socialists: Fourier, St. Simon, Cabet, Blanc, Proudhon.
e. The optimists: Bastiat.
f. The mathematicians: Cournot, Dupuit.

Sec. 48.   Development in Germany:
a. The eclectics: Jakob, Rau.
b. Expansion of old doctrines: Hermann, Mangoldt.
c. New theories of distribution: von Thunen.
d. The theory of protection: List.
e. The mathematical school: Gossen.

Sec. 49.   Development in America:
a. The statesmen: Franklin, Pelatiah Webster, Hamilton, Gallatin.
b. The text-book writers: McVickar, Cardozo, Cooper, Vethake.
c. The reaction: Raymond, Everett, Phillips, Rae, Tucker.
d. Free trade and protection: M. Carey, Colton, Dew, Gouge, Raguet.
e. Socialism and anarchism: Warren, Skidmore, Simpson, Pickering.
f. The philosopher: H. Carey.

BOOK VII.   RECENT DEVELOPMENTS

Sec. 50.   The Founders of the Historical School:
   a. Hildebrand.
   b. Roscher.
   c. Knies.

Sec. 51.   Scientific Socialism:
   a. Early writers: Marlo, the period 1840-50.
   b. Rodbertus.
   c. Marx.
   d. Lassalle.
   e. The revisionists.

Sec. 52.   Earlier English Writers:
   a. The mathematical school: Jevons.
   b. The rehabilitation of orthodoxy: Cairnes.
   c. Currency and banking: Bagehot and Price.
   d. Theory and practice: Fawcett.

Sec. 53.   Development in Germany:
   a. The extremists: Held.
   b. The Catheder-Socialists: Wagner.
   c. The ethical and historical faction: Schmoller, Bucher, Hasbach.
   d. The labor problem: Brentano, Schulze-Gavernitz, Sombart.
   e. The eclectics: Cohn, Philippovich, Conrad.
   f. The theorists: Dietzel, Schumpeter, Liefmann.
   g. Public Finance: Schaffle, Newmann, Schanz, v. Heckel, Lotz.
   h. The sociologists: Weber, Gottl, Ammon, Schumacher, Diehl.

Sec. 54.   The Austrian Reaction:
   a. The theory of value: Menger and Wieser.
   b. Capital and interest: Bohm-Bawerk.
   c. Transportation and finance: Sax.

Sec. 55.   The English Movement:
   a. The sociologists: Cliffe-Leslie, Ingram, Smart, Tawney.
   b. The historians: Toynbee, Rogers, Ashley, Cunningham, Unwin,
        Scott, Clapham.
   c. The critics: Sidgwick, Nicholson, Cannan.
   d. The theorists: Marshall, Edgeworth, Pigou, Keynes,
        the Cambridge school.
   e. The socialists: the Webbs, Cole.

READINGS

COLUMBIA UNIVERSITY
IN THE CITY OF NEW YORK

ECONOMICS 204

READINGS
IN THE
HISTORY OF ECONOMICS
BY EDWIN R. A. SELIGMAN

Secs.	*Book V*

32. Bonar I, ch. vi; Patten, ch. iv; Clark, pt. III; Boucke, ch. iii; Hollander reprints: Berkeley and Vanderlint.

33. Toynbee, chs. i-viii; Moffit, *passim;* Hammond, pt. ii; Ashton, chs. i, ii; Hamilton, ch. x; Heaton, chs. viii, ix; Marshall, *passim;* Unwin, ch. vii; Furniss, app. i-iii.

34-35. Cannan I, introduction; Haney, ch. x; Ingram, pp. 82-106.

36-37. Cannan II, passages *sub verbo* Smith in index.

38. Bonar I, ch. viii; Bagehot, ch. iii; Ingram, ch. v; Gide, book I, ch. ii.

39. Seligman I; Chicago Lectures, *passim.*

Research in the History of Economic Thought and Methodology,
Archival Supplement 3, pages 15-18.
Copyright © 1992 by JAI Press Inc.
ISBN: 1-55938-503-0

Book VI

40. Cossa, ch. ix; Rudkin, *passim*.

41. Bonar II, books I-III; Gide, ch. iii; Stangeland, chs. v, viii, ix; Patten, ch. v, para. 3; Haney, ch. xi.

42. Bonar II, book IV; Cannan II, passages *sub verbo* Malthus in index; Thompson, chs. i, ii, xi.

43. Whitaker, ch. i; Patten, ch. v, par. 4; Cannan II, passages *sub verbo* Ricardo in index; Stephen I, chs. ii, iii; II, ch. v; Haney, ch. xii.

44. Bagehot, ch. v; Hollander, ch. ii.

45. Stephen I, ch. vi; II, chs. i-iii; III, ch. iii; Patten, ch. v, pars. 5, 6; Boucke, chs. iv, v; Gide, book III, ch. ii; Haney, chs. xv, xviii, and xxii; Bonar I, book III, chs. ii, iii; Price, ch. iii; Whitaker, chs. vi, viii, ix; Raven, chs. ii, iv; Hobson, I, *passim;* Seligman, II, ch. iii.

46. Podmore, *passim;* Cole, *passim;* Seligman, II, ch. ii; Haney, ch. xxiii; Lowenthel, chs. ii to v; Hobson, II, ch. iv; Rosenblatt, chs. vii, viii; Slosson, chs. i, v; Beer, II, chs. i, ix; Hovell, chs. xii, xv, xvii; West, chs. i, ii, vi; Wallas, *passim*.

47. Gide, book II, chs. i-iii; book III, ch. i; Cossa, ch. x; Haney, chs. xiv, xix.

48. Gide, book II, ch. iv, and book IV; Haney, chs. xvii, xxi; Cossa, ch. xi.

49. Haney, ch. xx; Cossa, ch. xiv; Cliffe-Leslie, ch. xiii; Seligman, II, ch. iv; Turner, chs. ii-vi.

Book VII

50. Gide, bk. IV, ch. i; Boucke, ch. vi; Haney, ch. xxvi; Ingram, ch. vi

51. Gide, bk. IV, chs. ii, iii; Haney, ch. xxiii.

52. Boucke, ch. vii; Cossa, ch. ix; Price, chs. vi, vii.

53. Haney, ch. xxvi.

54. Gide, book V, ch. i; Boucke, ch. viii; Haney, ch. xxx; Ingram, ch. vii.

55. Haney, chs. xxv, xxix, xxxii; Price, chs. v, viii; Pigou, *passim;* Homan, chs. iv, v.

56. Haney, ch. xxxii; Gide, bk. IV, ch. iv; Cossa, ch. x; Moon, chs. i, ii, x.

57. Haney, ch. xxxi; Cossa, ch. xv.

58. Cossa, chs. xii, xiii.

59. Haney, ch. xxxiii; Homan, chs. ii, iii, vi; Cossa, ch. xiv.

60. Haney, ch. xxxiv.

References

Ashton, T. S.—Iron and Steel in the Industrial Revolution. 1924.
Bagehot, W.—Economic Studies.
Beer, M.—History of British Socialism. 2 vols. 1919-1920.
Bonar I—Philosophy and Political Economy, 1893.
Bonar II—Malthus and his Work. 1885.
Boucke, O. F.—The Development of Economics. 1921.
Cannan I—Adam Smith's Lectures on Justice, etc. 1896.
Cannan II—History of the Theories of Production and Distribution, 3d ed.
Chicago Lectures on Adam Smith. 1927.
Clark, W. E.—Josiah Tucker, Economist. Colubmia Studies no. 49, 1903.
Cliffe-Leslie—Essays in Political and Moral Philosophy.
Cole, G. D. H.—Robert Owen. 1925.
Cossa, L.—An Introduction to the Study of Political Economy. 1893.
Furniss, E. S.—The Position of the Laborer in a System of Nationalism. 1920.
Gide and Rist—A History of Economic Doctrines. n.d. (1916).
Hamilton, H.—The English Brass and Copper Industries to 1800. 1926.
Hammond, J. L. and B.—The Rise of Modern Industry. 1926.
Haney, L. H.—History of Economic Thought. Rev. ed. 1920.
Heaton, H.—The Yorkshire Woollen and Worsted Industries from the Earliest Times to the Industrial Revolution. 1920.
Hobson I—Hobson, J. A.—Richard Cobden. 1919.

Hobson, J. A.—John Ruskin, Social Reformer. n.d. (1898).
Hobson II—Hobson, J. A.—John Ruskin, Social Reformer. n.d. (1898).
Hollander, J. H.—David Ricardo. 1910.
Homan, P. T.—Contemporary Economic Thought. 1928.
Hovell, M.—The Chartist Movement. 1918.
Ingram, J. K.—A History of Political Economy. New ed. 1915.
Lowenthal, E.—The Ricardian Socialists. Columbia Studies no. 114. 1911.
Marshall, Dorothy—The English Poor in the Eighteenth Century. 1926.
Moffit, L. W.—England on the Eve of the Industrial Revolution. 1925.
Moon, P. T.—The Labor Problem and the Social Catholic Movement in France. 1921.
Patten, S. N.—The Development of English Thought. 1899.
Pigou, A. C. (ed.)—Memorials of Alfred Marshall. 1925.
Podmore, F.—Robert Owen. 2 vols. 1906.
Price, L. L.—A Short History of Political Economy in England. 1891.
Raven, C. E.—Christian Socialism. 1920.
Rosenblatt, F. F.—The Social and Economic Aspects of the Chartist Movement. Columbia Studies no. [1]71, 1917.
Rudkin, O. D.—Thomas Spencer. n.d. (1927).
Scott, W. R.—Francis Hutcheson. 1900.
Seligman I—Introduction to Everyman's edition of Adam Smith.
Seligman II—Essays in Economics. 1925.
Slosson, P. W.—The Decline of the Chartist Movement. Columbia Studies no. 172. 1917.
Stangeland, C. E.—Pre-Malthusian Doctrines of Population. Columbia Studies no. 56, 1904.
Stephen, Leslie—The Utilitarians. 3 vols. 1912.
Thompson, W. S.—Population: A Study in Malthusianism. Columbia Studies no. 153, 1914.
Toynbee, A.—The Industrial Revolution.
Turner, J. R.—The Ricardian Rent Theory in Early American Economics. 1921.
Unwin—Studies in Economic History. The Collected Papers of George Unwin. Ed. by R. H. Tawney, 1927.
Wallas, Graham—Life of Francis Place. 1898.
West, J.—A History of the Chartist Movement. n.d. (1920).
Whitaker, A. C.—History and Criticism of the Labor Theory of Value. Columbia Studies no. 50, 1904.

NOTES FROM EDWIN R.A. SELIGMAN'S LECTURES ON THE HISTORY OF ECONOMICS, 1927-1928

P.S. Allen

COLUMBIA UNIVERSITY
In the City of New York

ECONOMICS 203-204

LECTURES
on the
HISTORY OF ECONOMICS
by
Professor Edwin R. A. Seligman
(1927-1928)

Stenographic Notes Taken
By P. S. Allen

Reader's attention is called to the fact that although these notes have been taken down in shorthand and a reasonable amount of care and attention is given in preparing them, they have not been revised or corrected by Professor Seligman.

P. S. A.

Research in the History of Economic Thought and Methodology,
Archival Supplement 3, pages 19-206.
Copyright © 1992 by JAI Press Inc.
All rights of reproduction in any form reserved.
ISBN: 1-55938-503-0

HISTORY OF ECONOMICS

INTRODUCTION

PART I. PRIOR TO ADAM SMITH

Section 1. Economics

Economics is a science which attempts to explain certain phenomena in business society. Economic science differs very decidedly from exact science. We are dealing here with man and society. In the pure science one can deal with the phenomena the repetition of which can be accurately expected and through repeated experiments one can confidently express opinion. But when we are dealing with social science we are dealing with something which is not unchangeable, with mutable things. Life implies change. A man, a society alters. Exact repetition of phenomena is therefore not to be expected. As human beings live the system lives and the system changes. An individual investigator is necessarily influenced in such a science by his environment. In dealing with laws of economics every man is more or less influenced by condition in the environment that he lives in and above all by the institutions of his own age and his own country which differs from place to place and from time to time. Therefore all ideas of social life are dependent upon this change in time. We can say therefore that there is a mutual interaction, action and reaction between the institutions and the ideas. The subtle influencing of ones thinking by the spirit of the times necessarily influences the laws, principles and interpretations in the science. It is impossible to divert our gaze from the institutions in studying the historical growth of doctrines. There is an interaction of the facts upon the ideas of a time, and vice versa.

Economics of today is an explanation of our modern economic life and its institutions. Economic theory of today in the United States is different from what it was years ago, and it is different in this country today than it is in other places. It is a great mistake to think that economic theory is to be limited to recent and very recent times. It is true indeed that economics as science is a modern science dating generally from Adam Smith. What we have today in the last century is explanations of our age, capitalism, factory system, etc. The attempt to explain economic life takes us back further than the Physiocrat and Adam Smith. The history of economics is the history of the human being and their attempts which have been made from beginning to express economic life; therefore we have to go far way back. (This whole term will be devoted to study before Adam Smith).

While institutions have modified theory, there are on the other hand examples of theories modifying the institutions; the influence of Malthus Rousseau, etc., for example. This is a question of interaction and a question

f mutual influence. When we say we are dealing with the history of economic
theory, the question arises: What do you mean by economic theory? What is
n economic doctrine to be judged apart from? Value is connected to wealth,
ather than to welfare. In tracing the history of economic doctrine we must
e broad in our viewpoint of the subject matter. We must not be so narrow
s to refuse the concept of a social economics, and not so broad as to swallow
p all of sociology.

Section 2.   History of Economics

History of economics is a history of those theories and doctrines which
attempt to explain the real connection between the phenomena affecting the
individuals struggling to make a living. If that is what is meant, the next
question is what is the use of it all? Why should we bother about such a study?
Two reasons may be stated: (1) Makes you more critical towards ideas. It puts
you in a critical attitude to evaluate literature which appears upon a subject
economics. (2) More tolerant and more sane attitude towards economic laws
nd principles. Economic law or its explanation is necessarily something
relative—mutable, with changes in the times. There has been a progressive
evolution in the explanations themselves and the laws which have been
advanced at one time and place are not the same as those which have been
advanced at others.

The study of this development prevents one from being too conservative
or too radical. It has been said that with every progress in science the history
f that science becomes shorter. This is one attitude. We must distinguish,
however, between the old and the antiquated. It is important to see
explanations which held at one time and are no longer applicable today—that
, we should distinguish between the erroneous and the antiquated. We can,
therefore, quote: "History of any science is nothing but science itself in its
independent onward march for the truth."

BOOK I.   ANCIENT ECONOMIC THOUGHT

Section 3.   Oriental Nations

In the ancient literatures like that of the Chinese and Jewish there is to be
found general political and religious literature, primarily, and yet there is
enough to see something which throws light on the economic conditions at
that time. Dealing first, with the earliest oriental nations, Babylon, and we find
that religion and politics scarcely divided themselves. The state-craft and
morality was generally dealt with in the same work. We must not expect to
find any real economical analysis in the modern sense. We have learned a great

deal about economic institutions, agricultural conditions, banking conditions, commercial conditions, bills of exchange, etc. Until a short time ago we didn't have any literature. It was not until the beginning of the twentieth century that the great block was discovered by a French expedition which contained the code of law, Code of Hammurabi, and which was composed according to some writers between 2285 and 2125 or 2100 B.C. Now, it is worth while to dwell on that in order to get a glimpse of economic ideas at that time, which was about 2000 B.C. This is translated into English. It provides for the fixing of all prices and wages by law, fixing the service and price of cattle and how much rent you ought to pay to the owner of the land and how much to the State out of the agricultural produce. It is also interesting to notice facts in regard to ownership of land and cultivation of it. Any one who did not cultivate his land would be fined. Slavery, you will find existed at that time. Laws of inheritance stated that a man would divide equally what he has left to his children. The system of punishments were of a primitive civilization as people were drowned and burned for minor offences.

Again, we have the laws dealing with divorce and settling matrimonial difficulties such as that the wife and children were considered a man's property and he could sell them and pay off his debts. The idea of retaliation was applied all the way through. If a man took one eye out his eye would be taken out. Even a physician, if he operated on a patient and thereby the patient suffered a loss of arm or leg, the physician in turn had to lose his corresponding appendages. However, side by side with all these questions we have passages of the most modern and elaborate description.

With all these provisions of retaliation we find the essential modern view of an attempt to secure justice and equality where attempts are made to prevent cheating and overcharging—what we would call in this country an attempt to fight methods of competition. In a code of laws you simply find statement of injunction and provision and do not find analysis. Why should it be so. More recently another code of laws was discovered—the Assyrian code of laws which was found in the site of Assur. This code dates 1300 B.C., which came five to seven hundred years later than that of the laws of Hammurabi. This was studied by Professor Jastrow, who died a few years ago. It is very interesting to students of social life. Although they came 700 years later, they are of much cruder type than that of Babylon. In the Chaldean civilization we find certain agricultural treatises. These books were of clay tablets. We find the echoes of these early kinds of agriculture in the Arabian literature. However we know very little about it.

The same thing can be said regarding Egyptians. We have in this case a great many books but they do not amount to anything. Chief book refers to later period when Egypt was a province of Rome. They deal with fiscal and revenue methods. Breasted's history of Egypt, gives reference to economics and political condition in the fifth and sixth millenniums changing from early feudal state

o absolute state. All these we are familiar with. About the only civilizations
where we really find some interesting is India and China, and they have not
been worked up very much until very recently.

So far as India is concerned, it must be remembered that their state-craft
and morality, politics and religion were inseparable; therefore we must look
or a good many economic and social ideas in the religious and ethical
publications. Shilotri has published a number of volumes on Indo-Aryan
thought and culture bringing out thought between politics, economics and
religion, how economic and social ideas were influenced with some of those
religious doctrines, etc. We also find them in the code of Babylon, the code
of Hammurabi. The code of Muir was supposed to be the oldest in existence.
India of that day, for that matter India of this day, has been influenced by
the system of castes, and in its origin the castes numbered four in India. (1)
Brahmins, who were supposed to have grown out from the head of Brahma,
(2) Chatrias, supposed to come from his arm, (3) Vistas, supposed to have come
from the middle and (4) Sudras, supposed to have sprung from his feet. If
you consider that this system has lasted in India for thousands of years you
can realize what its consequences upon people and economic institutions has
been.

A few of the economic phases of the caste system are: First, it led to the
theory of private property, more absolute than anything we find in the
Occident. You can easily realize why that is so. It goes hand in hand with
another consequence of the system of caste; namely, the principle of
feudalism—of moral and ethical feudalism. Under this caste every man must
follow the occupation of his father and grand father because he is born in that
caste. There is no possible way of a man getting out of his caste. A goldsmith,
for instance, remains a goldsmith all his life—just the very opposite of the
American idea of changing from occupation to occupation and trying to
develop the best there is in one. In India you cannot change occupation. It
is a religious duty. The highest caste, Brahmins, cannot enter into trade. This
was true even in England until a generation ago. Only when deeply distressed
any Brahmin should support himself by trade. On the other hand the Somras
cannot become wealthy. No superfluous collection of wealth permitted to
Somras. And, thus when you study these deeply religious doctrines you find
that private property when it is amassed receives a sanction which otherwise
would be entirely impossible, and you have a gradation, division of economic
life, such as found no where else in the world. We have one other religious
doctrine which influence the religious doctrines: Transmigration of soul, which
is one of the most cherished doctrines of Indian civilization. The criminal under
this doctrine would be born as a worm, and for minor offences he would
probably [be] born as a bird and so forth in the family of the hierarchy. At
the time when this code was developed, agriculture was not very important.
If you take into consideration all these provisions in the book you find great

deal of light thrown on the general attitude to economic institutions. It is only that when his family is starving that a higher caste Indian would do work. If he is a laborer he would not be admitted to the court as a witness. We find all sorts of provisions attempting to secure justice between and among the economic classes.

There are a few books dealing with economical condition in ancient India. Law has a book entitled, "The Ancient Hindu Economics" which deals with the attempt to gain one's livelihood, and we have a work by an Indian statesman, Chanakya, the minister of Chandra Gupta, which deals with foundation of economics. This is known as Kautilya's Artazustra, which means the science of land. He deals in this large book of over 1500 pages with a great many economic problems. The last part discusses administrative system at that time designed to secure economic progress. Discusses the methods of irrigation and meteorology upon agriculture, the working of mines and manufacture. Devotes great deal of attention to management of different live stocks, e.g., superintendence of cows, horses, elephants, etc.

We now turn to China—the economic theories that were found in Chinese literature. We still know very little, only few things have come to us— translations and discussions that deserve mention. The great writer and thinker of China is Confucius. "Economic Theories of Confucius," was written by one of our students—Mr. Chin. Some other writer often associated with Confucius was Mencius who devoted comparatively small part of his discussions to economic and social discussions. He does give the advantages of international trade—trade in general, and international trade particularly. A book has been written by a Dutchman—Visserling. He wrote about Chinese currency, it is very interesting, having Chinese on one side and English on the other. In this book you will find a description, page 9, (all these out of Mencius), of economic conditions at that time with special attention to the agricultural situation— the private cultivation of land. It talks also about the revenue system at that time. It is a very interesting discussion, as in the modern terms we find a discussion of socialism and industrialism. These we find five or six centuries B.C., before any Greek wrote. They relate to the advantages of autonomy between individualism and uniformism, cooperative theory, theory of individualism in Chinese philosophy.

Paper money is discussed in China by Chow Ling. Even at that early age paper money is likened to flying money, such as Adam Smith's later reference: "The commerce and industry of the country, however, it must be acknowledged, though they may be somewhat augmented, cannot be altogether so secure, when they are thus, as it were, suspended upon the Daedalian wings of paper money..."

The concepts of Confucius are that all human civilization and all economic life and social life are subject to continual change and need change in order to correct evils and meet the newer existing needs. He finds three stages:

1. Disordered stage of humanity
2. The advancing stage, or somewhat tranquil stage
3. The great sanity or extreme peace stage.

*h*is development goes hand in hand with the development of the private *in*dividual. Confucius says, there are five social relations and therefore five *et*hical constants: Father and son; sister and brother; house [sic: husband] and *w*ife; friend and friend; and ruler and subject. And five morals: love, justice, *ri*ght, wisdom and sincerity. (Wealth and Justice—page 293). The real wealth *of* the state does not consist in pecuniary profits, but in justice.

Confucius first advanced the theory of laissez-faire doctrine. The best policy *to* follow was to leave alone the economic activities of men. Lead them on *pr*ofitably. Teach them. Regulate them. Do not interfere with natural economic *te*ndencies of men. The difference between the poor and rich is a result of this *fr*ee competition, which is one of the natural things in life. He also calls attention *to* the environment. In discussing the problem of prices he says, one must *al*ways consider the supply of the commodities. He gives the law of *ac*cumulation of wealth or capital. He says, one must not allow money to be *id*le. When prices rise to the extreme they will turn and go down again. At *th*e high price period you ought to get rid of your goods.

JEWS: We come now to the general economic and social theories as they *pr*esented themselves to the ancient Israelites. The literature of history is far *fr*om satisfactory, because of the fact that the few of the economists and *so*ciologists do not pay attention to economic problems. In the last few years *a* little more progress has been made about the cultural history of Jewish nation.

Economic and social development of Jews was migratory at the beginning *a*nd little attention was paid to commerce. The land acquired from other *c*ountries was divided among the warriors but there was no hardened system. *F*or many centuries the state was based upon agricultural system. Somewhat *la*ter, in 800 B.C., commerce was taken up by towns. The Jews were not in *cl*ose touch with the Phoenecians. A great deal was derived from the *P*hoenecian civilization. After private property developed we find the small *f*armer; then the small farmers begin to disappear and we find large land *p*roprietorship. In this early period there is still little attention paid to trade *a*nd commerce. Among the Jews usury was not permitted, they were primarily *fl*ock tending and commercial people rather than agricultural people. Still *in*dustry was very much frowned upon. Foreigners, however, were not *in*cluded in this prohibition. The usury therefore was allowed for foreigners. *E*ven in the case of strangers it is criss-cross, general attitude of the poor where *s*pecial arrangements are made where the men had gotten into debt. The point *t*o emphasize is that interest was not permitted within the country at first. *T*hen we find a difference (which is interesting)—a distinction made for loans *f*or consumption and loans for business. As regards strangers for business you could charge interest but when it was personal consumption it was different.

They got around the law, however, when the rabbis came, as they were law givers and they were able to square biblical prohibition with their needs. It was only by subterfuge that they therefore assimilated a contract. This business license was called Heter Iske. This subterfuge—the economic life within the state went on quite promptly.

By that time a good many abuses developed, such as that slavery developed for non-payment of interest. This caused an administrative ground for social inequality. Theories and projects of reform bring us to the time of prophets. General economic doctrines turned to the theory of property. Even though the land was sold, this transaction was not final and could be released as land was considered as being inalienable. Therefore hand in hand with this idea goes a very interesting idea, of a theory of redemption. This means that when you sell property to any one, any member of the family selling the property, if he so desired could claim it by repaying the price. In other words, sales were only leases. Difficulty arose in the cities. If you buy a house and fix it up and the original owner would want it back, what could be done? They were therefore compelled to make restriction and concessions, and they therefore limited this time of reclaiming to one year. The next stage of release was the jubilee. That is, after 50 years every man would return into the "possessors-previous" their possessions to the original owner. Strictly speaking this could not be done, as release came every 7 years and jubilee once in 50 years. 7 times 7 making 49. (We know that if work stopped today we will all starve in one and a half years.) Another reason apart from this was that this idea was never actually enforced. Talmud gives reasons why jubilee could not be enforced:

1. If the Jubilee were enforced we would close doors to rentals, for of course no man would rent if he knows he would lose his money.
2. Emphasis is laid on the ethical and moral consequences of the strict enforcement of the law.

The Jewish disputants were just as subtle as the Catholic divines. If the debtor and creditor agreed to pass the seventh year this agreement was valid, in spite of the fact that it went beyond the law—as long as it was not against the law

Jewish attitude towards poor: We find in Hammurabi and in some early Indian writings some references to the poor, but it is doubtful that apart from the tithe, that the Jews attempted what we would call nowadays the poor law There are many provisions in the bible which are intended to look after the poor, such as during the harvest period leaving part of the crop to the poor

Labor in the past was regarded as punishment for sin. We have nothing said in the bible as to the dignity of the labor. Laborers were barred from any kind of public provisions. In one respect Jews differed from any other nation that we have discussed, and that is in the high developed ethical and moral ideas that we find in this prophetic movement. Here we find a little better literature. Who were these men?

There are four men: Amos, who lived about in the middle of 8th century B.C., in the time of Jeremiah. He was a man without training. Then Hosea, who was, on the contrary, a priest. We find that he emphasizes the religious rather than economic decay. Isaiah came from the highest class and he was a great scholar. It was he that developed the idea of Messiah. Later on came Mica. Jeremiah, who lived 650-586 B.C., was rediscovered, recognized, and ntroduced. He came from a priest family. He stressed the idea of individual opportunity. He was followed later by Ezekiel. Later came Isaiah and out of exile and then different efforts were made to revolutionize the state. Again it was much later that we find in Apocaliptus, the last effort was made to influence these Maccabees. Amos first calls attention to the evidence of great prosperity and to the abuses whereby worship of gold was developed and the orgy of wealth. Amos in this gulf of excess saw nothing but paganism.

Hosea: His views on business ethics: "He is a merchant, the balance of deceit s on his hand." He says, to what purpose do you sacrifice unto me? Makes remarks on the rottenness of the political and business conditions at that time. He advocates social and religious education. We find a great deal in his passages calling attention to the differences of wealth and consequent abuses. Isaiah had to criticise women's dress, etc. His ideal of social and political felicity was to help the poor and feed the needy. In Micah who followed Isaiah we find similar complaints. It seems true that in contradistinction to the other oriental nations the Jews seem to be marked by essentially this modern spirit. (It is said: Christianity, religion of love; Buddhism, religion of thought; and Judaism, religion of duties.)

Section 4.   Greece

If we take a general view on old Oriental civilizations and try to understand the beginnings of their efforts we find very little scientific analysis. For that we have to turn to a very different civilization—the Greek Civilization. The and of philosophy, statesmen and science, the first cradle in the complete development of human mind—a development which perhaps has never been equalled. Here we find thinkers like Plato and Aristotle and that they far surpass any succeeding human beings. Therefore the study of Greek economic and social ideas will be one peculiarly interesting to us as marking a new chapter in human development.

We shall first say a few words about the development of Greek literature: recently we have had a very great addition to it. We have two books, both in the last 12 months, the more recent of which is the book of Calhoun— "Business Life in Ancient Athens"—drawn from the records of law in Athens.

The other is a translation by Glotz—"Ancient Greece," which on the whole is the best book on what Greece was like in ancient times. Alfred Aimous– On Greek Commonwealth, depicts political and economic life in the 5th century. We also have a great deal from Greek and Latin writers—books on Hellenic Civilization. This is the English literature. The more recent were in German, series of essays by Professer Meyer—two very good studies on economic development of Greece and development of slavery.

In French we also have two or three excellent books—Glutz (in French)– "Labor and Industries in Greece." There are two other French books– Guirode—"Private Property in Greece," Professor Francutte, on "Industrie in Greece." This is the chief literature on the economic institutions.

Best literature on economic theories: A very good book by an American scholar—Trevor—A History of Greek Economic Thought. In addition to this there is another French book by Souchon on the Economic Theories of Greece and by a German—Pohlmann, "History of Socialistic Theories in Greece."

Development of Greek Life

This is divided into four sections:

1. Homeric Period
2. Archaic Period
3. Classic Period
4. Hellenistic Period

1. Homeric Period: During this period we have a system of a primitive kind. There was no private property and the economic life was confined within the limits of states which were self-sufficing economically—the same as we find conditions in the Southern States in the pre-Civil War period in the United States. Stock breeding, flock tending prevailed. There were few slaves at that time. The work was carried on by the craftsmen and hired men, etc. Industry therefore, in the community was like the industries of a self-sufficing economic community, and only gradually do we find trade arise between the communities and between the larger groups. In this early period Greece was marked by great piracy, which was considered perfectly legitimate trade at that time. Oxen were used as money. An ox was thought to be very valuable at that time. There is no evidence of any precious metal being used as money.

2. Archaic Period: During three or four centuries great economic and social changes took place. In the first place there was a transition from common ownership to private ownership. With these changes there came a transition from flock raising to agricultural life, just as in the Southern States we have certain trading centers, so now they began these trading centers in Greece and the surplus crops were oil and wine. With the development of agriculture and

rade, wealth became more and more important and we find differentiation nto upper and lower classes. The trading classes now arose. They soon acquired 'ery great importance, and the land owner now tended to become the small nan rather than the big man. In the towns also we find the beginnings of ndustries on very small scale. The great change was with the growth of slavery. Population and land is the cause of slavery. In order to have cultivation we lave to have slavery. Slavery never disappears until these conditions change. During this time especially it began in Asia Minor and then spread into Greece vith the successful wars of conquests.

Another interesting development in that time was the gradual pressure of opulation upon the land and the development of two methods designed to neet that: One was ancient village of limited population and the other was olonization. The real theories of colonization and the states-manship were vorked out between the Greeks and their settlements, first to the north— 'hrace and then to Egypt to Cicilia and then to France. Development of trade nd commerce brought two changes: economic and intellectual—first use of netals, copper, brass, silver, and finally gold. Very beautiful gold coins were nade in Greece. We also find writing and beginnings of literature and rapid evelopment of the arts. The industry was still a minor question: potteries, ne textiles and marbles. But the work shops were all still of the household ype. With the reformation in the 6th century the seeds of the domestic novement were planted.

3. Classical Period: After the revolution of the 6th century we find a evelopment of trade and commerce and with it the growth of a rich ourgeoisie. In some of the towns a great deal of trade was carried on by foreign nerchants and we find among them banking and commercial classes. Judging om the names this was not confined to foreigners but also included the natives. : was during this period that we see the growth also of a great commercial evelopment both of import and export, so that we have pretty well developed conomic situation. The fundamental difference between the conditions in the ireek towns and cities at that time and in the modern times is of course that nere had not been any development of industrial capitalism nor machinery. 'he conditions in the big cities and towns of 5th century were very much like nose in the 18th century in France and England. It was called the domestic ystem, with a large amount of capital but no machinery, nor factory life. It as in the towns also that the slaves were largely found, because on the land ou had serfdom rather than slavery. During this period the farmer was rimarily, as a result of these reasons, a small man rather than a large capitalist,) that everything was predisposed to the development of democratic onditions. This was the beginning of democracy as against aristocracy and udalistic conditions. The environment was such as to lead to effluence [sic?] f art and music and drama, the like of which has never since been seen. The conomic life laid the basis for the advancement.

Summing up: Some years ago the general conception of Greek economic life might have been put under the term of oikos. The oikos idea was developed by German writers in the study of early taxation of Greece and Rome. As first developed the conception of oikos meant a house and the things that go with the house: the family household, wife, children and slaves. We have in modern times greatly differentiated forms of production—factories of production whereas in Greece, the system of oikos was such that everything that was produced in this state was consumed in the state and there were no separate classes. What was true of this oikos in Greece, was also true of the period in Rome. Consequently we must distinguish between modern and ancient life with that criteria [sic]. Meyer's essays were to the effect that Greece in the 5th century had an industrial life comparable to modern times.

There are two ways in which the word capitalism and capitalistic economy is used in modern times. When we talk of the middle ages and the introduction of capitalism we are talking about a great economic revolution. The change took place in the end of the 16th and 17th centuries when all the doctrines of Marxism arose under the stress of this national capitalism. When we speak of capitalism opposed to labor and socialism then of course we mean capitalism in its final development in the sense of factory system. There are various stages in the introduction of capital in the middle ages. There was very little capitalism. When it comes in, it comes at the beginning of industrial process and at the end of the industrial process. But in between the beginning and the end there is long interval, which deals with the tools and machinery, of the workmen and it is only the question of who owns the material and who owns the finished product. So, Meyer was right and he was wrong. He was right in calling attention to the growth of capital in the classical period where there was a great deal of capital invested in the industries and there was an international market for products. But Meyer did not know the domestic system and factory system as it developed in Greece. You never get a theory of distribution until you have capitalism all the way through. In fact Marx was much nearer the truth than Meyer. Marx distinguishes between commercial capitalism and industrial capitalism. Commercial capitalism existed in correspondence but industrial did not exist. Therefore why were oikos theory? It is essentially wrong and inadequate. And the objections raised by Meyer were only partly correct and in the light of this distinction we shall proceed to discuss some of the theories.

Calling attention now to the fundamental difference between the Greek idea and our own time: the conception of the state and political duties of the individual—the old conception of state was different from ours, because the state played so much more a role in those centuries than it does with us. Ancient civilization emphasizes the collective rather the individual opportunity, and we find this general conception by the writers. Although there were fundamental struggles in Greece, you don't find any such thing as socialism in Greece and there is never any socialism until you have capital permeating all the phases of economic life.

Pre-Socratic economic thinkers: Earliest speculation in Greece was rather along social than along economic lines. About this time we find doctrines on the science of eugenics. The idea of picking up your ancestors. Herodotus was regarded the first descriptive sociologist, but the attempt was made to explain rather than describe it. One of the most interesting of the early Greek writers was physician Hyppocrates, born in 460 B.C. He was one of the earliest writers to discuss the influence of physical environment upon the economic and social life of the community. His work has been translated. The fundamental ideas of anthropogeography you will find in Hyppocrates. He explains the economic and social life in terms of geographic changes. Some earliest writers, as Petagoras, Herculetes, Democretes wrote books on wealth, some of them wrote books, especially on agriculture. The work on wealth seems very much like what Ruskin put it in his famous indictment of the classical economic wealth as constituting the objects themselves owned by individual who uses the wealth. Another school of writers were Sophists, who developed for the first time the doctrine of an extreme individualistic system. To them the whole law of economics and ethics and the social life is an artificial creation which must be considered in the light of order, and the law of nature is opposed to the law of artificially created social conditions.

Economic Theories in Greece: Pre-Socratic writers and more specially the earlier writers on social, ethical and economical questions are characterized by extremely individualistic points of view and their effort to return to nature. Philosophers were opposed to slavery on the ground that it is not a natural institution, and also Stoics opposed slavery. There were few writers before Socrates who discussed primarily any economic question. We find however some very interesting forerunners of modern ideas such as the statement that and ought not to be in the private hands; and also some discussion in regard rich and the poor; that rich ought never receive any dowry and the poor ought never pay any.

As regards the works of Socrates, we are acquainted with these through Plato and others. There is a special book written by Erixias on wealth. It is interesting and shows the connection between the wealth and welfare. He starts out discussing the human wants, and points out that unless a thing is useful it will not be called wealth at all. Then, he goes on to contrast money and wealth and emphasizes his point by asking whether a house should be considered wealth. Socrates puts it this way: After all, the attitude to wealth is rather extreme. Increase of wealth depends upon the increase of desire and that the wealthiest people are deprived of a great many things, and from that point of view wealth is rather to be discouraged than encouraged. He has a great deal to say about demand and desire. He says, we want things most when we are ill, or when we are very poor, we feel the need, the lack. When people are wealthy they love themselves and they have a great many things. When rich do not get what they want they suffer more, but poor are free from the great worries to which the rich are exposed. That is the idea of Socrates.

We now will say a few words about Xenophon. He is responsible for a number of works, two of which are important. He calls one Economics and the other Revenue of State of Athens. Economics: He was the first to explain what was meant by ecos-nomos [sic]. He begins by asking, What do we mean by economic goods and wealth? He finds that the essence of it constitutes utility what he calls serviceableness. He says the important thing is not alone the cost of the thing but the cost of the man who owns it. (Ruskin quotes this idea of his.) Xenophon goes on to define that serviceableness of a thing is something that everyone knows how to use. It must be of objective qualification. He ends up by saying that if he would define wealth he would say: "Wealth is the excess of possessions over wants." and "If you are dealing with personal qualification that also is wealth." Marshall makes this same statement also.

Xenophon came to the conclusion that personal satisfaction may not be considered wealth, but the qualifications of an individual which enable him to secure material goods may be considered wealth. He says, certain services can be exchanged and if that is the case, then it is considered wealth. He then goes on to discuss the questions of various kinds of forms of wealth, and enterprise. He gives the earliest account of the advantages of division of labor He says, in small town it will be necessary for a man to know more than one trade, but in the cities one has to know only a part of one trade to get along He lays great stress on the importance of agriculture. As to trade and industry he says, sitting down all day weakens the body, whereas working on land strengthens the body. He devotes the last part of his book to domestic economy and the duties of the house-wife. His other book is Revenues on the State of Athens. He wrote about the middle of the 4th century and he shows the advantages of commerce, especially from the point of view of a rich city like Athens. He desired the government to start lodging houses and treat foreigners well to make commerce easy. He said, you must give them privilege but you must get revenue from them. He also says that law courts should be created in order to settle the disputes between natives and foreigners. He then takes up the question of price and says that the goods must be bought and sold according to their price. He points out that prices are fixed by the supply and demand, and that the values are always expressed in terms of money. He says too much corn is bad for the farmer as prices will go down, but if you are dealing with silver, the more silver there is the more silver mines there will be to dig out, because you can never have too much money. (In this respect he seems to be the forerunner of Mr. Bryan). He says that silver could also be used as a commodity, but even if it is not used as a commodity the value will always be stable. He thought gold was not stable but that silver was.

He asks, "What ought Athens to do?" He thinks that no private property ought to be permitted. The silver mines ought to be worked by the government. He advocated slavery to promote the working of the mines and thought that the revenue of Athens ought to come from these silver mines. He also gave the first statement of the law of diminishing returns. He said that mines are very different from the agriculture, as in the case of agriculture you can not go beyond certain limit and the productivity of land has definite limits, because some ratio cannot be increased indefinitely by adding labor or capital.

We now come to PLATO and ARISTOTLE: Plato, mightiest of all philosophers, who turns his attention to social topics. He has of course his Republic and Laws. As to his conception of wealth, there is not much difference between Platonic and Socratic ideas, but Plato was too a big man to be ascetic. He thinks that a competence for an individual is prerequisite for a good life. He says, poverty is just as bad as excess of wealth and a really sensible man would secure the medium between the two.

Plato's views about production and acquisition of wealth: He says, production is typified by agricultural industry, and things such as fine art, and the like bring something new into existence but the acquisitive arts don't bring anything new into existence, they simply help men to acquire from somebody else things which are already in existence, such as learning that pupils get from their teachers.

In regards to trade and commerce, he says there are two ways of acquiring goods: (1) Take them by force. (2) To buy them or exchange them. He says, of course the second is the better way. He says, you can also acquire goods by gifts, but if you acquired goods by sale, then, he says, you have to divide it into two categories: (a) You can get from the seller the things that he himself produces, or (b) you can get from the seller that which somebody else has produced. And, thus begins the whole subject of trade which is to be divided into retail trade, inter-city, or inter-political trade.

He says, there is another way to classify them: Principal or subordinate—fundamental to life or subordinate. Says, in all the activities of men you must consider the fact that they are subordinate to the activity of statesmen. It is the statesmen who weaves these minor things into that cloth of life. He subordinates economics to politics. He has nothing but praise for agriculture. He speaks about mechanical arts and industries. He also speaks of industries and good management and gives descriptions of labor and of economic and social life.

The most significant of these miscellaneous topics that Plato treats is the division of labor. He advances four reasons in trying to show the benefit of division of labor:

1. Product would be larger.
2. Not alone the quantity but quality will be better.

3. There will be less of strain to individual and things will be more easily
    produced and will be satisfactory to the nature and inclination of the
    individual.
4. Saving time.

What Plato does is to emphasize the matter of mutual interdependence, which
means economically, division of labor. (Adam Smith put this not in a less
defensible form)—(Sismondi thinks it is the best distinction of division of
labor.)

In the same way Plato gave a philosophical explanation of money. He said,
money is always the concomitant of exchange, and it is defined as the token
of exchange. In his work on the Laws, he enters a little more fully into this
problem, and points out that it is not alone a medium of exchange but also
value. He says, money changes products from being incommensurable and
uneven into the things that are commensurable and even, but he does not go
much further into the subject and has no conception that anything ought to
be paid for the use of money. He says, the usurer is a bee that is in search
to sting into his victim, thus poisoning others to improve himself. He finds
trade a greedy commercialism and he works out his general philosophical
attitude towards these things in his great book on State or Republic—one of
the most gigantic products of the human mind. This is really a book on ethics,
on justice. It is an attempt to trace out points of justice. One of the means
of attaining just human life is by providing this ideas [sic: ideal] state as close
as we can in order to reach that elevating conception from both the social and
economic bases of Platonic conception.

The origin of his system, the advantages of division of labor, etc. is with
him an entirely natural process and he says that in the course of time we have
a community composed of the following classes which represent the following
ideals or principles. We find three classes: Rulers, Soldiers, and Traders. These
three classes represent entirely different philosophical views. The ruler
represents the deliberation idea, the warriors represent what he calls aiding
idea, they help people to defend themselves, and the great mass represent the
money getting idea. He says, in the original conception of things, Providence
mixed different ingredients into the different groups. Into the rulers there was
put gold; into soldiers, iron to make him hard; and in the great mass of people
there was put simply brass.

He says, these three classes represent what we now call behaviorism. They
represent different incentives. The upper class is moved primarily by reason;
the soldier class is moved by anger and by hate, and the trading class is moved
by the feeling of desire, greed and lust. Thus we have the whole philosophy
of incentives in our actual life. Just as the individual, and anger and desire
must be subordinate to reason, so also this applies to the State. Plato had the
concept of an Ideal Unity. Also the Platonic idea of Communism is that you

could not have any ideal unless you have philosophic harmony—and that no one should be any different from any body else. In an ideal state all must grieve and all must rejoice alike. What does this mean? Of course it means that we should not have private property. As regards education, he says that the matter of education should be a state problem.

Plato says that the principle of justice in any community is common work and common training and on the basis of that he erects his whole theory of eugenics, the need of being well born, the need of looking after your progenitors. There is little controversy here, as he applies all these doctrines only to the two upper classes. This cannot be applied, he says to the money making class. Considering, however, his entire views it will not be doing justice to call Plato a communist.

The reason why Plato did not believe in democracy: In the 8th book he tells us of the different struggles of the forms of government. Democracy inevitably leads to oligarchy and it is a bad thing for three reasons:

1. Breaks the ideal unity of the state.
2. Diminishes the strength of the state.
3. It is bad because it emphasizes the ideas [sic?: ideal(s)] of money-getting and money wasting.

He says, tyranny is a bad thing and so democracy is bad. Why? In the first place, he says, everybody differs from his neighbor, and since everybody differs from his neighbor, everyone ought ideally to do the things for which he is best fitted, but democracy assigns equality alike to the equal and unequal. Says, some appetites are unnecessary as spending appetite, which results in unproductive action. His point is that democracy is a weak and inefficient form of government from the ideal point of view, and never can be efficient unless philosophers are kings and kings are philosophers and that there will be no ideal state in democratic government. He further adds that only when we are governed by our reason and not by our emotion can we achieve success.

In the book on the Laws, Plato attempts to work out his plans of a practical economic system. He still thinks that inequality must be guarded against, especially in the extremes. He says, luxury predisposes us to idleness and poverty produces mischief, and says that everybody must have land and that in this ideal community the artificers must keep very narrow watch on the merchants. It is true that merchants benefit the public but their benefit ought to be a moderate one. We must not allow advertising, he says. He calls advertising puffing and one should never use oaths in order to show the excellence of his wares. His ideal is a self-sufficient community. A state must be as far as possible self-sufficient and independent. He says that trading with other lands must be restricted only for political reasons.

We find in Plato most interesting discussion on population and slavery: He proposes very drastic means for keeping down population. He says the typical town should be 5400 houses. If more children are born—he was the first to advocate the birth control—and if this does not work they must be exposed. One of his methods was preventive, the other repressive.

As regards slavery he has not very much to say, but he does call attention to different notions that people have on slavery. He says people have entirely different ideas, they chastise them and make their souls many times as slavish as before. He says there are others who take very different views, and say that slave is a human being. However, he does not seem to disapprove slavery. Plato would have had greatest influence on the economic and ethical conditions at his time but they did not appreciate him as these were above their understanding.

ARISTOTLE: 384-322 B.C. We shall call attention primarily to the economic rather than the political views of Aristotle. He devoted a great deal of time along social science. He is the father of great many sciences. In the social sciences economics with him occupies a middle position between politics and ethics, part of politics and part of ethics. These are very distinctive points of views, and with him it means bureaucracy. Household economics, he said, should either be ruled or maintained. There are three relations in the way which is ruled—(1) house and wife, (2) mother and child, (3) relation of the master to slave. But not only household should be ruled but also maintained.

Aristotle gives us the first philosophical discussion of slaves. He says, slavery is a natural phenomenon, for the reason that in every man there is the body and there is higher element, which is soul. He says, just as there is this relation in the human being, so there is the same relation in the society. Some people are marked out for the soul life, and some people are marked out for the public life, some people can find proper use in the society only in their bodies and those people are natural slaves who must be subordinated to the mind and to the spirit represented by the master. As in the case of an individual his body must be ruled by the mind so in society body of peoples must be ruled by the ruler. There is such a thing as slave by nature. He says you cannot get away from this natural phenomenon. In the same way you could not get away from distinguishing between wild animals, some of them have capacity within themselves to become tame and some don't. He gets to the idea that slave is part of his master just as the woman is part of her master and therefore slave by nature. He further says that although slave by nature is the situation had as a result of phenomena, we have also had slave by nature and slave by law.

He says, from ethical point of view a man to be justly a master must show himself morally superior to the slave and must treat slave humanely, but if there should be a drawback in the attitude of moral superiority, and if slave is really not inferior to the master, and if he happens to have a soul then he should be liberated.

Coming to the 4th kind of attempt to manage the household, he says, as soon as you get into this discussion you get into problem of wealth. He then discusses wealth, starting out with genuine wealth which he defines as being private possession of useful things. He goes further and tries to give analysis of the qualities that make a thing wealth and says these are the characteristics:

1. It has to be something that is necessary to life and of greatest possible usefulness.
2. It has to be something that is capable of accumulation.
3. It must be something that is useful to individuals conceived of as members of society.
4. It must be something that is limited in extent.

Aristotle thinks of wealth more in the ethical than in the economic sense. Furthermore, his conception of utility is not like our modern views of utility. A thing is useful, he says, in that it serves the final good of life. He did therefore differ with modern economists. He says, the relation of wealth to happiness is the same as the relation of tune to a lyre. In the matter of value he gives discussions which have become classic. He says, every commodity has two uses and these uses are proper and improper or ex-proper uses. He says, for instance, a shoe has a proper use, as wearing it, but its improper use is to get something else for this shoe, say a hat. These are exactly what the modern economist calls value in use and value in exchange. This was known to Aristotle. He divides commodity into two classes, (a) Commodities may be used in order to get out of it what we would call today a psychic income—as running an automobile what one gets as delight out of it. (b) You can also use this to get money out of it. When you use commodities in order to get money income he calls it money income. The other one he calls psychic income, or pleasure income.

He further discusses the growth of economic society, where he gives his famous description of the qualities of man as being a political animal. As a consequence he says, there is the development not alone of society but also private property, which is natural. In the first place, he says, private property is a natural impulse just as in every human being we find the love of one's home, and just as mother and father love their children, man loves what belongs to him and the social consequences of private property are of utmost importance. He thought Plato was a dreamer in this respect. He says, in the first place, the private property makes liberality possible and the whole transformation of man is due to this economic fact. Kindness, he says, is another outgrowth and is a consequence of private property. He even says modesty is a consequence of private property, and says, the disadvantage of the opposite situation is equally plain. Communism, he maintains, will inevitably, in the face of natural inequality of mankind, produce discord, and says private property, not common property, is the salvage of mankind.

Aristotle shows his greatness as follows: "It is true that communism represents an unobtainable and in some ways regrettable ideal but still under the right moral conception with Plato, Is there not some way in which we recognize finality of ideal? Yes, there is a way. Property must indeed be private but its use ought to be as far as possible common. Certain things a man has no moral right to use for himself. Property should be private for purposes of production and its use common as far as possible in order to solve the moral problem involved."

Economic views of Aristotle: We have called attention to his allusion to value, and private property. That the most important method of acquiring wealth, the natural wealth is in connection with land. We then come to the typical view that agriculture is the really proper and natural method of acquiring wealth. Aristotle goes into detail in this. It is just that the benefit made is not from human beings but out of nature. Moreover, he says, the agriculture is free from objection, as it does not make the body weak, and does not make one do the mean and illiberal occupation. He says, How can you lead a life of virtue and be a mechanic? Most people are not virtuous and they attempt to make money otherwise. He then discusses money: First, he gives definition and description of money. Money, he says, is something which itself belongs to the category of useful commodities. Originally, says he, this commodity used as money was simply handed around, by size, weight and nuggets, then it was in bullion. It was only much later that it received a stamp and thus we have coin. He asks, How are we going to explain money?

First he tells us about barter as being simply the complement of one's natural wants. If we want something that somebody else has we get this by bartering. He says, when we are exchanging with other individuals we are dealing with unequal commodities, and we have to find out something which will make them commensurable. The demand is behind this all. Money he says, is nothing but a substitute for demands and renders commensurable those things which are incommensurable. This is stamped by government and it is called nomisma. That the first real function of government is to regulate method of making commensurable things incommensurable [sic]. He says, money can be used for exchange at present and at the same time has power to be used for future exchanges. This means it has a store of value. But, since money is a commodity, like all other commodities it is affected by instability. Yet it is the best kind of commodity we can pick out to serve as standard of value, money really has four functions:

1. Medium of circulation
2. Measure of value
3. Standard of value
4. Store of value or standard of deferred payments

Aristotle says, you must not confuse money and wealth, as money is wealth but wealth is not necessarily money. Of the different ways of making money it is very interesting to observe his views against the taking of interest and there is also the fact that the views he holds of interest are not the views held in the Middle Ages, or the same views as Shakespeare held in the Merchant of Venice, where he speaks of the Greed of Barren Metal. (Tocos—tectomi— Greek word for money.) Regarding four functions of money, when we speak of getting interest this does not belong to those criteria.

As regards wages, Aristotle says it is unnecessary to work if you can get somebody else to work for you. He says, to lend money is out of question. To try to earn money by trade and commerce was considered very undesirable, yet there is one passage in Aristotle which is a premonition of the future— he of course has no conception of capital. He says: If the cones were made to weave clothes by themselves, if the keys would strike the harp by themselves then the master would need no slaves. He discusses the problems of population. Unlike Plato he is not very drastic. His remedy of over-population is colonization. He thought there were still unutilized lands and as a result he advocated this remedy.

In speaking of the way of getting wealth, Aristotle says, there are three ways: By nature, by barter and by money. Natural ways: Agriculture, fishing, hunting, flock tending, and piracy.

In the other part of his works, Aristotle treats of Chrematistics as the science which deals with the acquisition of wealth. (In a different sense than he used this word before.)

CHREMATISTICS

Per trophen Natural or (proper method)		In between way Metaxu		Barter Capelike
	Ulotomia (woodcutting)		Metalutics (mining)	
Coa By keeping animals, bees, fish, etc.)	Georgics (Agriculture and arboricul- ture)	Emporia (Market place)	Tokesmas Interest	Misteria (Working for wages)

In the "in-between way" he suggests that although the lumber and metals are gotten from nature, they are nevertheless sold, i.e., a cross between "natural" and "unnatural" way of acquiring wealth.

There were, as we know now, a great many books and much literature in the ancient times but they were either lost or burnt during the big fire in Alexandria. Most of the discussions in these books turned about the relation between economics and ethics. We find three points of view, which are extremely analogous with the modern attitude. A very liberal attitude was held toward wealth by the Cyre writers. About principles of economics the idea was to get the highest pleasure with the least expenditure. There were many others who wrote. The attitude of Cynics was rather ascetic in their views; then Diogenes has been called philosopher of proletariat (of course this is absurd as there were no proletariats). They said, men who love wealth are afflicted by dropsy, desire of wealth was called the center of all evils. They said, How can virtue be the present of wealth? A third class of writers represented the middle class, that is Stoics. Instead of despising wealth they were indifferent to both wealth and poverty alike. They said that the real things in life were spiritual goods and not the material goods.

During the second and fourth centuries a great many books were written about Utopian literature. Descartes was the first one to give the idea of a golden age. Rousseau borrowed from him. A book was written to represent a community of barbarian nomads. Theopompus wrote a celebrated book of Meropian state with complete absence of money and private property. Hecataeus wrote the Communistic state and which goes back to earliest times in Egypt where all lands were equally divided. That was the basis of his Utopia. Euphemoris, in his sacred chronicle, refers to an island near India ruled by aristocracy and there were neither traders nor artisans. Jambulus, who wrote the first book entitled, Sun State, tells of the Isle of the Sun, or paradise of the sun, which was situated near the equator for the worship of the sun, where the trees never lost their leaves, human beings never lost their strength and women never lost their beauty. Collective ownership of all means of production, everyman in turn had to do every job, agreeable or disagreeable. This also applied to marriage relations. In this work modern division of labor was essentially inevitable.

Section 5.   Rome

Economic conditions: As to the literature there are no good books on the subject, very little in English. Kenny Frank has written a book, "Economic History of Rome." Professor Rotsetsief of Yale wrote a large book, and his ideas are most erroneous and he has not really contributed any thing worth while. Stenus Davis has written on the Influence of Wealth in the Imperial Rome.

The early Empire did not have private property. Money in Rome was in the form of oxen, pecuniary, pecus, meaning oxen. Gradually more importance was paid to the development of wealth. The history of Rome was marked by wo problems, slavery and public domain. The agrarian movement in Rome was made in 485 B.C. in which the attempt was made to get away from the Senate the control of public lands and put it in the system of occupation. The next century an attempt was made but failed. But big land conquests were developed in a large scale. In 377 B.C. this took three forms:

1. The interest that had been paid upon mortgage loans was to be deducted from the principal and the lease was to be paid in three years.
2. No one was allowed to have more than 300 acres.
3. In order to check the abuse of cattle growing, owners could not raise more than 300 to 500 heads upon the public pastures.

We know these laws were passed but enforcement was very doubtful. In the second century Tabirum Grasius succeeded in having enacted the laws of 133 which was the repetition of old laws. He added to these some new features, but he was assassinated. Ten years later his brother tried the same thing and he also was assassinated. These social movements brought about a division of class and sharpened the differences, which prepared the way for the decomposition of the Empire. In the meantime, as wealth multiplied we have the appearance of great companies which were then known as Societas.

Deloume wrote a book on the power of money in Rome. He speaks of shares and stocks at that time. That was a great commercial competition age and age of appearance of a class plutocracy based upon commerce, when the whole question of justice developed. The abuses became so great and differences so strong that this led to wars and bad results in the Empire. The system of fractional payment as we have today was very common in Rome and rested upon the transfer of rights in the title to land and especially of houses in Rome. Dealing in futures of real estate was found in Rome, and with it came the impoverishment of the peasant or the farmer. With the development of slavery we have also developed a landless poor class. The middle class—there was none. Plini said that there were only 6 land owners in Africa, in Italy there were only 6,000 land owners, with the advent of Empire, we have first, peace. We find a development of industries and commerce. Rome became more and more the center of certain form of industry and it began to reap all benefits of provinces, as Egypt, Asia Minor and Gaul. Commerce went to Great Britain and there was economic exploitation of England and Wales of Roman time. For almost two centuries there was no war. Never before was there such a peaceful development of human beings. Roads and buildings were built. Now, two things happened, especially in the later Empire:

1. The change of the system of slavery, which now, as population increased and cultivation become more intensive, gave way to a period of serfdom and colonade.

2. Gradual disappearance of fertility of the soil, pointed out for the first time by Professor Simkovitch.

The fall of the Roman Empire was due to the rigidity of the economic condition. The taxes were made hereditary and the men ran away to get rid of taxation, some were forced to come back, and the barrenness or exhaustion of the soil.

The whole Roman psychology was different from Greeks. Greeks were philosophers and artists, Romans were warriors and administrators. Never in Rome did there develop any science except the science of law. In their scientific attitude they were much influenced and depended on Greeks. Students from Rome went to Greece to finish their education long after Greeks lost their power. We don't find anything very great and original in Rome. Their views are reflections of great Greek writers, namely, Aristotle or Plato, or they were reflections to [sic] the economic problems as they presented themselves to the statesman of the day. There were earlier writers, but their books are lost. Other writers were Carthegenians, which literature also was lost. Cicero was not an economist nor philosopher, but he was a lawyer. We find a great many statements about economic topics and economic theories in Cicero. He was primarily an aristocrat and reactionary. In the doctrine of property he differed very much from Greeks. He tells us that private property depends upon various conditions and is due to various causes—sometimes ancient possessions, sometimes due to conquest, and sometimes it is due to contract, and sometimes simply to public constitution. He tells us that private property was created in order that men should hold and enjoy what is really naturally their own. He upholds private property and slavery. Being an advocate of slavery his views of the laborer are typically Roman and in the "Offices" Chapter 42 you find very interesting passage:

He says, merchants can never succeed unless they lie most abundantly. All mechanical laborers are mean, work-shops contain nothing befitting to a gentleman. Says, professions, like medicine, architecture, liberal arts, even teaching are honorable if they are suited to the rank or file who practice this. As to trade he says, if it is extensive and rich, if it gives bread to many people it is not despicable, and he places the agriculturer, a gentleman farmer, as really the basis of the whole body economic, everything else is to be frowned down upon. He realizes both elements in price: He discusses scarcity measure and the influence of utility and demand. He speaks in his Oration about money, as circulating money, and factors that make the good money, and he was interested chiefly in the problems of the day. He is opposed to the agrarian laws, does not approve of interest, of freedom of trade, has great deal to say of masses, of the community and of taxes. Cicero is far more interested in problems of production than of distribution and he joins with this, obligations to give security to the property owner. He was the representative of oligarchy and represents the economic point of view of reigning classes in Italy. He does not really add anything new.

Next, we take up Seneca who during the time of Christ represents the Stoic point of view. He is especially interesting because he calls attention to the dark side of slavery. He is often quoted because he has very beautiful passages. He explains natural advantages of one country over another. He gives function of trade as satisfying mutual desire for commodities, just as the views of Adam Smith. With this exception there is little in Seneca. Very much the same can be said in the case of Pliny, who wrote a great deal but did not add anything new. In discussing agriculture he wrote about the relative importance of large and small farms, on which John Stuart Mill spends much time 2000 years later. As regards precious metals, Pliny emphasizes the point of suitability, durability, malleability and rarity and other qualities of gold. He was of a character to look back and go the whole way.

Now we come to two typical Roman contributors to economic thought. They wrote of the gradual decay of agriculture and they recalled the Roman cities and emphasized the agricultural problems. They were called the writers on rustic affairs. These may be called physiocrats of Rome. Of these writers one was Cato. He wrote a large book on the subject called [De] Re Rustica, in which he describes the condition of the farm. This was the first attempt to estimate various degrees of profits in tilling different kinds of land. He discussed real merits of cereals and garden products. He thinks that either one or the other or both of them were more profitable than employing self in trade. Agriculture gives more honest population good morals, healthy persons and produces soldiers. About usury, he was much against it, in spite of the fact that he himself made much money by usury. There were two or three other writers who are important and are read even today:

Varro. Wrote libra [De Re] Rustica. He gives us very clear facts of the economic conditions of the time and the most important thing about this is that he is the first writer who calls attention to the economic disadvantages of slavery. He shows the inadequacy of slavery. Varro was followed by Columella, who wrote a number of books. He has a great deal to say about division of labor in different forms of agriculture and he is the first to discuss the evils of absenteeism, gives this as one of the reasons of decay of Rome, and points out the disadvantages of slavery. He also points out possibilities of garden culture near the great cities. One other writer, who was also very widely read, is Cato. There was nothing new in him, he only quoted his predecessors. They altogether tried energetically to stand this tide of agricultural decay, but in vain, as the whole movement failed and brought Rome into ruin.

Some other facts are to be found not in the economists themselves but in the legal writers. Corpus Juris. Their point was that the center of all prosperity is to be found in money, as it is important in the matter of trade. We find that in Paulis. He wrote of the origin and significance of money the accuracy of which have never been surpassed. Buying and selling originally consisted of mere barter, formerly there was no such thing as coin and therefore you could not call one thing a commodity and other thing a price. Everybody in those days changed his useful things, things that he did not need so much according to the necessities of time and place with the things he desired most. But since it would not always happen that you might have what I wanted and I might have what you wanted, a commodity was chosen which had public and perpetual value, and this coin did away with difficulties of mere barter by the steadiness of its quantity, by its intrinsic value and by its being a legal tender. He emphasizes the following two points, that everything had a value and except those things which could not be sold or exchanged and that value could be recognized in attempt to exchange. These writers discussed the capital but they never reached out [sic: our] conception for great many reasons.

Property in Rome was called familia. They made distinction between product and property. Things produced were property. Slaves are not property as they are not produced. It is the service of slaves that forms property and therefore productive forces of the community are put side by side with the products of the community. And the only distinction that the Roman writers made is between the parent stock and fruit of stock but they do not reach to our idea of capital. Pecunium idea which they reached as meaning capital which has had its significance both political, scientific and economically. This is a very important thing from economic point of view in that it helped to conver from industries of slavery into an industry of multiple capital. This made the laborer to a certain extent independent and added to improvement in the condition of agriculture, so that pecunium is an important topic of Roman thought of economic subject. The sors, capital sum, the amount—was the way in which circulating capital became as it were independent from this general mass of property. When money was loaned out in Rome the payment was called faluris, and it is interesting to compare the Roman explanation with our own. The Roman view was distinct from Mediæval and from our modern view of capital. They could not take the mediæval view which identified money with particular pieces of coin, because the Roman conception of property in general did not take our modern view as the Roman writers always identified the value as money value, not ideal value and capital price was represented in terms of money. Pecunia, as properly they called was the usus fructus— the fruit of the use and that sometimes was called usura—the origin of our term usury.

The use of money does not consist in its fruits because it is found not in itself but in something else, as a new contract, contract of payment of interest. And they looked upon usury as a penalty. Usury was not paid because of any gain to the person who gets it but it is inflicted on the debtor because of delay of payment, and the conception therefore is not an interest of capital but a penalty for non-payment. Interest among Romans was legitimate. Romans did not reach the modern conception of capital, so also they did not reach the modern idea of credit. There were two kinds of loans in Rome:

1. Loan for use—commodato.
2. Loan for consumption, which was called mutuo.

This proved to be the basis of the whole mediæval economic explanation. You find bankers in Rome, but they are only money changers, and not in the modern sense of a banker. The idea of conception of private property of Rome was entirely different from our modern theory. There have been several stages in our modern theory: Roman theory: You find the theory of private property as either being occupation theory or legal theory, either seized or state gave it. The modern stages or Teutonic idea as it is called is a more ethically proportioned conception and the idea is that laborer as a man earns his property—but the Roman idea was the seizure idea. Summing up the entire thing however, you find quite little of interest to the economist.

BOOK II.   THE MIDDLE AGES

Section 6.   The Church Fathers

We now come to the whole Middle Ages, regarded as the "Dark Ages". The best book is written by an Irishman, G. O'Brien—"An Essay on Mediæval Economic Teaching". Some other works are written by Frenchman Jourdain—"Beginning of Economics". Also Belgian, Brants. Also Andaman—"Economic Principles of Communism." More modern book Schreiber—on Economic Views of Scholasticism.

Christ has frequently been called a communist. He is often quoted from his teachings as showing communistic ideas. The economic meanings of Christianity are summarized as follows:

1.   Emphasis is put upon the promptings of spiritual life. The condition in Rome was pretty bad and the struggle seemed to be hopeless. The teaching of Christianity from the beginning tried to put some courage into hopelessness. The church supervised the contract to improve conditions of the average man.
2.   Did great deal in alleviating the situation of women, as women were being considered as property.
3.   Attitude of Christianity to the poor and charity. There were no hospitals in the ancient times among the Jews and other ancient nations. The whole idea of hospital is a Christian idea. The church looked out for the poor and acted as trustee upon them, helped a great deal to alleviate the condition of

the poor. Held the conception that a true Christian was obligated to help the poor.

4.   Doctrine of the dignity of labor as compared with the views of Cicero In theory at least the slave was the equal of the master, for in the church they were all the same. And, had it not been for the church at that time, the entir civilization would have been destroyed.

5.   Attitude towards slavery—the influence of the church upon th disappearance of slavery. This, however, was not so much direct as indirect Among the ecclesiastics system there was no difference between slave and lord It did a great deal for the improvement of slavery, since many were employee by priests or bishops. Later on if there was no other advantage, they coul at least buy their freedom. However, it would be a mistake to think that th Catholic church was the exponent of the abolition of slavery. In 1256 slaver was first made legal. But, slavery disappeared simply because it becam uneconomical. The teaching of the Catholic church however was in the lin for bettering the conditions or modifying their conditions.

6.   Attitude of Christianity to trade and industry, which will be discusse in next lecture.

A great many writers have argued and some have placed Jesus amon communists on the basis of his utterances as: "To leave the family and to leav the property and go after him .. ." The first Christians in Jerusalem were indee communists. "They that believed worked together and had all things i common ..." Attention also is called to Assinians the other communist sects Society in the time of Jesus was classified into four classes:

1.   Assinians who did not fight—ascetics, idealists.
2.   Pharisees who formed the bulk of the population and who were willin to fight and who were misunderstood.
3.   Zealots who were the more extreme on the one side while the Pharisee were the hard-headed enthusiastics on the other.
4.   Sadducees, small group of priests who controlled things.

Views of early Christians have been discussed, and the following should b emphasized: In the first place when we look to the references of Jesus himsel what he is objecting to is not the rich but the unworthy rich and his whol view is rather directed to the lack of idealism and morality irrespective o whether they have anything or not, as evidenced by the emphasis that he put upon voluntary abnegation, to the almsgiving, etc.

The argument that the early Christians were communists is true, but it mus be remembered that these early Christians were very poor people—peopl without any property. It is of course natural in such classes that such idea should arise, but as soon as new Christian communities started and whe

Christianity was introduced gradually into Antioch, Rome, etc., you do not find communism. Paul recognized private property. The argument as being essentially the communistic ideas of these sects is true but from the very beginning these were regarded as heterodox and they were opposed. It was more than 20 years after Christ's death that John opposed the agnostics; and they were opposed by everyone of the church fathers. In the 5th century they were opposed by St. Augustine. Simply because there were communist sects at that time among Christians we cannot come to the conclusion that the early Christians were communists. Another argument is advanced that when you are dealing with the patristic writers there you find nothing but communism. Who were these fathers? Turtillon 150, Cyprian, next century, Clemens from Alexandria and Oregens from Egypt, they all wrote in 200. Later on in the century came Lactincis, and Basil from Ceseria, Gregory from Nice, and Arosoten from Constantinople, add to these Jerome. Ambrose from Milan and Theodoricus, who died 450. Augustine about 430. This patristic literature has never been studied in English. There is a book but it is in German. It is written by Seiple, Chancellor of Austria now. The title of the book is "The Economic Doctrines of the Fathers of the Church." His idea of the church was communistic. Nitti in his book of Catholic socialism was translated to English so all American and English adapted that idea. In Belgium, his book on socialism is translated into English. Let us take some of the passages, as for instance the famous passage of Clement: "In strict justice everything should belong to all, inequity alone has created private property." Ambrose: "It is the order of nature that land should be in common and that all should have equal right to everything nature decrees, common property, usurpation has decreed private property. The saddest of all things is private property. Naked we come from the womb of our mother, naked we shall turn to mother earth, mine or thine are vain words."

If you take the book of O'Brien you find that he alludes to these so-called communist fathers under four heads:

1. In certain writers, the abandonment of all earthly possessions as a council of perfection.
2. Where alms-giving is highly praised and where the faithful loyal Christian exercises the charity that difference between rich and poor is eliminated. The emphasis is put upon charity.
3. Passages directed against avarice and wrongful acquisition of wealth as tainted wealth.
4. They almost always distinguish between the natural law and the positive law, the common law against the private property. So that it may safely be said that some way or other the early church was essentially communist is wrong. Of course every time when there is a great social movement you do find that the experimenters emphasize these ideas of divine law, natural law, common

property. Orthodox doctrine was the doctrine of church emphasizing the need of spiritual life and obliging all rich men to look upon poor men as their brother. So that doctrine of church fathers on private property is by no means radica

When we consider the teachings of church fathers on general economics an trade we find that their idea can be put very much like this: To buy cheap an sell dear, if that is any thing good. Jerome objects trade, he says, after all wha is advantage of trade? One man loses the other gains. Here again as in the opposition especially against usury, we find that they not so much lay dow economic doctrine but rather emphasize the spiritualistic ideas as over again earthly things.

After the Roman Empire went into pieces the Teutonic civilization starte from the bottom with an agricultural community, just as the Soviet Governmer of today. From 5th to 10th century you simply find the survival of the Roma Agricultural system and what little was left. In 12th century when towns showe themselves, the writers and thinkers had to take some definite attitude towar these new economic forces in trade and in commerce as seen in Florence, an finally legislation became necessary for protection. We thus come to Media val literature from 12, 13 to 15 and 16th centuries. It is true that in the "Dar Ages" we have not a single book. Yet there were hundreds of books writte We only have very few, like Jourdain, Stincy in Germany. We have very littl literature in English. Their views were arranged according to topics as valu usury, price, money. We have the literature from the following sources: Th Theologians, Canonist and Jurists. Theologians were moralists who had to dea with confessions from day to day which sometimes were of economic characte Canonists were dealing with canon law and had to interpret these things. Jurist the lay writers were dealing with the attempt of ordinary man to make his living

Section 7.   The Literature of the Thirteenth to the Sixteenth Century

Among the theologians were Alexander of Hale's, 1245; Albert the Grea who died in 1280; Thomas Aquinas, died 1274. Three or four others– Raymond Bonaventure, Henry of Ghent, who wrote a special work on trad In England John of Salisbury, and Richard of London. Two importar canonists—Goffroden and Dura died at the end of the century. In 14th centur there were not so many. The theologians discussed these problems in the "Summas." Among the other writers are Buridain of Paris, who is still livin In the 15th century, as this is a very important and active century, a great man books were written on various economic problems: Archbishop Anthony Florence and Bernard of Sina; in Germany John Nider, Thomas Vio. Amon the canonists the Lorentins of Rudolph wrote on usury. Among the leg writers, are Paul Gastro and Desias. In the 16th century when we come to th period of humanism there were still few survivals of mediæval writers. In Spai eologist and moralist Iotis Moline, German Azorus and Dutch Lescus. Most these writers wrote books on justice. Italian writers: Stracca and Scaccia, erman writers Marquad, Ralph of Turi.

Why and how did this literature come about? There were really two causes: irst, the basic explanation is the awakening of trade and commerce. With e beginning of the towns at the end of 12th century and with the development so of industry and machinery, trade and commerce, and first banks now gan in Italy. Hence the importance of capital. This period also marked with e development of art, architecture and building of cathedrals. A change took ace from primitive agricultural system to the infilteration [sic] of trade and mmercial spirit. In the second place the new trade acquired not alone a new agnetism but also a new law and new literature. It was at this time that schools jurisprudence started and in Bologna especially you find growing conflict tween law and theology. The whole religious movement was dominated by e question of hereafter and there was a great contest at one time, and the estion was, Who would dominate—church or state?

We will now say a few words about Thomas Aquinas. He was the greatest inker of the middle ages, born in 1226 [sic: 1225]-1274. We have very good udies on him and on his economic and political views in foreign languages. hief work of Thomas Aquinas is Summa Theologica. He wrote some mmentarism on Aristotle and above all he wrote special works on politics, vernment, and especially on usury. One sees the influence of Aristotle at e very foundation of his works. His views on private property. He thinks e whole concept of private property is superadded to natural law by reason d gives three causes, which we find in Aristotle, as to why private property rther increases continuous thrift; common property brings about confusion; d would lead to strife. He said that real economic property belongs to God. 'hat he meant by private property, is what he calls the right of using. As gard slavery he also follows Aristotle, as slavery then was just beginning to sappear. In the second place when you come to his general doctrine of dustry you find there that he looks upon the state as a self-sufficient organism d just as the state is to be self-sufficient so also the individual may be self-fficient. "It depends", Thomas says, "commerce or trade is of course to a ligious man not in a certain sense permissible, because the object of trade gain. Gain itself is not object of life, it is not honorable or useful as the aim life. Still it depends upon what you want to do with your industrial or mmercial activities and with your benefits. You may combine these things ith an aim which is in itself useful and honorable." He says for instance, uppose you are trying to earn money in order to support your wife and ildren, if that is your real aim and nothing but that, that is legitimate. But, ppose you trade to make money in order to devote your benefits to the pport of the poor, in this case one would have to be a very extreme man t to recognize the legitimacy of such an aim. Suppose that you want to devote

your efforts to public goods, that is also defensible." In other word, if you se
gain not for itself but seek it as incidental to some higher purpose it is n
illegitimate, and it may even become virtuous. In that way he finds a way o
of this difficulty, and combines the demands of religious life with exigenci
of every day existence. But there were two problems which set him thinki
especially, and these were the problems of usury and price.

As regards his doctrine of interest, his point was really misunderstood. Tl
whole theory of the Middle Ages has nothing to do either with biblic
prescription or with the Aristotelian, or Shylock merchant of Veni
explanation. The whole mediæval doctrine was a result of a very peculiar a
very difficult combination of legal and economic points of view with a ve
important social application.

We see that the Roman law makes a distinction between commoditi
according as they are fungible or unfungible. A fungible commodity might l
defined as a subject of obligation which can be paid off by turning over n
the thing itself but a similar thing. It is practically the same as we nowada
call the respective commodity, which forms our exchanges—wheat, coffee, ri
etc., are fungible things. The other distinction in Roman Law was consumptib
and unconsumptible commodities. A consumptible commodity is a commodi
the use of which consists in its very consumption and that it differs fro
commodities which instead of being used up are only used. What we are deali
with here are services. When you have this distinction between one use a
the other uses, you cannot consume it entirely by using it. Now we get to tl
point, what is gold and silver from the point of view of this distinction, fro
consumptible and unconsumptible, fungible and unfungible things?

In the first place, what is the difference between a coin and a gold vas
If some one borrows the vase, you want the same vase back, but if you borro
10 dollars, another ten dollars would be just as good. What is the proper u
of money? Money is here primarily to serve as medium of exchange and prop
use of money may therefore be declared its conception in exchange. Wh
therefore you lend any body any pieces of money the debtor pays you ba
an equivalent of money, that is all that economically and ethically can l
demanded, because when you turn over the money you are turning over
the other one the use of the money which is same as medium of exchange ar
you have no right to demand in addition to the return of the money anythi
for the use of the money, because the loan involves the use only and therefo
if you ask anything further you are asking usura, for the use which is a pri
of the use and that is equivalent to ask something over and above the thi
itself. In the asking of something over and above, and beyond something itse
therefore, we are doing something which is not right and this usura idea
a generic idea which applies to all dealings in loans and to all sort of thing
This is the fundamental basis and theory that dominated all minds witho
any question for centuries and centuries. What we call interest today, they call

ura. Usura was the price charged and not in the modern sense that we use
excessive charge. In the fourth place, we shall take up his Doctrine of
:asonable Price:—A man entering into economic doctrines he has to sell or
ty, etc. In the middle ages everything had to be worked out in detail. What
e these virtues? Is it right to buy cheap and to sell dear? The general answer
ven in the middle ages was negative.

Section 8.   Thomas Aquinas

Thomas during his discussions of any topic starts making an affirmation
d then he gives three reasons that might be used in favor of that proposition
d then gives three reasons to the contrary by quoting from some eminent
thorities. Then he goes back to argue every one of these three arguments
at he had advanced in the beginning, and in that way he gives very best
portunity possible for both side.

He makes a statement, as of the general sinfullness of trade, and gives three
asons. He says in the first place, Is it right to buy and sell for gain? In this
se one is acting like a merchant who was driven by Jesus from the temple.
the second place, that he thinks it is wrong to sell a thing for more than
u pay for it, and unjust to buy a thing for less than its worth. Now, he quotes
. Augustine. "The covetous traders curse at their loss and lie abominably."
te vice attaches not to the occupation but to the man. The conclusion therefore
ould be that if you trade for the purpose of making a gain then you are
vetous, but if you trade for other purposes, as charity, support of your wife
d children, that is very different, and he distinguishes between the gain and
st for gain. Therefore, the inference is that under certain circumstances it is
ssible and quite reasonable to buy cheap and sell dear. St. Augustine says,
you change the thing, improve the thing, and sell it for more, then you are
stified. Second, he says, if you buy a thing and keep it and sell it later on,
there no difference of time and place? There is always a risk, and something
ould be given as a reward for risk. And, in the third place, he says, a person
t only must not do wrong but he must be above suspicion.

The second argument is, Is it right to sell a thing for more than its worth?
ere you have this great view of Paul. He says, it is a natural thing for every
an to try to over-reach his neighbor, and the law does not object to this.
very body does it and certainly everybody wants to do it. Thomas says, what
common to all men must also be natural to all men. In the third place, he
ys, suppose you get a gift from a friend, you take it willingly. Now if you
rchase a thing, the seller also does not ask you to buy. But, still, says he,
de is for common advant[age;] you must trade to give and get equal values.
t there are exceptions. Suppose the buyer needs the thing very much and
ller would be injured by giving up for any less than certain amount, under
ese circumstances an additional compensation is legitimate. The third

argument is about friendship, which is a very different thing from trade
commerce. In friendship you can forget anything but in commerce it is differe
Since equality is the aim, and the object of all trade and commerce is to ma
gain, it is very doubtful as to whether it is permissible to sell a thing for mo
than its worth. Another question is, for instance, when a [man] is in busines
and the sales are held unlawful on account of some difficulty, the argume
is that if it serves to satisfy the wants of the purchaser even though there
a difficulty, why is it not right? In the second place people differ in their opinic
and also measure differs. In the third place, Who is there to tell you wheth
a thing is good or bad? Against these he quotes Ambrose. "To deviate fro
the truth in any respect is to cause injustice and to be guilty of deceit." Thi
argument is that each city government and town, must set the measure, a
as regards the export, it is said, after all a thing is bought for its use and t
qualities which fitted that thing, and properties and the qualities are eas
learned. It is therefore unlawful during a sale not to reveal the defects. Ne
question is, Is the seller bound to reveal the difficulty? The answer is that
must if the purchaser will suffer by concealing the difficulty.

Then we come to the question which soon entered into politics. Can a
one claim a higher price for credit than for cash? In general the conclusi
of Thomas is that this is illegitimate, because you are making people to p
more on account of lapse of time and time belongs to God, and as soon
you ask him to give back a payment over and above that credit, this is in oth
words a form of usury and therefore is illegitimate. This discussion leads
a question, What is a just price?

Fifth subject is the discussion on the problems of taxation: When the wa
were so frequent in those days that the prince found that ordinary sources
revenues were not sufficient he resorted to taxation. Up to that time kin
received gifts, etc., and they were beginning now to impose burdens up
subjects. The question therefore arose as to how far that was legitimate, a
the other problem that the kings of those days had to face was, Shall we ama
a treasury, or if everything else fails, can we afford to borrow? Thomas sa
when you lend money to a friend you are apt to lose both the money and frie
and when it comes to king we cannot lose the friendship of our king. Thom
wrote an essay to the Duchess of Berbezet, about the Jews. She was interest
to know whether Jews should differ or whether it was right to tax them, wheth
also it was right to sell offices. Sale of offices was considered legal and
approves of the sale, but, still, says Thomas, it is very possible that a man w
buys the office may not be just as good as the one who cannot buy the offi
He says, you should make sure of this first. The question as to what shall
do about the taxes, he says, if you have to tax there is no reason why y
should not tax Jews. But, if you have to, you can also tax the Christians, th
is if you have an extraordinary situation. He further says, a man who fig
for common welfare is justified to live at the common expense. In other wor

e duties of warriors are common duties and the state has brought them to
mmon defense. But while you have a right to tax both Jews and Christians,
•u must take from them as much as is absolutely needed for economical
ministration. He takes an idea from Aristotle, i.e., the distinction between
mulative and distributive justice—one applying to private and the other to
blic life in order to support his argument.

Let us now take up the question in the succeeding centuries. The chief
•ctrines, to show the changes that took place in the course of following
nturies, fall under four headings:

Section 9.   Mediæval Doctrine of Value

On the basis of what Thomas says the theory is worked out more elaborately
• a number of writers. In the 14th century, Buridain who was a Frenchman
•es into detail as regards the question as to what value is and how value arises.
e discusses wealth, the qualities of wealth, the bonitas, the goodness of a
ing which depends upon what you are going to do with it. Finally, he says,
e ultimate causes of the destination of all objects is to satisfy the human wants.
e calls it something supplementary to human lack of things and the means
satisfaction of what one needs. He says, the value of this supplement depends
•on the intensity of the want and that is why the utility of a thing in satisfying
ur wants is the real natural measure of all exchange. He goes on to distinguish
tween various kinds of utility. He distinguishes between proper use and the
•mmon use of utility. (We would now say the distinction between intrinsic
ility and value in exchange.) The use, he says, of a horse is the commutation
a horse, but he asks, Why do we buy horses? Simply because it is good
r riding, the common use of a horse it also may be said to sell them. Since
is is so money, therefore, is simply the intermediate. Real value, he says, is
e usus communis, and utility of a thing depends upon its usefulness. He also
scusses the question of individual utility, as over against social utility. It is
•t, he says, the want of this man and that man that fixes the value, but it
the group of people wanting these things that fixes it. Utility, he says, depends
•on intensity of demand and the want is greatly felt when the supply is scarce.
us, he looked upon this from the social rather than from the individual point
view. He says, prices don't depend upon the natural value, for then a fly
•uld be worth all the gold in the world. That the price is fixed according to
e degree of the utility which satisfies our wants and there is the whole idea
marginal utility. As for the moral question, whether it is right to pay less
•d sell for more, he also enters upon a very interesting point, i.e., how far
e whole element of price [a]ffects differences between the poor and rich, and
•hether the poor man should be compelled to pay as much as the rich man.
He points out that the rich man has money but poor man has nothing but
s labor. In order to get a commodity each man will give his surplus but the

poor man pays the smallest possible price, because he is in need of money
get other objects which he desires to secure. In the long run, he says,
equilibrium will be established between the condition of rich man and the po
man, and says the idea of resources and necessities should not be confuse
He says, there are two kinds of wants and therefore two kinds of value. Pover
in a certain sense means the feeling of a lack or of a want which a person cann
have. Now, rich man, he says, who has the money desires a thing very mu
and might not get it, he is in that sense a poor man. If poverty applies to t
absence of satisfaction in that sense there is some equilibrium between ri
who needs some expensive thing and the poor and thus an equilibrium
brought about in the market. A good many writers carry this somewhat furth
and attempt to explain further.

Bernard tells us that value depends upon three things:

1.   It depends upon what he calls vertus in the sense of goodness, its capaci
to satisfy wants.

2.   It depends upon the raritas, scarcity. He says many things of small pri
like water, nevertheless under certain condition may cost more than gold.

3.   It depends on the element. He calls placabilitas, pleasingness, or speci
attachment for a thing. So that these three elements always are to be observ
in case of price. He says, when you come to estimate the importance of tho
elements, the vertus, utility, depends upon the estimation. The question of rari
is influenced by want which is a problem of demand and supply, and whatev
is rare is dear. Furthermore, the third element in ordinary value apart fro
special attachment is what he calls the risk, the labor and the industry involv
in bringing the thing to the market. In the second place, for instance, wheat
to get wheat you have to work hard and wait a long time, the emphasis he
is laid upon the cost of production. If you take a general view of this who
mediæval doctrine of value we can get clearer idea if we remember these thing

In Aristotle it is more the demand side, the subjective view, that comes
the front and with the early church fathers more of the objective views a
considered (that the amount that is necessary for one's support). That is, write
from 12th to 15th century take a sort of middle ground but while they s
quite little of the idea of utility, in the main they emphasize more the eleme
of cost of production to support their theory of just or reasonable price. T
doctrine of reasonable price may be said from the mediæval point of view
be an amalgam for the two preceding views. When we leave this and com
to the next doctrine we find great many more practical implications.

Section 10.   Mediæval Doctrine of Usury

This is a subject on which we still lack a good book in English. When
are dealing with usury doctrine we must remember, like every other doctri

is doctrine also went through its history. First as rigid and unwielding but adual qualifications were made. Exceptions are permitted and it is found tie up the practical economic life with the rigors of really ecclesiastical ligations. Speaking of state, Thomas says, we must distinguish the views, d Council of Nicea 325, took a point entirely new, keeping up with biblical int of view, and in 12th century the councils made a general prohibition the manifest usurers. The last and this century mark the transition from e old to the new system. Peter Lambert emphasized the ancient, Alexander ale gave the new idea. Albert Great, Bonuventure and Thomas Aquinas all posed taking interest, but all put it in neutral ground, as we have already inted out. In fact the only writer who expresses real doubt as to this question Guso. The question as to how can you explain the growth of industry and mmerce in the face of absolute prohibition on all industry arose. How is possible? It is possible for agriculture, but it is not possible for trade and mmerce. The doctrine of usury was held as being one of the worst things wn to modern times. The only way to explain is to trace the history of the ctrine and to see the intelligence with which the Mediæval church treated is matter. It did exactly what the Supreme Court of the United States does day, making exceptions and distinctions. The church now began to make stinctions which were first opposed, then accepted by moderation. In the first ace let us remember that under no consideration at any time was anyone rmitted to derive any return from loan, but the first entering wedge of a ange came in through the concept of interesse—a payment that is made for an as a kind of indemnity for the interval and this concept the writers took om the Roman Code. This Doctrine of Interest had four states:

1. Doctrine known the emergent loss or injury—project being to avoid loss. other words, if one's property was less than when he would have kept it. his was really a fairly clear matter.
2. The ceasing gain doctrine—at first opposed, but after a while gradually ncessions were made in this matter. You had to prove an actual certain asing of gain. Paul de Castro said you can also apply this to a computed asing gain.
3. Doctrine of Mora—delay. Can you request compensation for delay of e money? It was said that there was a conventional doctrine and that was, u might agree on something as compensation.
4. Risk, the danger of losing your capital. Does the risk mean the risk of sing that particular thing or does it mean general risk of non-payment? eneral risk idea was not admitted at first.

So that when you take all these four things into consideration, you will get n immense literature as distinguished from usury. Finally, this was then put percentages, something approaching to the modern times. Now, there

developed the second series of exceptions or distinctions and that is knov
census, but in England came to be known rent charge and sometimes it w
called the lease. This rent charge implies the turning over from the one par
to the other of a piece of land that person in possession for use should p
the owner a certain part of the annual rent. Originally all such things had
deal with the land only but later on it developed so that it even dealt wi
an individual even if he did not turn over the land, and later on dealt wi
reserved land. In other words it was a sale and resale on conditions. Now, usu
that Henry of Ghent opposed in the 13th century, but later in 14th and 15
century it was differentiated. The question came out when a rent charge
that kind once created, Could you redeem it in some way? This doctrine
redeem went through three states: (1) Cannot redeem it. (2) The borrower cou
redeem it. (3) Later on either party could redeem or dispose of it, or sell
Finally the principle of rent charge came to be differentiated and even enter
into politics, about the beginning of 17th century.

For the growing needs of a trade these were not enough and so especial
in southern parts of Europe, in Italy, there developed in the third place tl
great doctrine of society, or society [sic], or partnership. This partnership ha
also three stages: (1) You have commenda. This had its origin in connectic
with overseeing the trade, the man who stayed at home and furnished wi
capital was called the commendator and the man who did the traveli
commendataris, the man in charge of the ship was called the practatro, mig
be the captain, owner, or temporary manager. The whole question was, Cou
you really show that the man who got the money got it at his own risk ar
the man who loaned the money really took a part in the enterprise? Th
developed, so that very soon they were called compania. When you do th
you subject yourself to the risk of unlimited liability. This developed the Joi
Stock Company, with liability limited according to the amount you put
which corresponds to our corporation. The question of usury depended upc
the question, Where is the real ownership? Usury is gain without risk, but
you let the thing go to such extent that when money is lost you lose it entire
and you have the basis of doctrine of partnership and out of this doctrine the
grew all sorts of abuses. Fourth distinction was made to provide land [sic
loans] and to open banks for the public loans. The banks became the monti
which meant collection and originally banker took in money only for deposi
The question was, Can the depositor be paid anything? When the system
forced laws [sic: loans] developed in the 14th and 15th centuries and whe
government was hard up and not able to raise money in the way of gift the
compelled rich individuals to advance certain sum with the expectation tha
they would be paid in the future. This was characterized as a free return f
loss and risk and the question was whether this free return given to the investo
as a return to his loss or risk was usury or not. But when Popes were compelle
to borrow money, this situation changed regarding this.

elopment of Usury Doctrine in the Middle Ages

During this period the theological and lay associations gradually began to
n money to the poor. This was a very interesting development. In the 15th
tury these were called Monte Profani but when you made small loans to
ividuals they were called Monte Pietatis. These public pawn shops
veloped very rapidly and paved the way for an immense development. Even
lay when you travel in France and Italy you see these Monte Pietas. This
o fell under the usury prohibition. Consequently there was an immense
olic discussion between Franciscans and Dominicans, and finally decided
it it was legitimate. In the later 15th and 16th centuries it became very
nmon to resort [to] what was known as triple contract, which became very
nmon in France and Italy. This was the combination of three separate
eements: (1) Contract of system. (2) A contract of insurance for the return
the capital, and (3) A contract of insurance against the loss of benefit. This
s called a sale of uncertain against the certain.

Section 11.   Mediæval Doctrine of Reasonable Price

Now we get at a point where certain things were accepted [sic?] from the
neral rule, but the general rule seemed to be all-embracing rule and these
re all exceptions. When the bills of exchange developed in the latter days
: question arose as to how far the usury laws was [sic] evaded in inland
change, foreign exchange, single exchange and double exchange, and what
call today accommodation bills. These matters were all hotly discussed and
was only toward that very end of the period that the idea was put forward
at after all a line of cleavage might be found, so that what is moderate was
itimate and what is abnormal was illegitimate. In England and very
dually elsewhere the development of the distinction between normal and
gitimate is interesting. It was considered that interest was moderate payment
d usury was the immoderate charge.
During reign of Charles II, a bill was introduced to prohibit excessive usury.
hat brought about this change? The fundamental explanation is the growth
capital, the growth and development of commerce and needs of business
der large scale. But hand in hand with that went the influence of the
eformation and especially of Puritanism. (This fact has been made familiar
us by R. H. Tawney.) They made us realize that Puritanism in its wider
pect was a social and economic movement, and that it was much more of
Jewish than Catholic system. One of the causes for that modern obsession
the whole Mediæval usury doctrine is generally traced back to Calvin.
What happened is that Calvin at that time (1564) was asked as to what he
ought of usury. Calvin did not take opposition, but he made certain
servations which may be interpreted as being a very much more hesitating

attitude. He stated that after all it is a childish thing to play with God a
that a great many aspects of the more important character must be obser
if you lend money to a man who needs it very much. There is no reason w
you should not ask him to pay for it, if you lend money to a buyer and
you are sure that the borrower is using it for producing something. But ev
then, says Calvin, it is better not to go into this business as a means
livelihood. Finally, most of the Reformers said, after all the lending mor
at interest must be considered imperfection, but man being weak, nothing e
could be expected and from that time on this movement grew up rapidly. T
spread into some Catholic writings, and De Moulin wrote a book, who we
further than Calvin. He opposed the whole theory of usury as a theory a
his point is that Mediæval writers were all wrong ... Then, Bacon came alo
in England. He says, it is better to mitigate than to believe in connivance.
the 17th century, German writers took it up and in the 18th century Holla
took the matter. Perhaps the greatest of the Dutch writers are Salmazi
Soumaise. He wrote a great many books on the subject, but it took Benth
to finally clear up the ground. Bentham says, capital must be free to ma
trade, and Turgot in France said, the same thing. So that by the 18th cent
the whole doctrine of usury was gone and all usury laws were consider
illegitimate.

Development in England

England was sort of backwater. France at that time was the center of
civilization, so that everything came to England much later. End of 16th cent
you still find in England the mediæval doctrine fully developed. Blacksto
wrote a book, entitled "Death of Usury." The strongest opponent of usu
doctrine is the book of Wilson, "A Description on Usury" (pages 289-29
There were four stages in the history of the usury doctrine:

1. So-called prohibition of all loans at interest.
2. The economic or Mediæval objection to a certain gain.
3. The distinction between legitimate and illegitimate rates.
4. Modern Stage. Bentham and Turgot, where the idea of freedom
   applied to the loaning of capital as well as to anything else.

One reason we keep our usury laws is that Bentham and Turgot doctrin
assume free competition and free competition assumes universal knowled
and intelligence. When a corner storekeeper lends to the ignorant negro farm
the fundamental conditions of the competitive theory are found lacking her
When there is any very evident lack of correlation between the two part
then freedom must be restricted and excessive rate of interest is to be frown
upon, and it is only partly because this idea still is prevailing in the agricultur

ates in this country, which is responsible for the retention of the usury laws n our statute books. You must consider the condition of the times as a basis f an economic theory. This worked out well for the protection of the gricultural community which was gradually fighting its way against the ommercial trading adroit capitalist class.

Section 12.   Mediæval Doctrine of Money

This is also a very interesting development for two reasons. Money in the arly Middle Ages was used as a lucrative prerogative of the prince and kings s the right of coinage was given to the rulers and the only way they could ake money was by debasing it. That was one thing. The attempt therefore f those moral reformers was to stem the tide of these governmental abuses, nd on the other hand there came the effort to understand what was going n, just as in the question of interest you find from what point of view it ought o be discussed regarding its nature. In the beginning of the doctrine of Thomas, e question was what is money: Is it a commodity or is it something that easures the value of other things? It was not until the 14th century that this uestion was taken up really in a very broad way, by a famous church uthority—Oresme, (1382), who wrote, "Origin, Natural Law and Changes of Ioney." And, his attention was directed to the situation created by the fact at in one day just before he wrote his book the current coin had been changed l times in value and that in one year 1360, on an average it had changed 7 times in value a day, and the maximum and minimum range was between .75 francs and 13.50 francs. And the chief offender was John le Bon. This ook is famous, but its fame is a little bit exaggerated because other men had iscussed the question before he had. Buridan also wrote a 700 page book on Iediæval theory of money.

There were three classes of writers who discussed the problem of money uring the Middle Ages. They were as follows:

1.   Canonist Writers. We find that they emphasized the fact that the bullion alue should be equivalent to money value, which of course would prevent e kings from having any revenue from coinage but they said that the prince ould make little gain, and whatever changes were made by king should be ade by the consent of the people. They also began speaking of excessive umbers of frauds, and so forth.

2.   Legist Writers. They discussed the question that the money should be onsidered as commodity rather than a sign, and the legal value must conform o the intrinsic value. Now began inquiry on the reasonable and just weight f money and they discussed false money or adulterated money. The legal riters were not concerned to uphold or to take away this money right from e feudal right of the king.

3.   Aristotelian Writers. His doctrine of money as a value and as a sig was taken up and they discussed how far public consent should be necessar for changes of this kind. Money after all, they said, being a public standar belongs to the community and not to the king and all money must have fiv attributes: (a) Material, (b) Weight, (c) Form, (d) Denomination, (Proportion or use. As regards the fourth, Oresme discusses in his book i Chapter 4, the matter of new money and old money, counterfeit and re money, really good and inferior money. Second point he discusses is th proportion of metal. Here we find the first discussion of bimetallism and peop were very much perplexed about this new idea. Oresme therefore was the fir one to discuss this question of bimetallism. He thinks that gold coin has mo natural value but that the legal value ought to follow the natural value of silv and gold. And he discusses in Chapter 10 the influence of output of preciou metal to their value in denominations, which he says ought to be accuratel fixed to prevent any confusion. The weight of gold and silver should be ju as to measures and weights. Finally he discusses the material, as to wheth in some cases you need a little more alloy. In Chapter 20, you find the beginnin of Gresham's Law—bad money drives out good money. Summing up: still i the main it is right to say that Oresme was the first to make a scientific stud of money problem. His influence was quite considerable in later year especially in Germany and in Italy, and we find from the 15th century on th protest against what came to be called in Germany "numerical disease." Th protest became pronounced when an astronomer, Copernicus published a boo in which he comes to the same conclusion as Oresme. So that, by the end Middle Ages theologists and other writers came to a definite conclusion to what money was and what money ought to be. But the relation of mone and price was not taken up as yet.

One more question which affected more than anything else was that whic led up to the problem of reasonable price. The question was not so very differe from what it is today in any particular aspects. In the Middle Ages there w no competition, they did not know what competition was and therefore th problem was how to protect the ordinary man—in view of the fact tha everybody tries to be monopolist. This led the very earliest writers, as Thom and Albert, to speak about reciprocity—that they must be equitable, they mu be in accordance with some kind of proportion as objective equality impossible. They said, what we have to deal with is the market price. Wh is going to fix this market price? Some of them called attention to the influenc of demand and supply and some of them to the cost of production. They sai there should be reasonable price for the consumer and also for the one wh sells these things. Henry Languirtein was one of the writers in France an Gerson was another; in Germany there was Biel. The problem is what real fixes the price and what is the just price. They argued that there were thre ys in which one must try to fix the price—they all agreed to this. Roman w was not at all satisfactory to Mediæval writers, because Roman law was ted to a very advanced community, but this Mediæval civilization was a fferent one. One of the considerations was that custom and tradition must followed. If a thing is sold customarily at a certain price, the presumption s that it was all right, but any deviation from the customary price was gitimate. Second was the agreement between the parties. This must be a e agreement which must not differ too much from a consideration of what fair to both sides. That is, where the writers cannot tell what consumer can y and what producer can afford to sell it for, they leave it to government fix this price which must be reasonable to all parties. The conclusion is, at the government has the right and duty to fix the price which will be between e minimum and the maximum. The Mediæval attitude was a huge economic mmercial design to bring about what was just and fair. No room was left r free market and competition.

Section 13.   Connection between Mediæval Doctrines and Economic Institutions

Summary.—Mediæval theory was a different kind of theory from our odern theory. This theory was, what ought to be? Our theory is, What is? nother thing to remember is that the whole Mediæval environment was one at might be summed up to be one for an isolated community—one which ill has barter economy, and economy of gain in a later stage. It was therefore ther an agricultural community which was rather of an undeveloped kind, r it was a community which dealt chiefly with small trade rather than holesale trade. Of course there were certain transactions which were wholesale character but they were exceptions. So far as industry was concerned it was ominated by a guild system which means absence of capital. The only fference between guild and primitive life was that under guild systems you ave only one class to produce and another class to consume, and the whole roduction was in the hands of the guilds. There were two very important roblems in the Middle Ages: (1) They did not know capital in the modern nse. (2) Usury and money doctrine. How was it possible for an economic fe to go on in the presence of laws against taking interest and also with the ebasement of money? The word capital is indeed occasionally met with in e Mediæval writers. They used the word capital, but what they meant was sum of money for the use of which a return is illegally granted. They did ot get to the idea of capital as a fund. Also, they used the word capital, but he thing itself did not exist. They had money and gradually utilized it in ommerce and trade, but even then it was not very important as most ransactions were done in retail. It may be said therefore that the word is not sed as in our conception in the modern sense. It is wonderful and in the second

place, it is puzzling to know how business could go on with all the
prohibitions against interest, etc. However, big men always got along, but on
the small men suffered. Great business men kept their account by artificial term
of money, which was translated into common coin at the end of the transactio
When you sum up the whole period of eleven to sixteenth century, called "Dar
Ages", we now know that it was a period of gradual progress and transitio
economically and socially. This was not a rigid change but it was a gradu
change, starting from a primitive agricultural community into which capit
for the first time came rapidly. The theoretical writers confronted the questic
that the people were concerned with as to how the individual and tl
government shall act in relation to these economic phenomena.

BOOK III.   THE MERCANTILISTS

Section 14.   The Transition in the Sixteenth Century

This is summed under the Renaissance and Reformation. If you sum u
the economic phenomena you will find the development of sea voyages an
the effort to find a way to get to India and Spice Islands, now that the Turl
had conquered Constantinople and had prevented the use of that route. A
a result of this series of sea voyages there took place exploration and discove
and the colonial system also began, at first by Portugal, then Spain, and the
other countries followed. Some acquired economic and political machinery an
developed the colonial system.

Two things happened as a result of the development of the colonial systen

1.   Sea voyages brought back from India not alone commoditi
themselves, as spices, etc., but also an immense amount of profit was heape
up on these old sea voyages and this accumulated capital was soon ready t
go into the other forms of enterprise.

2.   The discovery of silver in Mexico started another great movement. A
a result, within a few decades the existing stocks of precious metal wer
multiplied, the price levels change and this caused a record jolting of Europea
communities out of its [sic] settled ways. Then, as a result also of thes
conditions, you find the beginnings of both wholesale trade and more especiall
of the competitive spirit taking the place of mediæval customs or traditior
and hand in hand with that there came a great change in all forms of productio
in industry and agriculture. In industry the situation had been one c
predominance of the guild system as the same man was in control of the whol
operation from raw material to the sale of products. The guilds decayed o
account of the introduction of capital—and we find the first vestiges c
democratic system at this time. The system where the capitalist got contr

f raw material, retained the control of the finished product, selling it at holesale rates. The workmen were independent in working up the raw aterials at home into a finished product. Capital, in other words, now, comes to enterprise. In the same way we find introduction of capital into agriculture ith the development of the original village economy, which marks the whole liddle Ages. Now, in certain countries it became far more important to try • raise either wheat or wool for the foreign market, which led to the breakdown f the whole mediæval system of agriculture. All these things taken together ad much more important repercussions in the sense that it prepared the men's inds for the emergence of a national in the place of local organization. These eutral trades and industrial conditions required for their production things at were not found in the towns and cities and these were no longer united gether. In the colonies also we find the beginnings of national life and the reaking down of feudalism and introduction of absolute monarchy.

As a result of these changes several things happened. The whole period nown as mediæval times, which was distinctly theological, distinctly ethical nd individualistic, now began to become anachronistic. The usury system, le usury laws proved to be drawbacks to a new trading community taking le place of the agricultural community. The geographical distribution and the isurance to these forms of economic life led people to think less of heaven nd more of earth and the regime of theology became more and more restricted. ut, above all, the whole emphasis was now being shifted from the welfare f the individual to welfare of society—to moral welfare. It shifted to a newer onception, the conception of national wealth—not as an individual henomenon, but as social phenomena.

As soon as you get into the minds of men who lay the foundation of economic nderstanding, that this is simply an economic phase of the awakening of tellectual life of what we call Renaissance, they see how this period was onnected with the awakening of economic life. What we call Reformation 'as very much associated with this, and we see how one breeds into the other, nd what seems to be a purely religious spiritual field was mixed up with conomic and social field. We do know that the Middle Ages came to an end nd gave way to what we call modern times.

A good deal has been told us by historians about the mercantilists. We aven't a good book to explain this. A few points have usually been neglected > which I want to call attention. At least eight phases of the economic and ocial transitions have a distinct bearing upon our whole field, which is the evelopment of economic thought.

1.   Humanism. Erasmus (1467 [sic: 1466]-1536). The greatest Humanist. He 'as followed about the same time by another in Germany. I should say that here would be some doubt that it marks the separation of wealth from the

whole moral asceticism. The new idea is to consider wealth in itself and ;
legitimacy of material development as such, as we find it in the modern fisc
system of taxation. Humanism therefore emancipated economic life in a certa
sense.

2. Reformation. When we speak of Reformation we always think first
Luther. He believed in many things that Catholics believed. He published
great many sermons and treatises on economic subjects. In 1524 he wrote
separate book on trade and usury, and he discloses his great opposition again
trading companies and business. He says this is different from what Abraha
did. He thinks profits are bad things, as he says merchants get so big that th
can buy whole cities. He discusses just price. As to usury he says, devil invent
it and Pope gave sanction to it. In 1525 the Peasants Rebellion was consider
as a democratic message of brotherhood of man. Luther was in favor of th
idea. He called attention to the rapacity of merchant but when it came
outbreak itself, Luther wrote his exhortation to peace. Spoke of merchan
as hogs, and peasants thieves. He says, after all is it not true that an ass mu
be beaten by his master? Then the advanced reformers went a step furthe
as Calvin. So that when to all these things you add the consideration, name
the essential sympathy between Puritanism and Reformers on the one ha
and trade and capitalism on the other, you see a transition.

3. The Radical Movement in Economic and Social Life. The Radic
movement goes back to an earlier period in England. In the 14th century yc
find a discussion, how far private property among the priests is permissib
Wickliffe is sometimes represented as a complete communist. (Book of Poo
Illustrated of Mediæval Thought) Hernshaw, Social and Political Idea
Middle Ages. Wickliffe's idea is that the only title of private property
righteousness. Unrighteous men also unrighteous clergymen did not have rig
to private property. In the ideal scheme of things there ought to be no su
thing as private property, but this was not possible, unless everybody else w
ideal, while in economics theoretically it is so but differs when it comes
practice. It was his theory, however, that served as a basis for the theoretic
and practical men of that time. These radicals that resuscitated these earli
views on the Continent were, Sebastians, Neighbor Right Laws of Bohemi
The radicals had frightened Europe as much as Russia did for the past fe
years.

4. Utopians. They attempted to work upon men's minds by making the
think. First writer was Thomas More. His book was published in 1560. H
book was translated into every language of the world. Utopia started by calli
attention on some of the economic abuses of every day life of the unemploye
men and to the characteristic features of farming situation. Says, these existir
conditions are very bad and the whole order is made to check the limitatic
of wealth. The plan is that everybody works in Utopia, chiefly in farming, b
nobody works more than 6 hours a day, and all menial work is done by slav

d criminals. The consumer at large must content himself by simple things. uxuries are considered bad in Utopia. Grown-ups must be far behind dorning themselves and that is done only by children. Gold is used only to ake potteries or pay the mercenaries. In no town there should be more than 000, and no family should have more than 16 children. Every house will have garden around it, and the priest ought to be married. Another book was ritten by Hall, entitled "This and Other World." Francis Bacon wrote the ew Atlantis. Campanella wrote The City of the Sun. In his book he has the orking days only 4 hours. Then came Harrington, with his Oceana. There ere great many writers on this subject, and all these things prepared the way r further development.

5. Conditions of Trade: Foreign Trade and Exchange. The situation in ngland in 15th and 16th centuries was that everything, especially in those ays, centered around the question of precious metals and money supply and verybody was interested in preventing the exportation of gold and in order • do this they introduced methods, and these mediæval methods were of arious kinds. The chief question was to try to facilitate the coming in of the ullion and try to prevent its export. In order to do this they had the following heme:

(1) Staple towns.
(2) Institution of the Mint to prevent export, and to do this they had
    (a) Statute of employment
    (b) Searchers and exchangers.

Staple Towns. The word staple means to heap up, or those things that were eaped up. Staple commodities in England were wool, hides and leather, tin nd lead, and Courts were appointed to deal with these commodities in the esired way. The English Kings picked out certain cities in their French ossessions to act as staple towns. It was not until the middle of the 14th century 1at Calais was selected for this purpose. In this town there were staplers, amely, Mayor and the other officers, and they looked to it that when staple ommodities were sold that it should be paid for at once in good silver, or old. And, then, of course came the question of money. These metals were t once taken to the second institution, the mint, and in the mint the gold was onverted into English coin and sent to England. Now the question is, How re you going to keep it there? Statute of employment law of 1477 was passed hich provided that all moneys received by foreign merchants shall be mployed upon the commodities in the country. There were searchers of the ustoms who searched every foreigner to find out whether he carried away any oney with him. Finally there was the royal exchanger. Another question was, low should international debts be met? In the presence of this system it was ot easy to balance your account. Royal Exchanger's duty was to issue bill f exchange and see that gold is not exported but payment made by commodities. Under Edward III, the Royal Exchanger was created and liste in England until after the time of Charles I. In the 16th century, around 155 this question was very much discussed, and it was a very difficult thing t understand. Sir Thomas Gresham understood this matter and wrote a grea many reports about it and in 1560 he outlined it in few words in what is know as the Gresham's Law: "Bad money drives out the good." This system we ca the bullionist system, which was referred to in some of the earliest writers [sic on the subject. In England in 1530 Armstrong wrote a treatise concerning th staplers, which gives very valuable information on this system.

6. The Problem of Money. Money and the Level of Prices. Following th discovery of America, Europe was flooded with silver and on account of th prices went enormously high. Not only the debasement of money resulted bu also the increase of prices which could not be explained at first. Now you fin all manners of discussions, especially in Germany you find series of writing on this topic.

7. Agricultural Conditions, Husbandry. Now, writers began to pa attention to these questions. The first book was written in 16th century, the a few years later came a whole series of writers dealing with these problem: A book was published on "One Hundred Points of Good Husbandry." The came another book "500 Points of Husbandry", and etc.

8. Social Problems. Sixteenth century is marked by a very great intere taken in social development of the Nations. J. Latimer preached before Edwar IV and called attention to the difficulty, and abuses of the day. Latimer wa a great social leader and he was followed by great many writers, Simon Fisl Brinklow and Crowley.

Section 15.   The Leading Principles of Mercantilist System

There is no good book on this subject. First, what does the word itself mear The name has been made familiar to us by Adam Smith contrasting th Mercantilists with Physiocrats. One of the French writers used this word severa decades before Adam Smith. The term Colbertism as used in Franc corresponds to this term mercantilists. It was only in the 19th century tha the name mercantilists have [sic] become popular. The leading principles c mercantilism can be put in four categories:

1. The balance of power idea. What was that? This can best be describe by referring to work of English writer, Harrington, who wrote a book on th Commonwealth. He calls attention to the fact that the word balance is use in several senses: (a) Balance may mean an instrument for weighing, (b) Ma mean deficit, (c) May mean equipoise. We may consider the political situatio in the light of economic facts, and one can always tell the form of governmer from its economic balance sheet, or where land has certain importance, o

*i*ere trade is in the lead, as we see in Gothic, Aristocratic, or Nomadic *i*vernments. He explains these terms and also distribution of wealth, says *i*vernment follows this kind of balance. He says, the great object of all *i*tesmen in Europe is to prevent war, to make progress of all countries and *i*ep others in check which fact is looked upon as a kind of balance out that *i*gland was considered as being the pivot of the European balance. He says *i* great point in life is to keep this balance even, therefore the balance of *i*wer is important. He asks, How are you going to maintain this balance of *i*wer? He says, it is closely connected with the underlying factors of balance trade.

Mercantilists had an erroneous idea about money, they thought money was *i*alth and the only way to make a nation wealthy was to get as much money *i*o the country as possible. This idea is erroneous in a double respect: *i*llionist idea. It is not true that mercantilists thought that only money was *i*alth, but they laid great stress on money and coin. Even today we emphasize *i*is fact. What characterizes that is that you can measure the wealth of a *i*untry in terms of money supply, as they saw that prosperous nations had *i*ge amount of money. Whereas the bullionists believed in all graduated *i*ethods, the mercantilists said that there is only one way you can definitely *i* sure of abundance of gold and silver and that is by exporting more goods *i*an you import. If you export more goods you must get more money, which *i*ds to favorable balance of trade, but even this is by no means adequate to *i*plain this question. Professor Furniss wrote on "The Idea of Mercantilism *i* Labor and Population," and "The Position of Labor in a System of *i*ationalism." He has four points developed in this book. (1) Emphasis put *i*on the importance of working up the raw material in the country to secure *i*is favorable balance of trade—more workingmen, more production. (2) *i*nphasis upon large Population. (3) Connection between unemployment and *i*ck of money. (4) The theory, that might be called the economy of low wages. *i*hat mercantilists were interested in was the study of national wealth from *i*e point of view of production.

In various countries riots ensued. In France in the 1560's, the immense rise prices led Baudin to take up the matter. He published in the same year the *i*mous book on the state, "De la Republic." He has a great many books on *i*onomics and also devotes a separate book to fiscal problems. Matesteroit, *i*ho had become famous, attempted to give explanation of high prices and *i*audin wrote replies on the paradoxes of Matesteroit, because of the rise of *i*ices. He speaks of minor and major causes. Minor causes were: (1) *i*onopolies and grants of merchants, (2) penury, (3) ease with which all sorts *i*commodities and necessaries were exported, (4) high prices that the countries *i*d to spend, (5) undue luxury of the day, the changes in the value of money, *i*t [about; type illegible] all the increasing quantity of silver and gold. This *i* says, is the principle and almost the sole reason, and he calls attention to

the idea of banks. In England there was published a little before that a mc
fascinating work entitled the "Commonweal" in 1551. Pages 51, 128, 63, e

Section 17.   The English Controversy on Monopolies

Toward the end of 16th century great voyagers not only made their voyag
but wrote books. Sir Walter Raleigh wrote a book in which he calls attenti«
to the prosperity of England's rival Holland. The English writers tried to fi»
the secret of Holland's prosperity which they said was chiefly due to freedo
of industry. This led to a very interesting development because at this tir
there was a double movement going on in England: On the one hand car
the efforts of merchants' adventures and on the other hand was the Han»
merchants. Both of these institutions tried to maintain the trade especially wi
the East Indies. This was opposed by Mills, who called himself a custom
officer. He wrote his book in 1681, entitled, "A Customs Apology." His attac
were met by Wheeler who wrote a book, which he calls, "A Treatise
Commerce." He defends by this treatise merchant adventurers and also defin
the monopoly and further maintains that they did not have monopoly. At th
time there was a great movement to get a charter for the East India Compar
and the report of committee on free trade maintained that the natural rig
of every man to participate in trade should not be violated.

Section 18.   Balance of Bargain vs. Balance of Trade

There was a theoretical discussion of Balance of Bargain and balance
trade. This was a discussion on the merits of the whole system of the bullioni
as compared with a mutual system which did not yet have a name. The ch
writer of the whole doctrine was Malynes, who was a Dutchman and had co»
to England. Malynes wrote a number of works in the beginning of the centu»
and maintained all the fundamental principles of bullionist system. F
instance, he wrote a treatise in 1601, on "Cancer of the English Governmen»
He used in this treatise for the first time the term of over-balance of goo«
Over-balancing, he said, drives away the precious metals. In 1601, he publish
his State Budget in England. He says, "The Dragon now is the usury." In 16(
published, his "England's Few Unmasking Paradoxes of Baudin." For a deca
the situation was little better, but 1612-1615 things had come to a crisis
connection with the trade with East Indies. This led to a bitter attack on t
policy of the company in exporting bullion. Digges, who was one of t
directors of East India Company, defended the trade in general and tried
work out a theory. His theory was that it was not the prohibition of exp«
of coin, but rather export and import of commodities[,] that the situation cou
be met and the coin would take care of itself. Following this, two or thr
years later there were exchange of opinions between Malynes and Misselde

ix or eight books were written about the matter at issue and this represents
ne of the most interesting explanations of economic differences of opinion
f the day. Malynes had published a book, entitled Merchants Law. Misselden
rote a book to take issue with him. This led to some more books. Misselden
rote "The Circle of Commerce," and Malynes answered it by his book entitled,
The Centre of the Circle." There were at this time two opposing views, and
ese were bullionist and mercantilist arguments. This led to first real economic
ntroversy and which marked the dying of bullionist doctrine and beginning
f mercantilist.

Section 19.   The Founders: Thomas Mun

He is called father of mercantilism, which he was not, as the same doctrine
as very much more expounded in Italy before his time. His reputation arose
hen earlier writers were not known. "England's Treasury [sic] by Foreign
rade," is a book by Thomas Mun. He was director of the company. In 1628
 wrote a book entitled "A Partition and Remonstrance," but this book was
t published until 1664. He said, balance of our foreign trade is the rule of
ur treasure. He takes one by one all of the 144 doctrines of older bullionist
stem and shows how utterly useless they are. He says, real philosophy of
nation consists in having so much industry at home that you will export
ore goods than you will import, especially goods of thrifty kind to which
ale had referred. We can easily see therefore that Mun was one of the leading
riters of his time. Furthermore, he was a practical business man with a sense
' generalization and could put his ideas into good English.
Serra, an Italian writer, who wrote in 1615, must be credited for the
ercantilist doctrine. He had the same controversy in Naples as Baudin had
France. His work was a brief treatise on the causes of the abundance of
ld and silver. He wrote this book while in prison, and he discusses money
om three points of view. He has great deal to say about natural and artificial
ealth, and points out that the foundation of economic prosperity is the natural
ealth, as agriculture, etc. Then he has a book on the Liberty of trade in which
 says: It is not possible that any of the objectives sought to be attained are
ally of no use and that the rate of exchange far from being, as bullionists
aintained, the cause of the export of precious metals, is really the result. He
mes therefore to the great theory of freedom of trade. As absolute monarchy
as a step forward from anarchy and feudalism, so mercantilism was a step
rward from bullionism to freedom of trade. He says there is only one way
 increase the national wealth, that is to foster industry, so that this doctrine
 fostering of the industry depends upon the keeping out of the unthrifty
mmodities also finished products which may compete with the domestic
dustry. The mercantilists emphasize the need of free importation of raw
aterial, of free exports of gold and silver but of restricted importation of

manufactured commodities. Thus the whole theory of national wealth is o
of the assumption that in order to develop your industry at home you mu
have low wages, low cost and keeping out of the finished foreign commoditi
So that mercantilism while it marks an advance over bullionism both in theo
and practice at that time also serves as the intellectual basis of a ne
nationalism, just as the war a few years ago is sometimes ascribed to the ne
mercantilism.

In France we find two men: During the time of Henry IV, Laffemas w
the controller general of commerce from 1602 on. He expressed in his repo
very much the same set of ideas as the other writer—Montchretien did. Tl
latter is one quoted much more frequently because he was the first one
borrow from Aristotle the term political economy. In reality he does not deser
it, as he was not a great thinker or a great man. Most of his books are nothi
but plagiarism from Baudin and also from one of the German writers. H
book is, however, interesting because he brought into the foreground the nar
of political economy. He uses the term rather in its wider sense—as
represented the influence of politics and the government upon economic li
which was the theory of mercantilists. It was during this time that so mu
was done in the way of nationalization of weights and measures.

Section 20.   Development in England—From 17th Century to the Time of Adam Smith

During the 17th century you find perhaps 4 or 5 great names, men of fi
class ability and also quite a number of able second class writers, who prepar
the way for these others in the 17th century to mark a gradual transition
these original and rather rigid mercantilist ideas in double direction: (1) In t
direction of little more elasticity, little more freedom. (2) In the direction
a growing doubt cast upon the theory of the balance of trade itself. Duri
this period (17th century) took place in England the same thing that happen
in Spain in the 16th century and also what happened in Holland with t
extension of colonial Empire. England in the 17th century was sort of ba
water. In the contest with Spain and Holland England gained at this time a
in the 18th century England gained also over France. And, in another centu
over Germany. Gradual emergence of the new ideas in England has never y
been worked out and there were a great many different phases of it. We w
mention half-a-dozen writers:

1. Maddison, who wrote his book in about 1640, and who was s
    somewhat unmentioned in bullionist doctrine. The book worked its w
    to the middle ground between Malynes and Mun, who still were gre
    advocates of the doctrine.

2. L. Roberts, wrote in 1641. He was a great merchant of East India Levant Company, who shows his interest in more liberal aspects, although he emphasizes the need of state control.
3. Henry Robinson. His work is entitled, "England's Safety in Trade's Increase." He emphasizes what Holland has done in the way of greater operations.
4. Then you find an anonymous writer, "A Discourse on Free Trade," published in 1645. A great monopoly [sic] against merchant adventurers where free trade idea is very prominent.
5. Parker, who wrote great many books of discourse on Free Trade. In one of the passages he puts the question, How far a man should freely trade?
6. Fortrey—He wrote his England's Interest in 1660. This is a book which has been recently reprinted by Professor Hollander of John Hopkins University. He has good deal to say about immigration and coinage.
7. Roger Coke, has a large book, entitled Discourse of Trade, emphasizes the example of Holland. This whole literature grew up in the first half of the century.

Other group of writers devoted their attention to what was now becoming *agland's* great interest—woolen industry. They brought to attention the *assibility* of competition of England on one hand and the whole continent the other hand. Carter and Hyde dealt with export duties of wool and *luence* of woolen trade upon prosperity of England.

We now come to men of first rank: Sir Wm. Petty. His works have been *blished* in two volumes by Professor Hubbes of Cornell. Petty was born 1623, died 1687. He was a very remarkable man in his day. He was Dr. Physics, who in addition to all other interests was also interested in *ography*. He did great deal for Ireland. He is important because he was *e* first one to develop the quantitative side of this neutral science. He was *e* man who first paid attention to statistics, bills of mortality—(Graunt— *s* observation of mortality). Petty wrote a book entitled, "Political *ithmetic*." He says: "Method I take to accomplish the works is not yet usual *erest*, the use of comparative and superlative words and intellectual *guments*. I have taken in course ... in terms of weight, measures and *mbers*." He was also responsible to [sic] a large number of other works, as *olitical* Anatomy of Ireland, A Treatise on Taxes," and many other *ntributions*. He was the first one to work out the results of taxation and had to frame certain theory of production, and wrote a book on money. *me* of the main points in his theory are: He was the first one to use the *rd* oeconomics in England. He speaks of politics and oeconomics. He had *e* idea of economics as being a science, and he laid down the process. As *gards* to value, the question, he says, is to ascertain its cause. He says it is

not gold or silver that are wealth, but the real wealth is the enterprise of t
community and the results of labor. He points out that the real cause of val
consists in labor and the problem with this, he says, is, as he put it, to g
the par between the labor and land. Labor, he says, is the father, land is t
mother and the par between land and labor is the one important problem whi
you have to settle before you can make further progress. He calls attenti
to natural price of commodities. He points out that if they [sic: there] are tv
commodities upon which the same amount of labor is expended, their pri
is referred as natural price. He has great deal to say about the influence
labor upon wealth. Then he gives a good account of fiscal situation in Engla
at that time and also gives account of the different kinds of taxes.

Petty takes very strong ground against further displacement [si
debasement] of the coin. He was also responsible for the idea in which he te
us that increase of production depends upon increase of consumption. I
developed also his doctrine of super-lucrition. He has a great deal to say abo
the practical problems of his day. Economics to him is in certain way mo
or less a natural characteristic, and for that reason it will be doing very go
justice for Petty when we call him the first scientific economist, so that he h
very great influence in succeeding times.

Child: He was a great merchant and was one of the directors of East Ind
Company and a Tory, also a very wealthy man. He was a businessman w
was able to put down his ideas clearly and put it in a book form. First bo
he wrote was "Philopatris," in which he made a great plea for freedom
exporting of gold and silver. He wrote another work, entitled, "Observati
of Trade and New Discourse of Trade." In one respect he put the cart befo
the horse. He speaks of low rate of interest being the cause of prosperity. I
points out that in Holland the rate of interest was very much lower. Low ra
of interest with him was the mother of frugality and tried to reduce the inter
rate from 10% to lower rates. He also points out the benefits of high wag
Many thought low wages meant low cost and low cost meant low export. I
says wherever wages are high throughout the country it is a sign of riches a
wherever wages are low the country is poor. He was a great advocate of hi
wages. As regards the balance of trade, Child says, there are two things enteri
in the matter, although the notion also enters in it, it will appear doubtful a
uncertain as to general trade, and particular trade is apt to be erroneous, y
cannot tell for certain whether you have the exact figures. He was the fi
writer to point out the invisible elements of the trade. Doctrine of gene
balance of trade, he says, is doubtful and the attempt to apply this doctri
to trade with any particular country is erroneous. He says, law of balance
trade is true only in general balance of trade, but is not true in particu
commodities. The real way to find out, says he, whether a country is getti
rich or not, is to see the increase and diminution of shipping. So that Ch
marks a step forward.

). North: He wrote with reference to money situation, as the condition of nage was very bad in England, but he pointed out that one must not bother iself about the supply of gold and silver, as the supply will regulate itself. says, lack of prosperity does not show lack of money and true wealth does consist of gold and silver but it consists of industry of people, then he adds— ich for all the world sounds like the most advanced view of extreme rnational free trades—the whole world would trade with nations or peoples. says, money is a merchandise and there may be too much as well as too le of it. That people cannot want money if they found industry. Money, s he, expended in trade is increase of wealth, but spent in war is so much overishment, and all favor to one trade against another is an abuse and t the real principle is to look not at the individual country but at the world a whole. He looked upon interest not as a cause but as a result, and he s one of the very first writers to look upon interest as the payment not for ney but for stock, and he pointed out that interest should be put in the ie category as the rent of land.

Nicholas Barbon: Was the last of these writers, who was unknown until of y late years. He got interested in land bank idea, certain commodities, and d. He wrote two books which are very important, from the general point view of economic theory. He describes in his writings the trade of 1690. his discourse on money in his controversy with Locke, he brings in four nts:

.   Doctrine of value, he says, not so much depends on labor but upon wants of mankind, or utility. He was first one to speak of value by virtue, and that the price of a thing depends upon virtue as well as value.

?.   His doctrine of interest is that he takes same idea as North. He says, interest is the rent of stock and it is just [as] legitimate as the rent of land.

i.   As regards trade, he says that balance of trade doctrine is wrong, gold and silver are commodities. The balance of trade, he says, depends upon the rate of exchange, different from rate of bullion.

l.   The reason why he was so little heard was because of his 4th doctrine of money. He pointed out that value of money was entirely due to law, which was contrary to the ideas of Locke.

Locke: He was primarily a political philosopher. There are two things that de him important for economics at the time. There was great trouble in ney situation in the colonies. He was also the head of plantations of ierica. His books were partly on one and partly on the other topic. In his itical philosophy he deals with the aspects of private property. He is ecially important for founding the whole labor theory of private property. says, the labor of man's body is his. How to apply this theory to land?

He says, the property in land is acquired as other properties. As much a
man improves it for use, so much is his property, by this way man makes
common property his own. This also applies for the man who does not wo
as in the case of a person who inherits the property. So, no one question
the foundation of the theory of absolute private property and Locke theref
was responsible for this. Of course, modern doctrine is different from this wh
is the social utility idea rather than the other.

Locke has a good deal to say about value, making distinction betwe
intrinsic and marketable value. Then he goes on with his theory of money
fact part of his theory of labor. Locke has made four contributions
economics:

1. Doctrine of value.
2. Doctrine of money.
3. Theory of distribution.
4. Theory of taxation.

Money: He distinguishes between the quantity of money [a]ffecting the pri
and rapidity of circulation. He was in certain sense father of quantity the
of money. He calls attention to the influence of rapidity of circulation. He sa
it depends not only on quantity but also on quickness of circulation. He bri
these doctrines into very interesting correlation. He was really the first
introduce the theory of rent and theory of interest. He tries to point out
connection between rent and interest. In his discussion of interest he
forerunner by 200 years. In his theory of taxation he marks also a new epo
He originated long before the Physiocrats the doctrine that all taxes were bo
by land. The point about Locke was that he was a commanding figure b
in political and philosophical point of view. What he said carried great wei
with [word not legible]. So that Locke by right can be considered a landm
development in the economic life. He was no less important than Newton.
was in favor with mono-metallism and was a mercantilist in that respect.
did not differ much from any of the others, and rather sided with Engl
merchants in their anxiety over the competition with colonies.

Charles Davenant: About the end of the century he wrote great deal, w
at this time England was in war. He was one of earliest writers to discuss w
and means to carry on war. It may be said that they brought the mod
conceptions from Holland, and Davenant was one of the foremost writers
discuss these problems, and on the whole he was in favor of ideas of Holla
He became the advocate of excise. Davenant was a Tory and therefore he
the main sided with mercantilists. He is still in favor with free trade with Fra
and other countries, he does not agree with Locke as regards incidence
taxation, and at times he has acquired great reputation by printing the fam
calculation of Gregory King who was important business statistician

ngland. He wrote his "Nature and Political Observation of England," and was Davenant who published with interesting comment. One of the points scussed was that prices rise in greater proportion, with more increasing oportion than supply. Altogether Davenant was a practical financier who d great deal in the way of advising government how to make both ends meet. e also wrote a book on the Balance of Trade and on General Mercantilist eory, in fact he practically held the boards for a decade or two.

Gee: He was a merchant and wrote a book on trade and navigation. This as read great deal up until the time of Adam Smith. This marks the later ews of mercantilists. This does not by any means exhaust the whole universe. nere are in addition, at least six or eight different economic fields in which uring 17th century and half of the 18th century that important works were ne.

We shall now say a few words on the question of social problems. Socialism its broader sense during the revolution started out with political revolution, d it was not long after that was followed by Levellers and by the Diggers. ey, however, finally turned economic in character. They held that private operty was illegal and then extended that general idea so as to say all property as illegal. Then came the Quackers who also exerted a considerable influence, ch as John Millins[?], Peter Chamberlain and others. On money and finance ere is very interesting development which started out with the opposition the bullionists and they took up problems connected with debasement of oney and the recoinage of 1696. This brought forth at least two or three rks. The mint report of I. Newton which appeared at this time has never en adequately studied. Banking, too, at the time is not studied. In the 17th ntury the plans culminated for land bank project, bullion project and bank England which was projected by Patterson. On the other hand there is the estion of interest dealing with its neutral phases. In the third place there s discussion about general theory of trade and you find a number of teresting writers. Yarranton, sometimes called father of political economy, ote a book and called it England's Improvement. Tryon also wrote a book trade where you find the first idea of modern conception of consumption d importance of consumption and development of standard of life. Temple o wrote a book. All these discussions were in the direction of freedom of de and modification of mercantilist ideas. John Kerry, and Roger Coke also ote several books in this same period, dealing [with] much the same estions.

Agriculture: The agronomic and agricultural problems were also discussed d what was true for second half of 17th century was much more true of st half of 18th century.

Before Adam Smith there were at least six important topics that there was thing done to study these. What were these problems?

1.   General problems of Trade: There was a controversy about the Ea
India Trade, as to whether it was good thing for land or not. The mo
important problem was the controversy over the treaty with France in 171
That is marked by scholars who took both Tory and Whig sides. A schola
who was a Tory has hundreds of pamphlets which have not been studie
Charles King has three volumes on British Merchants Point of View. Th
is on the general trade question.

2.   The Public Debt and South Sea Scheme. This debt was the war det
There is a whole lot of literature on the public affairs, and the leader w
Hutchinson.

3.   The matter of wages and poor laws; labor cost and subsistence theor
The high wages theory and low wages theory. We have these problen
discussed long before Ricardo 1718-1725.

4.   On agriculture where you have a literature which introduced all neutr
methods in France.

5.   Fiscal problems and tax problems. These discussions grew up fro
practical and everyday problems. Jonathan Swift wrote a book on separa
Coinage for Ireland, and the mercantilism of the whole time was supplemente

Section 21.   Development in France

Development of economic thought in France in 17th century and early pa
of the 18th century was marked by the abuse of fiscal system. It happen
therefore that most of the writers devoted themselves to economic proble
and attention was called to worst of abuses. It resulted in two works.

Boisguillebert, who wrote toward the end of the century a very detail
description of France in which he pointed out the situation as he found it a
attempted to call attention to some remedies. He did not agree with t
mercantilists about the importance of money and balance of trade doctri
and went so far in his criticism of that problem as to give vent to very extrei
enunciation [sic: denunciation] of money. He says, if money is not wealth
is a pledge, you must not make ideology of it, and the wrong conception
money, in fact, is going to lead you astray in your whole view of econon
life, it likely does more harm than good, instead of being slave of money tl
view makes a tyrant. He calls money a criminal thing. He suggests mc
freedom to stop preventing consumption. He says nature created liberty a
it is for mankind to conform as far as possible to these natural ideas. Sor
thought that he was a free trader, but in reality he was a very small part
that. He was only interested in creating supply and preventing famine. I
recognized the scandal of financial ways. He says, low price of wheat is wo
than high price of wheat. High price is worse for consumer but low price doul
so for farmer. What he wants to do is to try to make the lot of peasants a
farmers more satisfied in France, and says you can do it in two ways:

reedom of export and (2) Agrarian protection, in so far as the import of raw
*a*terial and food products are concerned. Summing up: We find that he was
great apostle of industrial protection, rather agrarian protectionist. He is
*i*teresting in this respect that the origin of term laissez-faire is ascribed to him.
e then discussed the whole problem of finance and pointed out the
*i*terdependence of different classes of society. His views are very similar to
*i*e man that we are now going to take up. He had great influence but on
*cc*ount of his radical views he had to escape from the government and his
*oo*k was burnt.

Vauban: He was a great soldier, he was Marshall of France. During one
f the combats he got interested in the condition of people and came to the
*o*nclusion that the situation was terrible. He wrote essays and also a book
*e*titled, The Royal Tenth. He gives a very sad picture of the existing conditions.
e says one-tenth of the people are beggars, five-tenth can pay absolutely
*o*thing. Of the remainder four-tenth, three-tenth are in bad circumstances.
i France, he says, there are not more than 10,000 people who are truly well
f. The condition in France was very much worse than that of England. He
*s*cribes the reason for the whole trouble to the fiscal situation. He says, taxes
*r*e excessive and in the second place they are absolutely unequal, as, he says,
*c*h escape and poor are made poorer. He starts out with the universality of
*a*xation. He says, the universality of taxation is desirable because it is the
*a*tural obligation of all men to contribute, and all exemptions are unjust, and
e suggests the idea of simply taking one-tenth of all proceedings, and also
*o*e-tenth of the rents of city houses and earnings of ordinary business man.
e still keeps the gabelle and the import duties. In his general economic ideas
e is still mercantilist, that is when he exaggerated the importance of gold and
*l*ver. His book was very popular because he was a prominent man. Had he
*o*t been a prominent person it would be very bad for him, as the way it was,
e was almost exiled on account of his views. This threat put a check to all
*a*tempts to further social reform in France for a certain period of time.
*E*verybody spoke about economic conditions and when the king died, it was
e embarrassment of France that now led to that remarkable episode when
a Scotch adventurer by the name of John Law made his appearance.

Law was a most engaging acumen of personality, he was not only a lady
*i*ler, but also killed many men for the ladies. Such was John Law and his
*M*ississippi Scheme. He was the cause of issuing paper money by the Mississippi
*C*ompany. People got rich overnight, the price inflated and everything crashed.
n the matter of balance of trade doctrine Law was a staunch mercantilist of
*m*ercantilists. He says, all political power depends upon wealth, all wealth
*de*pends upon population and bigger industrial prosperity, all these depend
*up*on trade and trade depends upon money. So that you must make distinction
*be*tween the intrinsic values of things and the additional values of things. Now,
*m*oney is not the value for which things are exchanged but it is the value by

which things are exchanged and the important thing in money is the addition
value conferred upon it by government. Since the real value of the money
the additional value that government can confer, this additional value can l
conferred upon other things than gold and silver. This can be done by issuin
paper money. He was not successful in Scotland but was successful in Franc
He was the first to develop the idea of credit and money. We therefore con
to his theory of credit and money. Money, he says, is in the state as bloc
is in the human body. Without circulation of the blood you die, so does tl
state. Credit, however, acts as the soul and subtle part of the blood. Mon
depends upon credit. Credit therefore is not a transaction but is an object,
thing. Since, he says, credit has almost this objective reality the granting
credit is tantamount to the creation of capital, and credit thus becomes a
additional, a separate and independent capital. This was an attempt to reali
the value of credit. But he went further than this and said credit is independe
from capital, and then he came to dangerous spot. In a loan, therefor
according to Law, it is the debtor who convenes the favor on society. He sa
the chief in a community is the king, therefore it is up to the king to conf
credit. As a result of this theory which goes to this very dangerous extrem
there developed what is known "The System." However, in Paris his syste
was dissented and there was formed Anti-system. The situation in France w
pretty bad at this time.

There was, at this time, a prominent church man, Saint Pierre. He goin
back again to the ideas of Boisguillebert and Vauban found the real troub
in the fiscal situation. He now comes forth with an entirely different kind
plan. His plan was adaption of virtue which was a suggestion of a proportion
income tax without fear or favor and without any of the exceptions whi
existed under the system of taille. In the main, however, if you take a broa
view of situation in France so far as general theory is concerned of tl
mercantilist doctrine only one or two men need be mentioned because it w
their views that represented the policy of the government.

Chief writer was Melon. He wrote his Political Essay on trade in 1734. Tl
chief point for which we have to remember Melon is his opposition to slave
when even in England this idea had not appeared. He is noted for the o
phrase. He realizes the danger of the whole "System" of Law. He says, h
Law insisted upon emphasizing the good side of public credit and if kept
certain limits he would be successful. Melon's phrase: "Public credit is real
innocuous and not dangerous, because, public debt means the debt from rig
hand to the left hand."

Dutot continued the work of Melon and he seconds the work of Melo
and apologizes for Law.

Two other men at this time dealt with economics incidentally: One w
Montesquieu and the other more eclectic writer, Forbonnais. Forbonnais w
responsible for some good economic and fiscal history both of France and

pain. Just about that time the whole economic condition was taken up by
great physician and because of his position as the body surgeon of Louis,
e had great influence. So that, as we see in France they were now getting
:ady for a new era.

Section 22.   Development in Italy, Germany and Spain

The views we have learned now in England and in France found
:presentatives in all the other countries. In Italy only two names may be
:entioned. Two very important things happened: First, Genovesi, who was
:lectic writer and who filled the first chair of developing economics and the
:her was Galiani, who was very well known and widely read writer. He wrote
:ooks on money and free trade question. He is noteworthy because he was
:e first one to emphasize the objective [sic] side of theory of value. He brings
:e idea of value of utility. The other point is that during the 18th century
:e German writers approached the whole problem from a different point of
:ew and also you find mercantilists in other countries. The wealth and welfare
f the princes depended much more largely not upon taxation but upon their
:usbanding or housing of their properties and large part of the wealth in
:ermany in the 18th century in the form of forest lands were still in the hands
f potentates. Private initiative in Germany had been killed by the 30 years
:ar. It was the religious war of the 17th century which ruined Germany more
:an anything else. The writers who began to discuss this question were most
f them practical administrators. They dealt with government property and
:id down the rules. Since the committee dealt with these they were called
:hambers, and we call them Cameralists, who did in detail so far as general
:overnment is concerned what English and French writers did for France and
ngland.

Section 23.   Criticism: About the Mercantilist System

Their theory went through three stages: (1) There was restriction, as balance
f bargain system of bullionist. (2) Balance of trade doctrine, early mercantilist
: its orthodox form. (3) Bringing in neutral ideas, invisible export, etc., which
:sulted in the classical description recently, as to how situation can best be
:presented by the term equipment of commerce. Mercantilist writers begin
om the end and approach to the other end. Invisible elements were very much
:ss important than they are today. You must remember the importance that
:oney had in those days, as to that matter it is important even today. In those
:ays you find in colonies high prices and abundant raw materials. Whereas
:e older countries had comparatively little money and prices were low. Older
:ountries thought they were in danger of disposing their commodities at these
:w prices, whereas in new countries they would get high prices. The situation

appeared to them reverse of today. Today countries with low price have a advantage. The chief point that ought to be made clear about mercantilis doctrine is that as over against the modern ideas the laying so much stres over production, and one thing seemed of most fundamental importance wa the increase of production. That is why we find so much importance attache to fishing industry and agriculture in England and above all to the growth o population. We can realize the economic basis of neutral nationalism and yo can understand why every statesman was a protagonist of mercantilist systen And, the writers attempted to explain what was going on. They did analyz this from the same point of view as we would do today. As capital becam more abundant, the conditions changed and what was more or less defensibl in the beginning of the movement and of the 16th and 17th centuries becam less and less true as they went on. The fundamental fallacies of the whol mercantilist doctrine from our point of view was their doctrine that what on country loses in trade another country wins. Nowadays, we see that bot countries may win. Still another phase must be laid stress upon. Th mercantilist theories were built on the ideas of constructive restriction, an the restrictions existed in the local economy were taken by national econom)

If you take a broad view, which is admissible in interpreting history, w would say that mercantilism really marked a great step forward to economi and political thinking, it dealt with national and social wealth. It was true o mercantilism that capitalism received more support from, and this was decided step forward to civilization. In fact mercantilism as absolutism wa a step forward to the advance of civilization. Furthermore, mercantilis separated economics from ethics. Mercantilism was not as much movemer in thought as in action. Toward the end of the period, by the middle of 18t century it had become anachronistic as every system becomes so when it come to the end. Now, in the 18th century there was a fresh wind that began to blo\ and we find that this represented the Physiocratic movement in France an the other movement initiated by Adam Smith.

BOOK IV.   THE PHYSIOCRATS

Section 24.   The Transition to Physiocracy

Most of the writers in France in 18th century might be called later mercantilist There are two writers among many which must be picked out. Economi condition in France was going from bad to worse, which led to an attempt t improve the administrative system. Gournay is spoken of as founder o physiocratic movement. He was nothing but a skilled administrator, who di not write any book at all. He wrote only memoires and he was not founder o laissez faire and laisser passer, but still he was a very liberal man. He saw th shortcomings of the guilds and in his opposition to the abuse of guilds he ha een misinterpreted. But you do find something different in D'Agenson, who was Minister of Foreign Affairs at the time. He was only known in international olitics and his journals were published after his death. He is responsible to this hrase: "To govern better you should govern least." He wrote anonymously in famous economic journal, which was translated into English in 1751.

Section 25. The Founder

Quesnay—founder of Physiocratic movement. He was brought up as a hysician, surgeon, and he later became surgeon of the king. His attention was alled to some of the sad conditions of the day. From every point of view France was in a bad condition. In the first place bureaucracy was corrupt and xtravagant; the farmer was ground down by the feudal banalite the noblemen ould compel the peasant to work for him few days a week or month. The ndustry was checked in every way by the guilds. Trade was hampered by the xport and import restrictions, and taxation was so enormous and so unequal hat everybody who had property lived in continual dread of tax collector. Quesnay started out to think over this condition and came to the conclusion hat what was needed was more capital for the farmers and more equality for hem. He then began in the 50's to write about farming wheat, later on in 1757 e met famous Mirabeau. Quesnay became great advocate of the ideas of Mirabeau, and developed great many other ideas. In 1758 Quesnay composed conomic table about the whole theory of economic production and istribution. He wrote dialogues on business and his great book on natural aw. Quesnay was the author of the terms Physiocrat, or Mercantilist. When Mirabeau published his theory of taxation in collaboration with Quesnay, Mirabeau was impressed and led Quesnay to keep quiet for 2 or 3 years. After hat he started again and at the end of 1763 he and his school dominated the whole country and they were called for the first time the "Economists."

Section 26. The Cardinal Principles

The doctrine of absolute liberty is expounded fully in his book of natural Law. He says, "There is a law of nature in the sense of physical and natural novement of star, same dominates also with morals, and this natural law has pplied to men." He defines natural law as the right to those things that are ecessary for his enjoyments. This natural right, he says, is primitive and pontaneous, it is a product of nature itself, it is not ideal but it is actual, it s universal and in this system there are two kinds of natural rights. (1) Right f property, (2) right of liberty. What are the rights of property? He divides nto three, (a) Property is something that one owns, slavery therefore is unnatural. (b) Property multiplies itself because of labor. (c) Property in land. But more important than property is the liberty. He goes on summing up what liberty consists of and says that the positive law is what to be the attempt to realize these abstract rights. He says, there are two things however. First, he still believes in usury laws as did Adam Smith and, second, in politics he think the ideal government is found in China.

How does he develop his economic doctrine? He begins with agriculture and he points out that all capital invested in agriculture has to deal of cours with the force of nature and what you could do is to put your materials in the ground and you got certain expenses attached to it, then by the action o nature upon the soil what you get out of the land is more than what you pu in, and therefore you have this net product which is a result of wise investment Now, in the case of manufacture, he says, the thing is different. You may hav in all industry a price which is higher than what you put into this and plu the wages, but this is not a surplus as it is in agriculture. In industry this highe price is due to three things: (1) Privileges enjoyed by the producers, the unjus privileges, monopolies, etc. (2) Due to economics, sometimes breaks in wages (3) and chiefly speculation. So that in the main the higher price in industria produce is something purchased at the expense of the farmer or agriculturist All trade and commerce depend upon this principle, an exchange of value fo equal values and that has two important corollaries: (1) It involves the whol mercantilist contentions. (2) It involves the barrenness of all trade an commerce and industry as over against agriculture.

He finds society divided into three classes: (1) Productive class—the farmer (2) The sterile class—useful but economically barren—workmen, etc. (3 Proprietor class—class of land owners. The basis of all he finds it to be th peasant. He says, poor peasant, poor king; poor king, poor kingdom. Thus he says, everything depends upon the prosperity of farmer. The practica conclusion is that since the net surplus exists only in the case of the soil, sinc the social income depends upon farmers' prosperity, therefore support of th community depends upon this and therefore there should be only one singl tax on this surplus of land. And, every thing else will be indirect tax. He says all indirect taxes cost more than they are worth, therefore, the solution of whol problem of the condition of France is to impose a single tax on land. Thi being his single doctrine, he works out great many ways and great man ramifications. In his table he works out by figures how this net produce is turne over to the classes and being spent by them again for commodities, which flow back to the productive class but cuts the surplus. Very much importance wa attached to this economic table, it was considered one of the 3 greates inventions.

We have called attention to the fundamental principles of Quesnay, an particularly over and above the general ones. So far as the theory of economic is concerned he has had quite a little influence, and he developed his idea about value and price. He first made familiar the distinction between usefu wealth and things which are sold, corresponding to value in use and value i xchange of Adam Smith of the commodities and wealth. The value in use eferred to wants of man whereas the value of exchange refers to market. We lso find another thing that he discusses, which is the natural price and market price, and his whole economic table dealing largely with this topic is an attempt o bring these into correspondence. Theory of population with him is much he same as Malthus. Physiocrats further opposed to mercantilists in their heory which naturally refers to population. The mercantilists over estimated he importance of great population. On the other hand he is no special pponent of the poor laws. As to theory of wages, in Quesnay, we find the ubsistence theory of wages, but he differs again from the mercantilist writers n that he wants for the sake of producer—the farmer, high prices. He says, igh prices, high wages.

Those being the general ideas of Quesnay, you can understand why in the ace of growing difficulty in France, as periodic financial difficulties and specially in view of the fiscal difficulties that he should attract great deal ttention. Whether they should have free trade in coin or wheat was important roblem in those days. In 1756 they took agricultural journal and made official rgan of the school. Young men, as well as prominent farmer scholars, got ogether during their meetings. Adam Smith spent a whole year in Paris and vent to these meetings every week, and he became very devoted to Quesnay nd other Physiocrats. In the following year they took the Daily News of the itizens and then especially his followers now began to write very freely. The nost famous were 4 or 5 young men who had fiscal ability.

Section 27.   The Followers

Mirabeau. He had written a book and who was now converted and he and Quesnay wrote a book on taxation. This book points out among many other hings, the cruelty that was evidenced by the tax collectors to common people.

De la Riviere: He wrote a book, entitled, "Natural Order of Society." He ays he wanted to make the distinction between the legislators and legisfactors. Ie became so famous that Catherine of Russia sent for him to get his advice. Ie was interested in commerce and labor. He elaborates the necessary price deas. He caused so much stir that Voltaire now wrote a little satire, entitled, The Man Before Crowns."

The next writer was Baudeau. He wrote the first introduction to economic hilosophy. In this book he calls Quesnay Confucius of Europe. He says, his oints are proven just as problems in Geometry. For the first time you find n his book the term, laissez faire, laissez passer, which was the motto of his chool. He wrote work after work in the 80's in which he emphasized the hortcomings of the whole system. He is a man who has never been adequately tudied. He was the author of at least a dozen of works, and was a very emarkable thinker.

Letrosne: He wrote two volume work on social order in reference to economi value. One of the Physiocrats had come out with a subjective theory of value whereas the Physiocrats emphasize the cost theory. He emphasizes also th principle of equality in exchange as over against mercantilist point of view an in practice he did good work by showing up weakness of colonial system whic at that time American colonies were breaking away from England.

Dupont de Nemours: The most famous and the most important amon Physiocrats. He wrote a book, called Physiocracy. He was so enthusiastic tha he even edited some of Turgot's works. He was great popularizer of Physiocrac and after the downfall of the school in 70's he played a relatively even greate role than Baudeau. He worked through the revolution and became one of th leading men in the revolution. He tried to do away with all indirect taxes. H had to flee to United States and here he founded the great family of Dupon returned to France only for a time, always kept his interest in economics. H is responsible for 15 or 20 books, they have never been studied.

Section 28. Turgot

He is one of the great thinkers of world. A man in economics, second onl to Adam Smith and in some ways more important. His nine volume book have never been translated into English. He came to France from Scotlan He was the youngest son of his family and was intended to be a priest. Studie in the school but soon outgrew the idea as he was mostly interested i philosophy, literature and science, and as a young man when he was only 2 or 22 he wrote his essays on paper money. In 1761 he entered upon politic. career and soon became governor. Situation at that time was very bad in Franc and he had learned enough economics to attempt reforms. At that time th situation was very much like that of China today. He introduced certai reforms, did away with forced labor, built canals and altogether improved th conditions of peasants and did find time to write his great work. When th king died Louis XIV came to the throne and Turgot was made Minister c Navy and Minister of Finance. He started out at once to work and durin the short time of his office he brought about some remarkable changes. H mapped out a plan of nine reforms, and if they had followed his plan, revolutio would not have been necessary. His plans are as follows:

1. Free Trade
2. Abolition of forced labor
3. Abolition of guilds
4. Complete reform of taxation
5. A severe code for whole France
6. A comprehensive political reform based upon representativ government

7. A religious reform, separate church from state
8. Complete liberty of thought and expression
9. Abolition of all remains of feudal system.

Whenever a new law was given in France a reasoned explanation, a philosophy of reasons was necessary as to why the law is passed. Turgot wrote each motive and pointed out that each one on the theory of economics that these edicts were based upon. As regards the abolition of the forced labor, he made exception for the clergy. Complete destruction of guilds, and others which dealt with certain reforms of taxation and certain local situation in Paris, arose a serious objection. However, these soon died, so that everything seemed promising. In the next few months he completely reformed colonial system, and brought some improvement in finance. On May 12, 1776 he resigned and wrote to a friend, "Now as I have liberty to use my library ..."

As soon as he resigned old abuses returned one by one. He lived for a few years, and died in 1781. He wrote a work entitled "Formation and Distribution of Wealth," in which he laid the foundation of his theory. Then he wrote his very interesting theory of both production and distribution. He wrote essay on value which is exceedingly interesting. He makes distinction between the subjective view of value and cost theory of value. Then he wrote about free trade which gives foundations and further development of whole doctrine of international trade and freedom over against mercantilist abuses. He wrote memoires on mines and quarries. He wrote prelude to the abolition of guilds and he wrote a special treatise on his American friends on indirect taxation. It was in this work that he lays down his famous theory about what is known of right of labor. Perhaps the most familiar thing about Turgot is the right of interest. He says the payment for the combination in the difference of time the interest. But in his theory of trade he first calls the attention to the work of foreign trade, which is less important compared with internal trade.

I will say a few words about the little book of Turgot. This book is entitled, "Formation and Distribution of Wealth." It was written for the edification of Chinese prince who was traveling through Europe at that time. In making general statement about wealth, on pages 7 and 8, he uses the phrase that later on became famous, "What the farmer creates would be the fund for the wages of the labor." On page 8, he uses the statement which later on also became famous: The subsistence theory of wages by means of which he gets only his livelihood. On page 14, he divides all economic classes into three: (1) Productive class. (2) Stipendiary class, people who receive wages. (3) Dispository class. Things that we can dispose of. On page 27, the second part. He says, there another way to get rich beside tilling the soils and that is through the use of capital, trade and commerce. On page 50 he gives his famous definition of capital: Any one cultivating the land gets surplus. If he saves this surplus, this is called capital, and he discusses how capitals may be employed. On page 54, he defines the capitalist, entrepreneur, merchant and employers. On page 6? he begins his famous treatment of interest, pointing out beautifully that interes is paid not for money but for use of capital, and gives very remarkable statemen in connection with low rate of interest upon welfare of society. He says, pric of interest may be looked upon as a kind of revenue behind which all labo agriculture and commerce come to an end, like a sea spreading over a vas area. If this sea rolls back ... On page 81, he gives five different methods o investing capital: (1) To buy land; (2) To lease and work the land; (3) Inves in the industry; (4) To invest in trade, and (5) Lend it out on interest.

Whether Turgot was a Physiocrat or an economist, he shared with ther certain ideas, but he was entirely too great a man to be satisfied with th conclusions of the physiocrats. When Turgot wrote to the Journal, Dupon tried to change his views. He was in agreement with physiocratic doctrine, s that from every point of view in method and content, accuracy and profoun analysis, Turgot marks a very decided step forward in the history of economics It can be said about Turgot that he was the first scientific economist. Howevei everything that Turgot did politically was undone by revolution, whereas hi scientific analysis was preserved for future.

Section 29. Opposition

Voltaire never took much stock in them. Then, Mably wrote at end of 60's He expressed doubts to philosophical economists, and he is among the greates communists. He maintained that private property ought to be commor Forbonnais was a great eclectic mercantilist but his criticisms are no important. Galiani was a brilliant man and a witty writer. He wrote his dialogu on the wheat trade in 1770, in which he opposed the physiocratic doctrine He developed the subjective theory of value. Furthermore, after a while ther came a split within the ranks of physiocrats themselves. Condillac now wrot his famous book on trade and government. He broke out with Quesnay o the following two points: He could not swallow (1) the doctrine of sterility (2) He opposed the whole doctrine of value. On the onset, however, the view of Galiani, as well as Condillac were neglected, as the years passed by.

Section 30. The Development in Other Countries

In England the situation was not at all favorable for such ideas as physiocrat expressed, as they were forging ahead in trade and in industry, and so far a doctrine of single tax was concerned, an English writer, Asgill, had emphasize this from another point of view. There was at this time a very interesting write who was a Frenchman and who lived in England and wrote in English. Thi was Cantillon. He emphasized also the importance of land and land condition and physiocrats and all benefited very much of the writings of Cantillon an

uesnay. During the 18th century there was no repercussion on physiocrats
England, but on the other hand the single tax doctrine was favorably received
Germany, especially by Charles Frederick. He decided to introduce single
x system into three little towns in the 70's, and the experiment lasted for
few years, which later on was abandoned. So what was advanced by
hysiocrats relative to single tax, was tried by Charles Frederick and was given
p. Mauvillon expressed the same idea. But, there was a real man in Italy that
e find repercussion of French idea. This was Leopold of Tuscany. He tried
popularize the new idea of economics. Just about that time they started
conomic chairs. However, scarcely had economists had [sic] produced any
fluence elsewhere on the continent, Adam Smith predominated. The times
ow were ripe to loosening up the clamps which were put by mercantilists and
at is why physiocrats had been succcessful. Summing up therefore the real
ontribution of physiocrats made to economic thought.

Section 31.   Influence of Physiocracy

Three distinctions were made: (1) Opposition to mercantilists. (2) Ethical
actor. (3) Positive views of production and distribution.

Ethical factor interests us very much. Their conception of natural right
atural order is something which is eternally true. It is valuable as being
omething as an ideal natural justice—the ideology element based upon justice.
Iow they attempted to solve the social problems which would mean the
econciliation of wealth. Of course, that lies with their whole conception of
ature and natural law, which plays a great role with Adam Smith. They said
ature can be conceived in its three phases: (1) Original constitution of things.
2) Nature embraces physical and animal world. (3) Nature includes the
onstitution of universe, including men, living things, as well as other
henomena. Therefore in their views you find a full realization of individuality
f human beings, the natural right of every human creature to seek for himself
nis realization. This conception is often misunderstood. They said, law means
our things: (1) A body of constitutory usage, (2) A statutory enactment, (3)
t means a rule of action, (4) It means statement of relation of cause and effect.
his explains the conflict. The idea of law has something in harmony with
ne universe, and at that time law in scientific sense was statement of cause
nd effect, because their whole analysis of economic and social life was based
pon the attempt to develop a scientific explanation. You must, again,
istinguish between production, specifically as it stands, we no longer believe
this today. Of the sterility of commerce, soon came the breakdown, and
vith that we see the disappearance of the whole edifice of single tax. But, in
nany other respects they made a step forward. In their theory of value they
nade a step forward, although they started things out in the wrong direction,
s they emphasized supply. Also in their doctrine of capital and above all in

their theory of distribution they, for the first time, attempted to mak
explanation as to what is meant by law of wages, interest, law of profit. And
finally as a result of this theory of distribution they gave the theory of incidenc
of taxation which was entirely new and original. Two things, marked their cla:
to enduring fame:

Practical side. Just as mercantilism emphasized at the bottom the infiltratio
of capital into trade and industry, so the physiocrats tried to apply capitalis:
to agriculture. They did not believe in small proprietors of land, they believe
in large farms, and their whole practical aim was to attempt to apply capita
to agriculture on a large scale. This marks a stage in the development c
capitalism. This is practically and theoretically important for it sounds th
keynote of individualism and represents a reaction against the old trend c
thought in Europe at that time. What physiocrats did was a part of the grea
work that was being done by other leading thinkers in France in the 18th century
They attempted to do in economic and social life what encyclopedists were doin
in religious fields and what Rousseau was trying to do in Political life. Roussea
advocated going back to nature and laid special emphasis on reformation c
politics. Physiocrats, however, were the protagonists of what you call natura
economics as over against historical economics. They must be called first schoc
of scientific economists. It was the combination between the two that made
so attractive to Adam Smith—the combination of critical, constructiv
opposition to the whole mercantilism, constructive in the sense of theory c
distribution which they were anxious to give, favor of thought, ideology an
passionate appeal to nature. All these things physiocrats have done and rendere
immense service up to the present day. They contributed a very remarkable ston
to the edifice of scientific thought and to general well being.

PART II.   SINCE ADAM SMITH

BOOK V.   ADAM SMITH AND HIS
IMMEDIATE PRECURSORS

Section 32.   The Precursors

It is a well known fact that Adam Smith first studied philosophy but late
on switched over to the study of economics. In order to find out, therefore
what he might have learned from the contemporary and preceding philosophe:
one must know something about these men.

Bernard Mandeville was one of the philosophers who lived about th
beginning of the 18th century. Mr. Kaye wrote a two volume book abou
Mandeville, entitled "The Crumbling Hive." Mandeville had written a poe:
about a society of bees—an analogy with the human beings. He tries to sho

that the bees were prosperous as long as there was vice and luxury around them. In 1714, Mandeville published a new edition of this poem—"The Fable of the Bees, or Private Vice and Public Benefits." This new edition started a stormy discussion, because the people realized what he was hinting at. His economic views are as follows:

1. All virtue is nothing but selfishness. He expressed this view to Schopenhauer. He claims that we give alms to beggars only to save us the trouble, and that every act of ours is prompted by selfish motives. Of course, he does not mean to say that there is no such thing as altruism, charity or philanthropy, but he claims that most of our acts are prompted by fear of shame, or desire, or pride. Reason, he says, is the plaything of our emotions, and this is true even today.

2. Luxury, he says, while a bad thing for the individual, is a very good thing for the community in general. Savings are injurious to the community, but in this respect his theory is purely an economic fallacy. Mandeville thinks that by spending more money people will have to work accordingly.

3. He deals with the poor laws, saying that it is prudent to try to relieve the wants of the poor, yet, he says, it is a folly to try to cure them. He says, in every society ignorance is a necessary thing in the admixture, as otherwise there would be no simple people to do the hard work. He says, one must therefore pay them little, in order to keep them working.

4. Labor: Mandeville is the first to allude to the question of the division of labor among the bees, and it was this contention which aroused the storm against Mandeville.

5. Mandeville's doctrine of laissez faire is that he maintains that the bees—or rather people—should be let alone, and one should not try to reform them.

Another important philosopher is Francis Hutcheson (1604-1746), of the University of Glasgow. When he retired Adam Smith you remember occupied his chair for a while. Hutcheson's philosophy, as well us that of Adam Smith, had been influenced by that of Shaftesbury and Locke, particularly with regard to the doctrines of Natural Law and Private Property. About the theory of natural rights, Hutcheson gives a much more detailed account, and does the same thing with reference to private property. In speaking about the division of labor, Hutcheson calls it "Advantageous rights of man", while later on Adam Smith changed its name to "Advantages of Society." Hutcheson's idea about private property is that he says it all depends upon the Public opinion of the particular country. But he is strongly opposed to communism. In Chapter 7 of his book, "Principles of Economics and Politics," he speaks of value or price and says, it depends on the utility of the particular commodity, yet prices do not follow the real use of the commodity. He says, they depend upon the difficulty, or scarcity of getting the goods. He says, the prices increase in two

ways: (a) Natural profits, which are the wages for superintendence an
management, and (b) Contingent profits, due to fortunate actions of the marke
In Chapter 13, Hutcheson discusses the matter of interest, and he is one of th
earliest philosophers to get away from the mediæval idea that interest is
punishable crime. He accepts the legitimacy of interest and claims that it vari
according to the state of trade and the amount disposable. Adam Smith followe
these views and took up the matter just where Hutcheson had left them.

Besides these philosophers, we are interested also in the economists wh
preceded Adam Smith. At the time most of these men were imbued with th
prevailing mercantilist doctrines, but half a dozen men are of special intere
to us in order to enable us to understand Adam Smith.

We will first say a few words about George Berkeley, Bishop of Irelan
He published in 1720, a rather gloomy essay trying to picture the future i
very dark colors. Soon after, he published a small book entitled the Queris
which of interest to us.

George Berkeley's great work set everybody thinking in England. Th
attention is called to the fact that his theory is that the real foundation of wealt
is to be found in industry. Also his views with reference to balance of trad
Query, 556, he doubts the universality of the rule, Q. 559, whether it woul
not be wrong to draw money in the country and keep it there in gold but n
in industry. Q. 562, whether the amount of gold and silver will increase wealt
of a country rather than the industry. Another point where he marks a gre
step forward. People were beginning to talk of the advantages of banking an
paper money. Q. 219, whether the absence of banks and paper money is ju
objection. Q. 233. Whether all public funds be in a mine of gold to Englan
and finally Q. 247, whether great evils of paper money in North America ha
sprung overland of rents issue of paper without discretion and legislation ..
In other queries we find in Berkeley first statement of the doctrine that attaine
very great proportions. Knapp wrote a famous book on money and said th
chief value of money did not come from coin but stamp of the governmen
Berkeley says in his Query 23. Whether money considered to have intrins
value or whether the idea of money as system is not altogether that of a tick
of a counter, and whether money be not in truth a ticket for conveying c
recording ... Then he paid great attention to economic evils from which Irelan
was suffering. He says, standard of life is not result of prosperity but prosperit
makes it possible. Q. 59. To provide for the poor, look after poor and see th
all people will be well. Q. 107, whether comfortable living would not produc
industry. He questioned the right of the eldest son for the education, an
whether a worker with earth was beneath a gentleman, property acquired b
birth, etc. By means of these questions he set the people thinking.

Another writer was Vanderlint. Karl Marx says, Vanderlint was the on
thinker who influenced Hume. Vanderlint wrote a large book, "Mone
Answers all Questions." His points are as follows: In the first place he wa

, great advocate of the quantity theory of money. He says, that large amount of money will make trade flourish. That prosperity is not proportional to the quantity of money and that the important thing is to increase product by increasing the amount of commodities in relation to money. He says, where prices will fall and wages will fall. If wages fall England will be able to compete more successfully with other countries of Europe and become more prosperous. So that according to this theory the increase in raw produce is far more important than all these projects advanced by mercantilists, and it is the foundation of the whole prosperity of England. He says, this is argument for restriction of trade. Make things cheap enough and everything will go well, real advantage is to produce cheap goods to export large quantities of goods and with that import similar quantities of raw materials. Although he seems to be an advocate of low wages, he in reality is an advocate of low prices. He, like Berkeley, emphasizes the importance of increase in consumption as well as the increase in the quantity of commodity. And, it must be mentioned that he marks a new step forward. He advocates the removal of all taxes on commodities.

J. Massie: He was a critic of Locke and Petty. His chief work is, "Essay on Natural Causes of Interest"—1750. This is the first scientific work on the causes that regulate interest. Earlier writers said interest depends upon money. Even Locke thought so. Massie is the first one to point out that interest is always in close relation to the profits of trade. He says, the actual rate of interest is not difficult to determine. If men pay interest for what they borrow they must make profits and interest must be governed by the amount of profit. That his first contribution. He was a great writer in 18th century. He is also of great interest because he was the first English who made great collection of earlier books on the subject. He devoted his attention to the problem of taxation, to the problem of poor laws, also to trade, and it is very interesting to observe that he called attention to American colonies. He said that instead of colonies being help it is a hindrance and England would be much better off to get rid of them. Passing over these rather insignificant writers we come:

Hume: He was a great philosopher and teacher of Adam Smith. Hume is more noted for his philosophical works. His economic contributions were few in number but they were very remarkable. They were published in 1750 under the title, "Political Discourses." This is not a book of definite arrangements, is rather haphazard work on different topics, but after all he was a great genius. He called attention to a few points in which he made impression on Adam Smith. He emphasized the need of general economic laws. He says, that they may fail in particular things but they may be all right for general things. He says, everything in the world is purchased by labor and are causes of labor. Hume gives the very interesting treatment of luxury. In olden times these were treated from the ethical point of view, but only in later years that it is expressed by Voltaire and Hume that luxury ceases to be innocent when it becomes to be dangerous. It was pointed out that luxury must be looked upon not from an absolute but from a relative point of view. Voltaire developed this idea and Hume marks a step forward.

More important than this is his contribution to the theory of money. H does not mention Voltaire but he was very much influenced by him, and h refines upon the quantity theory. He says, it is not merely increase in quantit of money that leads to increase in price but primarily it is in the interval betwee the increase of money and increase of price that makes it profitable. He work out this theory very interestingly. Furthermore, he developed his doctrine o money. He comes out to opposition to mercantilists. He says, there are tw circumstances of any importance: (1) Gradual increase, (2) Thoroug concoction of circulation. He takes opposition to public credit, which lead to more theoretical discussion of interest. He takes all the points of Massi and makes a well known, widely accepted theory that low rate of interest ha got nothing to do with the supplies. His conclusion is that in international trad it is not the question to get money, but the question of getting goods. All effort to impede the natural flow of trade from one country to another countr deprives nations from free exchange, he says. Hume is perhaps best know for his doctrine that taxes instead of being a burden upon the community ma be an advantage to the community, and he gives this argument: "Since natur necessity or disadvantage may be thought favorable to industry, why may n artificial burdens have the same effects?" It would be very wrong however t accuse Hume of likening taxes with the natural phenomena, because mos people forget that he followed with much important qualifications. But tha exorbitant taxes destroy the industries.

In these writers we have a number of steps in advance. There was, howeve one other writer, who had a great deal of influence because of his positio This was Dean Tucker of Glouster, who lived in a trading town and calle attention from the beginning to these matters, about American colonie Tucker wrote a great many books. One was a kind of guide book intende to give instructions for travelers. This was a book to tell the English travele on the continent what to look for in the line of economic things, observation etc. Tucker's contribution falls under four headings:

1.   Possibility and need of real science of general economic principles.

2.   The doctrine of self-interest, and plea for freedom. He claimed that a trade is carried on for the sake of self-interest and that obstruction to it a to be deprecated.

3.   Analysis of human wants and the proof of the fact that by developin wants you develop industry and will develop prosperity. He was the first on to call attention to development of machinery and says, instead of machiner being bad for laborer it is really a good thing. The first philosophy of machiner and high wages is found in Tucker.

4. Philosophy in exchange. The idea of England being nation of shopkeepers. He says, shopkeeper will never get more customers, by refusing serve his customers. So that he was a man of real perspicacity and had very reat influence for changing the view of men about him. Industrial revolution as just beginning at that time in England. He was perhaps the last immediate recursor of Adam Smith to mark a distinct progress.

The name of a remarkable French merchant who lived in England must be mentioned here. Before he died, he wrote a book, which was published in 1755, nd was entitled "Essay on the Nature of Trade." This man was Richard antillon, the influence of which was especially noteworthy for two reasons:) That in his general point of view he had a very great influence both on hysiocrats, also upon Adam Smith. (2) He was a very prominent business man. He was one of those practical men who thought and tried to explain money trend, exchange, credit, etc. His book was reprinted by Harvard niversity a few years ago and in the beginning of his work he starts out with discussion of wealth and different manifestations which came to disclose themselves. In that very first chapter, he says that the earth is the source from hich all wealth is derived and labor is only the form which produces it. He makes statement which is very remarkable, that all the wealth of men in a state re assisted or they enlarge themselves at the expense of the landlord. Mirabeau aw this statement, so that in certain sense it may be said he is one of the orerunners of the edifice that was erected to physiocrats on the land side as ocke on the fiscal side. This is, however, of secondary importance.

It was Cantillon that made popular the distinction between the intrinsic value r price and market value and who attempted to work out what he calls the quation between land and labor and there is no doubt that not little of it is ound in Adam Smith. He has more or less influenced Adam Smith's measures. the last place, long before Turgot wrote, Cantillon used the word ntrepreneur, page 75. He says that all other classes such as entrepreneurs and orkmen are dependent on land owners. But he is also of importance from the double point of view of population and of money. It was Cantillon who rings the population very close contact with the means of subsistence. He makes this statement and brings in close touch these two factors. In his second ook he deals with the problem of money and amount of money that ommunity needs. He does not at all agree with those writers who give the ore primitive statement of quantity theory. He says, introduction of double mount of money does not double the price of goods. He says, if you double he amount of water in a river it does not flow twice as fast. Of course, as successful practical business man he could not believe that interest was ependent alone on money and long before Massie he calls their attention to the connection between interest and capital. As regards international trade his ook is perhaps the best one that had yet been published. This is a large book, and he understands better than all preceding writers. But we must n understand that he was an epoch-making person. We find that he still believ in the balance of trade. The influence he exerted upon Adam Smith was n the more liberal attitude but it was rather in those fundamental points of origi of wealth and some of the problems connected with money.

Steuart is another writer who ought to be mentioned. He is to be mentione however, as one who aroused Smith's reaction rather than sympathy. Steua who lived (1712-1780), in 1768, he wrote a two volume work, longest wo on the subject, entitled, "Enquiry of Principles of Political Oeconomy", an if it had not been for the speedy appearance of Adam Smith's great wor Steuart would have attained prominence and would have retained it. His poin were very modern and was eclectic mercantilist. He made very decided progres In the first place it must be noted that he is very much given to the historic treatment. He is all the time paying attention to the historical developme of institutions that he describes. There are four points in theory in which h is specially to be noted:

1. His doctrine of population. Again, completely overshadowed by th work of Malthus. He supposes of generate faculty of mankind as a sprin loaded with a weight. He devotes quite a time to description of the connectio between population and food supply and limits all population by the foo supply. On page 208 of the first volume, he makes distinction betwee multiplication and propriation which later produces political and econom misery. He raises the question, How to get rid of these difficulties?, but in th explanation is at a loss.
2. His doctrine of trade and industry where brings out the point of wh he calls the balance between work and demand, between production an consumption. Professor Patten finds in Steuart real forerunner of his ide in relation of production and consumption.
3. His view on money and credit. Steuart takes exception to the views Hume. Karl Marx estimates Steuart as being the highest of all the economis of the 18th century in England. He says prices are regulated not by quantit of money but by relative proportion between commodities and wants.
4. His doctrine of taxation. He makes a very fresh and original distinctio based upon his own view of shifting and incidence of various taxes, betwee taxes and alienation and taxes upon possession. Taxes upon alienation, he cal proportional taxes where taxes really assessed upon the things what we ca indirect tax. The other, he calls cumulative taxes. We find in Steuart the fir of the full study of the influence and effects of taxation. His conclusion do not hold water. He raises problems which have not been raised befor Altogether Steuart was a man of considerable ability and did not howeve have sufficiently great originality to break with the old. He still belongs moderate mercantilists. So that, in this little list that I have rapidly ran ov

u find quite a deal economic thought which might give Adam Smith
ssibility to look at the subject from fresh point of view.

Section 33. The Economic Condition of England in the Eighteenth Century

Adam Smith was not a creator, but a creature, and we have to find what
nd of world Adam Smith was living in. Our knowledge of the situation was
ry much enhanced. In the last few years, almost a generation ago, A. Tawney
sthumously published and gave it the title of "The Industrial Revolution",
d this phrase has become very common. We don't realize this. There was
such thing as revolution, if you mean by revolution a shock. He limited
attention primarily to what was going on in agriculture, especially to the
tton industry. But after all they were relatively inconspicuous part of English
uation. Special investigation shows that there are two things: In the first
ace, that the change took place in some industry rather rapidly and other
terprises and industries very slowly. In the second place, we now understand
eat deal more than what they understood a generation ago, that there was
such thing as dramatic change coming in capitalism in the 18th century
d 17th century. We find a good deal of capital, certainly in its incipient form.
me of these books that have been published a few years ago, books like
hton on the iron and steel in the industrial revolution, or books on pottery,
d especially by Mr. and Mrs. Hammond. We have no adequate books on
s topic in English, but two best books are to be found, one in French and
other in German. The French book is by Montous, the German book is
Solomon, under the Life of Pitt, which gives the best view of conditions
England that existed at that time. Let us try to get a bird's-eye-view of what
s going on.

The transition in the 18th century was a transition from agricultural to
lustrial state, and this was very slow. You may trace from the end of the
th century a kind of league between the large land owner and large merchants,
large clothiers and it was this coming in the capital, in that sense explains
development of the later mercantilism. During the 17th and beginning of
18th century in England trade and commerce was rapidly increasing.
lonies of Spain and Holland were becoming less important as markets and
dually industry began to assume larger proportions, a factor which is not
been adequately treated was the influence of conquest of India—the capture
alone the Indian trade but confiscating immense treasures that had been
assed during the past centuries. Thus in a double capacity India played much
re important role in what we call Industrial Revolution: (1) In the
largement of the markets, and (2) The provision of capital. These immense
ms of gold and silver which came in Great Britain, which was an important
tor in stimulating very great changes in agriculture. The fundamental point

was disappearance of open field system and introduction largely influence convertible husbandry.

Now, so far as industry is concerned the old farms still survived. Y remember that the guild system had broken down a century or two before a that gave rise and became known as the domestic system. And, by the domest system we mean the system that developed primarily in the textile industr in England in the 18th century. The system where capital coming in at ea end of the process, raw material bought and owned by capitalist. But, ra materials were being worked out by individual and his family, working at hom That was true in textile and true in some part of other industry, as brass industr and some other industries. There was good deal more capital element and si by side with that there also came a complete development of small or ha industries, as wrought iron or cast iron, etc. If you contrast this system w the guild system, it was a system in which the forms of industries were mo and more apportioned into growing capitalist system which meant four thing

1. System of apprenticeship.
2. The regulation of wages. Under the old guild system the wages we regulated primarily in the interest of the consumer, when later on the regulati came rather in the interest of workers. Each of these forms are still found through the 18th century.
3. You have the marks of the whole mercantilist system: the legislati protection, import duties, prohibitive system to develop incipient industri
4. We have the survivals of liberation of garment workers. What happen this time was the development of new industries—cotton, silk, the change the methods of the potteries, etc. The new inventions in iron, for instance. The new industries tend to create in the neutral towns where they could be fr from these old regulations of guilds and legislators. The improvement transportation was scarcely beginning but real improvement came later on a the whole frame work of the system when Adam Smith was writing was s that of mercantilist state, that is the reason why Adam Smith places so mu emphasis, and tries to point out how much better England was than Fran and his estimate of different social and industrial classes are important. T capitalists of the large trader type appear rather wise and acute and forwar looking. The landlord was still nobleman in both sense of the term and t laborer did not amount to much either theoretically or practically, a industries were increasing most rapidly, if about 3% every year previously n perhaps increasing at the rate of 6%. But, still not very great, and the wa were not very low and utterly bad. The condition as a whole was satisfacto and colonies were still a considerable source of profit to the mother count but we find opposition showing itself even in the ranks of the various class In the first place between 1763 and 1776 when Adam Smith wrote his bo there were good many unsatisfactory symptoms not alone in French wars, a

merican trouble but also there was very bad circulation of capital, prices of
od were very high, and above all there were appearing now a rift in the class
industrialists themselves. You can compare, for instance, East India
erchants with the manufacturer of silk and iron and etc. The situation in
ngland was very much like that of Penna. today. There are manufucturers
iron in this country today who no longer are interested in the least in the
otective system, those that have reached a state where they can compete with
reign traders, if they were permitted to. Furthermore, we find splitting up
th the Liberal Party.

The same rift appeared in England, the rift between neutral industries that
ere in need and older industries where they needed larger markets and cheaper
arkets rather than protective system. Tucker represented all those who
anted freedom from the old way. So that the general doctrine of system was
ll mercantilist system still in large significance and you find these beginnings
opposition in England. Now, if you compare all that with what I told you
out the philosophical antecedents of Adam Smith you can easily realize what
e general conditions were found to be in that of a man who was influenced
any such thing as great industrial revolution. A great revolution certainly.
hen Adam Smith wrote, you remember James Watt made his discovery in
at very year and it is only after 1776 that real great development of very
eat importance took place in iron and other industries. Adam Smith was
ought in and influenced by the later mercantilists and developed democratic
stem where capital was beginning to be of considerable importance and it
w became chief significance to sound the note of dissent with the prevalent
licy of restriction and of selfish mercantilism. From that point of view we
n proceed now to study Adam Smith.

Section 34.   Methods of Adam Smith

We shall say a few words about the significance of the work. As regards
significance with which the book was received as it is always the case in
man nature you find most extravagant phrases and also most deprecatory
character. For instance, Buckley tells us that "Wealth of Nations" is the most
luable single contribution that was ever made by the human mind to
termine the true principles of government. McCulloch says that the "Wealth
Nations" exercises a power and beneficent influence on the public opinion
d on the legislation of the world absolutely unrivaled in the history. Adam
nith, it is also said, not only founded it but almost completed it. Read the
Vealth of Nations" as it deserves to be read and you will easily realize that
fore him no political economy existed and since nothing has been done. Now,
s is extravagant. On the other hand a writer called Adam Smith a half-breed
otchman who violated the laws of God, and damned the creation, etc.

The book itself was published in 1776, same year the Independence America, and discovery of steam engine. Five editions were made during life time. It was translated into almost every foreign language. First Americ edition appeared in 1789. The editions after his death were very numerous a some of them were very different. Playfare's three volume published in 18 In 1814 four volume by Wakefield. Four volume edition in 1834. One volu edition in 1863. T. Rogers printed two volume edition in 1869. In 1880 seco edition. The Everyman's Library two volume edition is probably cheapest a convenient. Two volume of Rogers is about the best.

Adam Smith—political economist and moral philosopher, was born Kirkaldy, Scotland, June 5, 1723. His father, a lawyer and customs offic signet writer, died before the birth of his son, who was brought up throu a delicate childhood by his mother. During his early childhood it is said t he was stolen by gypsies. At fourteen he was sent to the University of Glasgc where he came under the influence of Francis Hutcheson, and in 1740 he w up to Oxford as Snell exhibitioner at Balliol College, remaining there till 17 After leaving Oxford, he gave lectures upon English Literature and Economi and in 1751 became professor of logic, and in 1752 of moral philosophy Glasgow. The reputation won by his lectures was increased by the publicati in 1759, of his "Theory of the Moral Sentiments." Little later he worked his Moral Philosophy which is divided into four parts: (1) Natural theolo (2) Ethics, (3) Justice, (4) Police. In 1763 he was appointed as traveling tu to the third Duke of Buccleuch, went to Geneva and spent a whole year Paris 1765-66. Adam Smith met Quesnay and whole school of followers, acquainted with Turgot. He used to go to weekly meetings at Quesnay's ho and speaks of fellows under Quesnay. Then he returned to Kirkaldy and star to write his book spending 6 years at home and then he transferred to Lond taking altogether 9 years in writing a book, nine years you remember. A result of his book he was appointed a Commissioner of Customs, took a ho in Edinburgh, where he lived quietly and at ease and after his mother's de he retired and died July 17, 1790.

The Book itself. His Methods: Adam Smith of course is generally celebra as the founder of great many important theories. The book is based prima on inductive method, great deal of historical facts connected with economic Perhaps one of the more [or most] attractive things is his practical exampl the illustrations that give Adam Smith quality of a very learned and erud man. He collected a great library on the general subject of economics a politics. In fact we still have a catalogue of his library. We see that Adam Sm read several languages, perhaps all of the European languages, as Fren Italian, Spanish, German and other languages. He had good knowledge literature, he was not alone a scholarly man but also an open-minded and ma sided person. Intellectually he liked to look every problem from all possible en This, however, was not of advantage to him but disadvantage. It led him onsistency. Finally we might call attention to his views of what political nomy is. Quoting him: "System of political economy considered as a branch science has two distinct objects: (1) to provide revenue or subsistence for »ple and (2) to supply the state with the revenue under which service to public »ossible and the process to enrich both people and sovereign." He calls it :ience but looks to its teleological side.

Section 35.   The Lectures and the "Wealth of Nations"

Analysis. Before we take up the "Wealth of Nations" itself we must say a words about the lectures that he delivered on the subject for several decades ore he wrote. He lectured on moral philosophy. A student of his took very »d notes and those notes were discovered sometime ago and edited under title: "Lectures on Justice, Police, Revenue and Arms."This is a book which very interesting historically. In order to prepare the way for adequate :ussion of "Wealth of Nations" I call attention as to what there is and what re is not in those lectures. What he got from Physiocrats. Important thing o learn is that most of these lectures deal with non-economic problems. t two, Police—this word is used in the sense that Germans used it. The t division of this Police, what he calls cleanliness and security. He says police ;inally meant policy of government, only inferior parts, as cleanliness, urity, cheapness and plenty, and also he gives a discussion of opulence and Ilth, etc. He tells us that opulence arises with the division of labor, how ision of labor multiplies the product, what gives occasion to division of or. What circumstances regulate the price of commodities, and here he says, re are two different prices which although seemingly independent points connected, that he calls natural price, and market price. Natural price, he nts out, is the price received by laborer sufficient to maintain him during time of his labor, which depends upon labor and cost. Market price is ulated, he says, by quite other circumstances, as demand, scarcity, the riches, power of those who demand.

That leads him to consider the question as to what causes rise of price above natural price, and this gives rise to a short discussion of monopolies and es. He then discusses money, money as measure of value and medium of hange. And, he quotes Hume, bringing home the fact that national opulence s not consist in money. He gives an account of the origin of money and y industry is more important than money. Balance of trade, he considers ry absurd doctrine, because, he says, all commerce carried on between two ntries must necessarily be advantageous to both not simply to one as the doctrine indicates, and therefore all prohibitions are harmful to both ntries. Then, he has a chapter on the South Sea Scheme. He has a short sage on interest where states that interest is paid not for the use of money for use of stock. He discusses exchange limitations from country to country,

then finally he concludes by a very interesting and philosophical account
the causes of slow progress of wealth; points out why wealth increases so slo
and gives a historical account of what was happening in the Middle Ages
influences of taxes and monopolies.

Then we come to part three, which he calls Revenue. This is a gene
consideration upon taxes both direct and indirect, showing advantages
disadvantages of both, and what he calls stocks, by which he means governm
bonds. Now, we see he discussed topics just as Hutcheson did. Those w
his famous lectures.

The Discussion of the Book itself: In the introduction the first sentenc
perhaps most important sentence in the whole book: "The annual labor of ev
nation is the fund which originally supplies it with all the necessaries
conveniences of life which it annually consumes, and which consist alw
either in the immediate produce of that labor, or in what is purchased w
that produce from other nations." Then, in Book first, Chapter first, he gi
the definition of division of labor, that is, simply working out in far gre
detail than what we find in his lectures. Because he calls attention not al
to division of labor but also now some of the disadvantages of the divis
of labor. For instance, Chapter two, he discusses the principles which g
occasion to the division of labor, and here he finds the real cause not in
thing else but in the inherent propensity of human nature, the barter, excha
one thing for another. He says, it is not from the benevolence of the butcl
the brewer, or the baker, that we expect our dinner, but from their regard
their own interest. We address ourselves, not to their humanity but to tl
self-love, and never talk to them of our own necessities but of their advanta;
Then in Chapter three, he points out how division of labor is limited by
extent of the market, and then we also have rather interesting statement
what really are the disadvantages as well as the advantages of the divisior
labor. Then, he goes at once, next to money—origins and use of money. W
he says is perfectly true. This then leads to discussion of value, and he s;
values have two different meanings. It sometimes expresses the utility of
object and sometimes the power of purchase of other objects. One is va
in use and the other value in exchange. He starts to investigate the princi
that govern this. And, in Chapter five, he deals with normal price
commodities. He tells us that value of any commodities is equal to quan
of labor which enables him to purchase or command labor, therefore, it is
real measure of value, and yet although labor is real measure, it is not the th
by which values are commonly measured, and that is money. But, he trie;
point out that money is a very defective measure as compared to labor
since labor is responsible primarily for producing raw materials
commodities, this leads to a very interesting discussion. He finds corn or wh
a better measure, as money values vary to a greater extent.

In Chapter six, he considers the component parts of price, where he starts
t and says that at the beginning there is nothing but labor and laborer, and
refore wages, and that only after a time when private property develops you
ve profits, and also land becomes private property and we also have rent and
refore, he says, there are three parts constituting the elements of price: (1)
ges, (2) profits, (3) rent. Chapter seven is another most important chapter
ause he discusses the natural and market prices, and he identifies natural
es with the ordinary or average rates. He says, the natural price is central
ce towards which price of commodities naturally gravitates. He then goes
to explain what other causes are responsible for deviation of actual price
d average price, and he discusses monopolies as well as other causes. Then
goes more particularly and more in detail than in his lectures into each one
the elements and devotes a chapter, first to wages and then to others.
Socialistic elements of Adam Smith as regards labor that the whole profits
labor belongs to laborer when he does not consider the landlord, but, he
vs, as soon as land becomes private property then comes the rent. He makes
st discussion from the point of view of profits of labor, second discussion
m the point of view of progress of labor and then finally we come to the
nation in modern times where wages depend not alone upon the employer
h his profits but also upon the landlords with their rents. Then the relation
employer and laborer is discussed, and while he agrees that wages would
turally be at that point just to enable the workmen to live, still he says, there
other circumstances and causes which enable wages to be higher. He then
es on to discuss its causes. He says, in young countries like American colonies
oduce is large to afford high wages, and calls attention to the connection
tween number of people and amount of employment, and he also finally calls
ention to differences of standard of life, the difference between Great Britain
d other countries. Two things in this chapter are important: (1) He shows
y decided sympathy with the laboring class. He says, no society can be happy
y greatly when part of its members are poor and miserable. (2) His discussion
slavery especially in the American colonies, which he points out that the work
ne by free men comes cheaper in the end than that performed by slaves. He
vs, this is found to be so even in Boston, New York and Philadelphia. So
t his discussions of labor are actual problems of the day.

Section 36.   Adam Smith's Originality

Not very important but rather interesting to those that claim that he is the
her of system of economics. It would be surprising to know, what we now
ow, those whole proceedings in this course and dealing with problems and
ics upon which Smith based himself. I shall just mention a few points, some
which known, others are not well known. We find Smith's great argument
inst early bullionists, that of course, we have already found in mercantilists,

in Petty and Mun. We find statements and discussions about the nature
wealth in general, about the conditions and relations between labor and l
which are more or less familiar. From Petty Adam Smith has taken
conception of labor and measure of labor. From Child and Culpeper
discussions of advantages of low rate of interest. From Massie and subsequ
writers his discussion that interest is paid not for money but paid for the
of the capital. In Locke and Newton we find what he has to say on curre
and what he says about both taxation and public credit. In Tucker, no dou
he has taken his views great deal with reference international aspects
commerce. In "Cantillon and Law" we find much what he says about the
of credit and currency. Marx points out that one of the most important passa
dealing with division of labor that it is copied almost word by word, 10
15 lines from Mandeville. He took great deal from Berkeley and Hume a
acknowledges indebtedness to them.

There are two other points. Lesler, in German monogram [sic] of Wea
of Nations finds 15 pages deadly parallel columns, 50 or 75 instances the alm
exact statement and imitation by Adam Smith from preceding writers. Seco
point is, still exact indebtedness of Adam Smith to Physiocrats. Indebtedn
of Adam Smith to French writers of the 18th century on problems of taxati
and public finance. Adam Smith bases his entire public Finance to Fre
writers. The whole Adam Smith's treatment is contained in the French wri
before 1776. The other point is that his indebtedness to Physiocrats was hear
debated until the publication of his lectures.

Now, we know what there was in these lectures. What there was before
went to Paris and after he came back from Paris: Economic Freedom—T
he did not get from Physiocrats, because you remember we find it in his lectu
In his lectures Adam Smith bases his principle upon expediency. He knew
work of Pufendorf on Natural Law. Adam Smith was very much influenc
by Hume and Montesquieu. What the Physiocrats did was to supply Ad
Smith with a fully developed philosophy, with a fully developed basis
philosophy and it was after their exposition that he went back probably to
work of Locke and Hutcheson, so that in the main while he could formul
from Physiocrats, still if Physiocrats never lived it would have been the sa
thing. In the second place, however, the theory of distribution is taken fr
Physiocrats. We don't find it in his lectures at all. It is true the distinction betwe
profit, wages and rent was expressed in English writings in 50's and 60's,
there is no doubt that much fuller exposition by Physiocrats gave shape to Ad
Smith's mind. In Canon [sic: Cannan] books you find the parallels.

In the third place, the emphasis is put upon the consumers interest and wh
theory of wants. When we were speaking of mercantilists the stress was laid up
the producer, now Adam Smith emphasizes rather the whole problem of la
and product, which was leading to his primary cause of consumption and he
not absolutely certain, but probably that he was considerably influenced

ysiocrats, perhaps it is likely that reaction to mercantilism would have brought
n to this point of view. In his lectures these were treated very scarcely.
Fourth: Discussion of stock—What is meant by stock? Its characteristics,
ture, its employments as well as distinction, productive and unproductive;
re is no trace of that in his lectures, and therefore all this is due to
ysiocrats. So that, you see, there is a great deal to be said, that Adam Smith
s a student a follower of Quesnay, even though he does not share their
rticular views. He tells us in comparing different schools of political economy
ile he does not agree with the conclusions of Quesnay as regards the net
oduce and sterility of industry, yet notwithstanding that fact they certainly
ched the truth more closely than any other preceding writers. In 12 different
ces it shows the influence of Physiocrats upon his thought. (Professor Patten
es to minimize the influence of Physiocrats upon Adam Smith. The
nclusion is that Patten is all wrong.)
Summing up: Adam Smith owes great deal to his predecessors, yet what
ference does that make? Marshall put it up this way: "Although undoubtedly
borrowed much from others, yet the more one compares him with those
o went before and those who came after him the finer his genius appears,
re broader his knowledge and more balanced his judgment." I think we
st all agree with that. We now leave the question of originality and come:

Section 37. Smith's Defects

Some of the special doctrines. In the first place, as a general proposition
e of the shortcomings of Wealth of Nations is its lack of all systematic
rangement. In the second place, we find very great weakness in definitions.
dam Smith was not much from the point of view of definitions. But when
come to the doctrines we reach to a very interesting point.
Theory of Wealth: That of course is very important point. The annual
oduce of land and labor, wealth in terms of exchange value, as regards the
nual produce of land and labor, instead of emphasizing the money side of
oblem common in his predecessors he stresses the idea of consumable
mmodity. That was a great step forward, yet even in this concept of wealth
u find number of points to query. In the first place nowadays as you know
differentiate between capital and income as measure of wealth. Adam Smith
metimes speaks of progress and annual progress. In the second place there
nothing in his whole discussion which enables us to distinguish between the
gregate wealth and average wealth. Is Belgium richer or poorer than
gland? and, Is a Belgian richer or poorer? is another thing. There is nothing
Adam Smith to throw light upon that. But, there is still another more
portant point which is the discussion of wealth. That, of course, has to deal
th whole topic of production and labor. The idea as to whether wealth is
be restricted to material objects or to mere consumable commodities, or

to commodities having a money exchange value, a price, or whether wea
to be looked upon the broader sense of welfare. Those different concepts p
great role in the whole modern discussions.

Adam Smith was quite satisfied to identify wealth with consuma
commodities. This is not sufficient for us, but it was sufficient for his tin
His doctrine of capital was borrowed almost entirely from Physiocrats. Ada
Smith makes distinction between stock and capital. His conception is t
accumulated mass of commodities. There are good many points that is to
considered. He divides this stock into fixed and circulating capital and ha
great deal to say about the characteristics of each one, which as time we
on showed little importance in the practical importance in economic life.

Then, we come to his doctrine of the relation between increasing stock
community and division of labor. His argument, there, is very far fr
convincing. He does not prove his point that there is definite connecti
between the two doctrines of employment of capital. You see, how much
was influenced by Turgot, and then he shows the influence of Physiocrats wh
he concludes that capital employed in agriculture is more important th
anything else, because in agriculture nature works along with men. That wh
discussion is meaningless. This is the influence of Physiocrats. He maintai
agriculture is more productive, at this time. You can tell that it depends up
the conditions. At one time commerce was considered more productive, a
so was agriculture. This changed rapidly from year to year according to t
treatment. This theory is very unsatisfactory today.

Fifth Theory: The theory of value. It is very remarkable that everybody w
discusses the question of value always goes to Adam Smith, socialists
otherwise, they find something to prove their points. In the very beginni
we find it is stated that value is governed by its cost of labor, that is dear whi
it costs much labor to acquire. He works out the theory that later on becai
known as labor cost theory, which is the foundation of Ricardian economi
On the other hand almost in the same paragraph he speaks of value being t
quantity of labor which it enables a man to purchase or command. This theo
became known as labor-command theory. Controversy between Ricardo a
Malthus turned around this point. We find both of these in the same paragrap
All of these that Adam Smith tells us exists in the primitive state of socie
and therefore whole treatment has been characterized by Whittaker as he ca
it philosophical theory. Adam Smith tells us that after a while the who
proceeds of labor no longer goes to the laborer, and gradually as land becom
private property rent goes to the owner, then we have profits of stock; a
that value in exchange, therefore, in modern times is no longer in proporti
to the labor cost. The real value will be the different components measur
by quantity of labor. Then labor measure value reverses itself to labor, prof
and rent. You can realize without going more into detail that his doctrine
value is an undecided doctrine and not clear cut doctrine.

Sixth Doctrine. Productivity of labor. This is the most unfortunate and least isistent part of his work, as he is thinking of wealth only in terms of material nmodities. Productivity of labor with him necessarily meant only that labor ich embodies itself in such material commodities and every other kind of or is considered unproductive, as lawyer, physician, musician, servant all them unproductive labor. It was an error on his part, and which theory production bases itself entirely upon this theory of productivity of labor. is led to a great many implications.

Seventh Doctrine.—Theory of Wages. Here again we find two absolutely posed doctrines in Adam Smith. On the one hand he starts with the sistence theory of wages. He states that we have those wages which cannot pushed by the employer below the point of subsistence. You also find he s attention to the supply and demand theory of wages, and that, he says, ges therefore are regulated not so much by the cost of subsistence but by demand and supply. He again started here two entirely different schools.

Eighth Doctrine. Doctrine of Profits.—Here there are two interesting things be supposed: that Adam Smith thinks of profits only as an average return, re is no difference in his mind between the laws of wages and laws of profits, re are normal wages so there are normal and average profits. Profits, of course the return of capital. At the same time he says, interest is paid not for the of money but for the use of stock. He did not get any further. Profits to n meant double interest, but interest he says, is a part of profits and in theory re is not much difference. He calls profits a compounded interest. He talks ut the rise and fall of profits also. Second point is that, he looked at it from ew point of view you find Adam Smith in agreement with the Marxian theory surplus profit. In primitive society, he says; got the whole, but as soon as ciety developed he got part of it and some of it went to the owner of capital. en he goes on to discuss the relation between wages and profits.

Some of the Special Doctrines of Adam Smith: Let us now study his doctrine land, his theory of rent. The interesting distinct feature of Smith's discussion that in the first place he calls attention to the fact that land in almost in y situation produces a surplus. He agrees with the Physiocrats in this respect. d, the fact that land almost always produces surplus over slow growth of pulation. Then the distinction that he makes between land that always yields ent and land which does not yield a rent. By rent he means the price paid money for the use of the land and that, of course, must be in some proportion real produce of the land. The rent therefore is the money rent which is nditioned by the fertility of the soil and the price regulated by the demand ich is in the case of food always high enough to give a surplus. Therefore ce land alone can produce a physical surplus and since food produces a ney surplus, namely, all land yields a rent and rent therefore is to Adam ith virtually a monopoly price. A return for the use of land, in view of the t that quantity of land is limited and amount of population is not limited

in the same way. On the other hand, land which does not produce food d
not necessarily yield surplus. It may or may not yield a surplus, and whet
the rent enters into the price or not depends upon the scarcity of food
reference to population. Demand for clothing over against the food is differe
This is not always such as to insure a price which is higher than that nee
to pay for the labor and to replace the stock with ordinary produce wh
Adam Smith thinks. Therefore distinctive feature of Adam Smith's r
doctrine is between the land that must yield a rent because of monopoly a
the land which does not yield a rent. We shall see that when this problem
taken up by his successors that some of the weaknesses of this theory
pointed out both by Malthus and Ricardo. I call attention to the fact that the
of Smith as regard to rent is least satisfactory and lasting than either his the
of wages and profits. Even they are not satisfactory for modern times.

If we were to pass our estimate of Adam Smith, he did not stand as h
as we put him. The reason why Adam Smith stands so high is because of
general philosophy, his general points of view. Therefore, we leave this rat
unsatisfactory, but never the less necessary criticism and try to elucid
[illucidate in original] his general principles.

Section 38.   His General Principles.
The Theory of Self-interest and Theory of Natural Law

The Theory of Self-interest. That you remember we traced, back
Mandeville and all those who are familiar with the literature of France of 1
century philosophers can see that these are very much elaborated in the wo
of Helvetius [Helvicius in original] and others. It was more or less comm
idea that the liberal self love constitutes life and power. So these writers y
remember pointed out that liberality and prevalence of unselfishness wo
be death to competition and destruction of all activity. Some of these write
you remember, tell us that prevalence of unselfishness would reduce the wo
to barrenness and to barren waste. It is different with Adam Smith. He h
very different opinion. He bases his theory upon sympathy. In Wealth
Nations he emphasizes the economic life and economic action influenced
self-interest. You find numberless passages in his book emphasizing the gene
principles that the best results can be attained by every man looking out
himself. You will find quite a number of passages in Wealth of Nations wh
this point is put in a least decisive point and expressed as a probability.

Take for instance, Chapter two, Book four, where he speaks of the influer
of the trader: "Every individual is continually exerting himself to find out
most advantageous employment for whatever capital he can command. It
his own advantage, indeed, and not that of the society, which he has in vie
He neither intends to protect public interest, nor knows how much he do
But the study of his own advantage naturally, or rather necessarily leads h

) prefer that employment which is most advantageous to the society." Here e points out that when a man works for himself not necessarily and inevitably, ut frequently helps along the community. In the same passage you find when e refers to interference of government with what he calls freedom of individual, e says, that this is in almost all cases either a useless or hurtful thing. Still is conclusion in the main is one that it identifies him with the advocates of ublic and private interest. Most writers however have overlooked the passage a which Adam Smith calls attention to the possibility of disparity of interest.

Take Chapter ten, Book one, where he speaks of the combination among ne merchants. In Chapter two, where he speaks about the actions of the manufacturers as over against the country gentleman. After making allowance or all these points the general proposition of the whole book is found in Book our, Chapter nine, where he puts in this way: "All systems either of preference r of restraint, therefore, being thus completely taken away, the obvious and imple system of natural liberty establishes itself of its own accord. Every man, s long as he does not violate the laws of justice, is left perfectly free to pursue is own interest in his own way, and to bring both his industry and capital nto competition with those of any other man, or order of men." One of the results of this doctrine was to identify the activity of the individual and results f individual activity with the ways of providence, and it is here that Adam mith brings himself in the line with the work of Physiocrats, and he stresses ne doctrine of natural liberty. The liberty of nature which comes to a man y the very constitution of the universe.

He speaks continually of the beneficent and equitable economy of the world. Ve find frequent reference identifying the ways of providence and natural berty. You all understand how this work was at peace with the development f idea of natural law in other domains than economics. The natural law was f course not anything new. You find it all the way through the Middle Ages a Roman times, in fact even in the Greek philosophers, starting out with the hilosophical concept with nature of universe and applying to man as well as ature. You are acquainted, of course, with the way in which the Roman octrine of natural law developed, which was very much like what happened a England of the doctrine of equality, the idea of commonwealth and of law. nd, these forms some times are exceedingly difficult to understand. When tome became a great trading center and people of different nationalities began) have commercial dealings with each other, the forms used in legal system f different nations were entirely diverse. The Roman lawyers had a judge who vould deal only with these cases, and they called him judge of the foreigners, nd when he came to look into all these different forms, in trying to find out ne form which was common to all, he found them very widely different from ne another. He finally hit upon some one thing which seemed to be the basis f all these diverse forms. He came upon the idea what he called the law common) all nations. These particular things which were common to all nations, and

in the endeavor to make those acceptable to Romans, he now took from th
Greek philosophers this concept of nature and identified the law common t
all nations to what was really common to all man and gave to mankind. Th
developed in Rome what came to be known as natural law, or called the la
of the nations. This has nothing to do with our international law.

In the course of centuries the whole early rigid system of the Roman seve
law was modified and completely changed by this system of natural law whic
was identified now with universal justice. Same thing took place in England. Ear
laws were modified in the 12th century by system of justice and equity and
took number of centuries before the identification of this new system of equit
upon the whole rigid common law brought about a situation which Blacksto
refers to as crystallized justice. When philosophy of 18th century began to de
with political economic questions they also countersigned by this chaos. In Fran
every town has its own law, as weights, or whole system of money, but the
was not any system of loan. In England owing to its Island situation that can
little early but all over the continent you had also a chaos of economic and politic
system. Therefore all the reformers whether in law, politics, simply did as eve
reformer would do, that is they tried to find out what was really fundament
basis of these proceedings which were common to all, and they identified th
with the law of nature or the natural law. Lawyers did that, philosophers d
that, political philosophers did that. Starting with Rousseau and what oth
writers did in these lines, Adam Smith and Physiocrats did in economics.

In those days it was not realized that law and politics are different phas
of a larger social science. We find this idea develop only recently. They we
all working toward that concept but they had not reached it in the form
a separate science. And, it was therefore entirely explicable that Adam Smi
who should identify the principle of sensibility with the general disposition
man in general, that he should identify self-interest with the economic wor
as an outgrowth of the same idea. That, you see, is the idea of his attitu
of questioning and opposition to everything that was going on. It was this th
served to influence the whole Europe and which explains why Adam Smith
work went like wildfire all over the continent then. It was much needed the
than England. Two great things followed as consequence of this principle.

1.   Opposition to the entire policy of the mercantilists, and for that matt
of all Europe so far as internal reaction of industry and activity was concerne
It set people free and pulled down the rotten fences.

2.   That as regards the international trade the whole theory of mercantilis
was considered false, because mercantilism bases its doctrine, says Ada
Smith, on the idea that may be good to prevent other people doing certa
things, whereas the only truth of natural law, which is that letting things
in their own way and letting every nation enjoy advantages which was accord
to it by the creator.

Here again, as in the case of self-interest, when he came to deal with practical problems he was not any more extreme. It may be said that there are at least half-a-dozen points in which Adam Smith tells us that interference with this natural liberty may be desirable. As regards free trade, for instance, he calls attention to the desirability in certain cases of restraint of importation. Chapter two, Book four. "There seems, however, to be two cases in which will generally be advantageous to lay some burden upon foreign for the increase of domestic industry is desirable. The first is when some particular sort of industry is necessary for the defense of the country, as a large Navy in the case of England is absolutely necessary and for that reason Navigation Act by no means is to be criticized. It is not impossible indeed from many reasons from the point of analysis, but they are as wise as if they all have been dictated by all mighty wisdom." You will find that Adam Smith permits interference for the sake of health: "Interference with the individual in the interest of community, not only desirable but necessary." Third: In the educational field to examine candidate for the profession seems to be interference of the liberty, but, he says, where would we be if they would not be examined. Fourth: In the case of protection of labor he has very interesting reference of anti-trust acts. He says, all these things ought to be prohibited. Fifth: He considers it desirable and necessary to lay restrictions upon the activity of banking, because of great influence of currency upon the country. Sixth: So far as import duties are concerned if you have a system at home internal duties which leaves some hardship on industry you can be justified in imposing duties on foreign goods to protect the home industry. Seventh: Where he discusses the functions of government and desirability of interference, calls attention to the inability of individuals to accomplish results, and he says, it is entirely legitimate for government to step in. So that in every one of these cases Adam Smith shows that he is really broader from all of his followers.

Section 39.   General Estimate of the Value
of the Work of Adam Smith

You must realize that he was after all like every great man only the child of his times. After all, great men are both creators and creatures. They are creators in the sense that they lead the community to recognize what their real fundamental doctrines are, but great men must be more than leaders, They must be leaders of what is really felt by the community. A great man is a man who paints a picture which must be framed by a community, which he is painting. Adam Smith was able to get together the thoughts which were almost ready to be accepted.

BOOK VI.   THE CLASSICAL SCHOOL

Section 40.   Economic Writers, 1776-1810

We will now begin our discussion with rather neglected chapter.—The writer of half a century that followed the "Wealth of Nations." Most individual writer on the history of economics jump at once from Adam Smith to Ricardo an neglect the time which has elapsed between Adam Smith and Ricardo. I wi now give a hurried survey of this period, because we find very little informatio in the books and too, because not little has been done during this time whic has paved the way for later writers. We have to speak about a series of writer on different phases of practical economics—the economic problems of the da during the last quarter of the century. I would like to put this under six head There are of course, no writers during this period to be compared with eithe Adam Smith or Ricardo, nevertheless, there are some original scholars.

1.   The problems connected with agriculture. There are at least three name that must be mentioned in connection with change that was taking place i 18th century in English agriculture. One was Marshall, who was in one of ver long list of men that made detailed survey of the way things were actually bein done in farming operations. He made many suggestions as to the improvement in agriculture. Toward the end of the period there was very detailed surve made and published by government from 50 to 100 volumes by experts of ever county in England, every one of these data serves as a landmark. They dea with the agronomic questions. There were two more in addition to Marshal One was Sinclair, who devoted special attention to conditions in Scotland, an stressed also the relations of the agricultural labor to the land owner. An then, Arthur Young, a man who perhaps among all others achieve international reputation. He began a few years before Adam Smith with th so-called farmers' letters and published new volume every year. Altogether 3 to 40 volumes during his life time. Only recently that a good study of Arthu Young appeared and gave excerpts. Two important works of Arthur Youn should be mentioned: His Political Arithmetic, published in 1774. He took u the name from Petty and attempted to solve problems of agriculture. It is book which deserves great deal more attention than it has received. He the went to France after the outbreak of Revolution and published his famou Travels in France. So that his name has been very familiar on the continen and his very acute observation on agricultural conditions as well as economi and political conditions in France compared to those in his own country wo for the book a reputation which is very very great indeed. This book has bee frequently re-edited in this century and it is one of the most charming book He wrote until the beginnings of the 19th century and all his writings dea with the practical problems of agriculture.

2. We have, especially after the completion of American war a series of rks on trade. Among the writers that stand forth is Lord Sheffield, who gan writing before American Revolution and wrote for 50 years. In 1783, wrote a book on Observation on Commerce of American Trade, which is y important from statistical point of view. It dealt with our relation to Great tain at that time. He was also interested in Ireland, and United States. His servation on the manufacture and trade of Ireland is important. His position s very interesting one, in general he was conservative and did not agree with am Smith. He thought there was great deal of value in colonial system. says, that the United States would continue to be dependent upon England 1 political separation would make very little difference than economic. He vocated policy of agricultural protection. At the time of Ricardo and althus he still advocated corn laws. As to the relation between England and land he maintained that English policy was unjust but also uneconomical m English point or view and that it was wrong to kill all industry except en industry. He was a great advocate of more liberal policy of England vards Ireland; also advocate of liberal policy towards industry and nmerce. So that, he has a very great reputation as a writer of great many oks, who is more opportunist than theoretical writer. He wrote on Trade ation which was connected with East India, and what England should do h India and East India Company and how far England would benefit from l benefit the country. This was a political literature, and therefore, they were t of fundamental importance to economic theory.

3. This literature appeared in connection with discussions of high prices England at that time, which was beginning to be subjected to the influence capitalists. The growing capitalist system began to feel the ups and downs cycles of trade, prosperity and depression. Passing over the others I will er mainly from 1795 to 1800. And, of course, prices went up exceedingly h especially in agricultural products and industries. First outburst of rature appeared in trying to explain the causes and consequences of all this, l here again study will have to be made and there is the origin of good many as. There were large number of men at this time who were interested in case of the treatment of the poor.

4. There was a different problem now. The situation was becoming very ficult in England, and the movement largely of all so-called outdoor relief ich started whole system of public relief to supplement wages in this nsition period from domestic system to factory system. You find that the ges of the ordinary workman gradually being pulled down. Competition machine was such that workman found very hard to make a living. It was vorse period in the history for the workingman who had not yet adjusted the new system. We have large problems of poverty and conditions of the or. There are three names which would stand out prominently: George Dyer, lely read. Wrote a book in 1793, entitled Complaint of Poor People of

England, where he tried to analyze the sad conditions. What he did for cit
and towns was done by country by D. Davies, who wrote a book entitl
The Case of Laborer and Husbandry. He attempted to suggest remedies
agricultural evil. Both of these books overshadowed by Sir F. Eden, wh
book was entitled, State of Poor. This is a large three volume book a
published in 1797, which was a very remarkable analysis of the social conditi
of England of the day.

5.   Problem of public debt, which was worrying great many people.
happened that about the time that Adam Smith wrote a Dutchman who l
lived long time in Paris came to England. He wrote a book which was full
and best and still remains today the greatest, especially of the theory of
public credit. This man was Pinto, whose English book was published in
70's, entitled, Essay on Credit. And, he was a most extreme advocate of
beauty and advantages of public credit and wrote that England now
following example of Holland could prove that public debt could be a m
of gold. Pinto's work is still today the most extreme decided exponent
advantages of this new thing which England was only beginning. The mat
was taken up at that time by Price, who now became responsible as being
father of Sinking Fund Idea. Says, after you attached to public credit t
characteristics you are bound to succeed. He says, first, public loan must ha
the principle of inalienability, and you must apply to this debt inalienabi
and the revenues you must not divide; secondly, this inalienable revenues m
draw a compound interest and you can borrow as much as you like and
aside sinking fund and provide for its payment. Finally Alexander Hamil
in this country adapted this system. So that, although Price was opposed
good many people he soon acquired great reputation and influence. As a res
of American war the debt seemed to stagger. Adam Smith was very cauti
about public debt and great many people opposed it, especially when war bro
with France. So that you have during the 90's very interesting discussions
which hundreds of writers wrote as to whether debt should be encouraged
otherwise, to conduct the war.

6.   As a consequence there was the discussion of taxation—the practi
problem of taxation, which led to theoretical discussion. Then the great wo
of another Sinclair appeared which was on the history of public revenue. T
was a three volume work, which was a landmark in English literature. Th
it was followed by two events about two years later. An anonymous wri
published a volume on the principles of taxation to complete the work of M
and Adam Smith on social body economic. Finally, came Pitt, who utili
the great war with Napoleon to introduce income tax, and that produce
literature most abundant and interesting as regards theory of public revenu
which no doubt, had its influence upon Ricardo. (Still more important practi
problem, which is the money question we will pass by for a moment). Th
is very interesting problem of theory advanced on these practical econo

>blems, on which you find a considerable number of writers, most of whom
re more or less influenced by Adam Smith who started out an independent
e. That was first group. Second group dealt with underlying philosophy of
>nomic and political life and who are known under the name of 18th century
licals. A few words on the radicalism of the time:
The radicals were many in number. We will mention half-a-dozen men who
racted universal attention, and who gave rise to the reactionary movement
thought. These radicals were: Priestley, who published his work even before
am Smith. It was a treatise on civil government of 1678. He was keenest
l very crude materialist. He attacked religion and who in politics was very
ich influenced by Rousseau and who accepts the doctrine of natural rights
l natural law. This is interesting to us for many reasons because Priestley
s teacher of Bentham and Bentham was the teacher of Ricardo. His
oretical conclusion is to let everything alone. Now, in this respect of course,
idea was not so entirely different from idea of Adam Smith, but the new
>arture was that this system if followed would bring about perfection in the
iverse, a panacea for all human wants. His words: "The end will be glorious
l pass beyond what our imaginations could now conceive." He founded this
v system and thought that here we find the great instrument of civilization.
In the same year that Adam Smith wrote, Price wrote his dissertation. He
s a minister, a man who had great sympathy with American colonies, and
s opposed to colonial system, he was discontented with the economic and
ial conditions of the day and the motto of his book was "In a free state
ryone is his own legislator." Government, he says, must never trench upon
· natural independence and the remedy for all the difficulties of England
the day he finds in a very radical change in all economic and political
ıception.
Thomas Paine, who you remember, was in the public service and came to
s country in 1774, got acquainted with Franklin and others, and in 1776
sent the whole country into flame by his work entitled "Common Sense."
demanded complete separation from England and helped raising the
ndard of revolt. He followed his first publication by another work, entitled
risis", published every few months, books on direct revolution. As a result
his efforts he received several important positions from revolutionary
vernment. Later on turned his attention to economic topics, as banking,
>er money, etc., then when he returned to the continent he was interested
the French Revolution and now while in France and while a member of
:nch Constituents he published his most famous book, "Rights of Men",
1792, which among other things is remarkable because in it we find that
at defense of graduated taxation which was soon to take an important place
French Revolution. He followed that book by another, called, "Agrarian
tice." He entered into the system of English primogeniture of land. You
o find in this book the first demand for old age pension.

Thomas Paine whose effort was to make this country independent, after
finished his political organization in this country and in France, and while
prison in France wrote his "Age of Reason" which became a famous wo
and quite undeservedly he was called infidel, atheist, and etc. even by Presid
Roosevelt. He was of course nothing of the kind. After he was released throu
the effort of the American Representatives, he wrote his final work in 17
entitled the Decline and Fall of English System of Finance. It is a very ac
and elaborate criticism of English System. His book on religion was a
attacked and he lost all his friends, he lived here quietly and died in absol
poverty in 1809 in this country, but his work lived after him. He found a v
distinguished biographer, who wrote a two volume work, which is about
best we have.

We now come, especially two writers who attacked the stronghold—
English Land. One is Ogilvie, who wrote anonymously, an essay on Right
Property to Land. It is a very interesting work. He tries to separate and
analyze the value of land into three parts: Original or fractional; the access
or improved value; the contingent or improvable value. Now the first and th
elements of value belong by natural right to the community and to individu
says he, as to the second part and the first part they are subject to taxati
perhaps also the third. He gives us very radical criticism, as he was a scho
and he gave a criticism of English System. He maintains that the situation
independent cultivator is the one which is most favorable to virtue a
prosperity. Property in land he considers a pernicious monopoly. Rent, I
interest he says should be regulated. Monopoly renders the whole situat
stationary, and is responsible for poor returns and altogether, he says, i
a very regrettable situation. He advocates a progressive agrarian law that ev
citizen 21 years old ought to be able to have 40 acres in England, 200 ac
in this country, and they ought to be entirely content. He works all these poi
out in detail and emphasizes them. He is not to be considered a commun
He emphasized the small proprietorship of land instead of large l
ownership. He became very popular, but he did not follow his suggestio
a very proper way.

This was done by a writer, Thomas Spence, shoemaker, illiterate man,
he had good mind. In 1775 he gave a lecture at New Castle, which was l
on printed. He calls it "Meridian Sun of Liberty, or Rights of Man." The lect
was published two decades later. He laid down the principle of natural rig
of every one. He said, property in land as well as liberty ought to be eq
among all men, land actually being suffered by demi-gods who call themse
aristocrats. He takes Locke's theory and shows that this was not applica
for land. He says ignorance and usurpation created private property. He
together few people to join him to develop Spencerian system. He follo
these up by series of other work in the 80's. He wrote a poem, and spoke
the swinish multitude, pigs meat, or food for swinish multitude, and later

*llowed by some such other works. He published also the Ideal of Privilege
` the Commonwealth. Origin of Society to its Natural State. Last work was
*ry extreme and he was arrested and tried in 1801 and sentenced for one year
prison. He published more works after he got out of prison.

We have now first good survey of Spence and his followers. Spence
*veloped an idea of natural right to property and later developed still more
*dical views. This was taken up now by Godwin and his daughter. Godwin
*mself started out with an inquiry concerning political justices. He published
*large two volume work in 1893, which was inspired by French Revolution.
*cond edition was little moderated. His views of the government was that
* was originated for the purpose of protecting unjust acquisition of private
*operty. Since, he says, private property is evil all governments are evil, and
* got to follow the inherent law of reason. He says, age of reason is an age
*thout government, and private property is really responsible for every thing
*at is bad. It has produced vanity, ostentation, poverty which goes hand in
*nd with private property. Property, he says, stunts the mind and turns human
*ings to slaves, it loosens the reason and destroys mentality. He says, justice
*n be attained only when we have aggregation of free and independent
*inciples, living under the regime of communism. But his views are very
*egular about what will happen if people were left alone without private
*operty. He says, elision will come only to those who are stunted by private
*operty and government. The inquiry of 1798 was published, in which he not
*ly took the ground that poverty was the root of evils but also pointed out
*e economic aspect of situation. He held that machine and manufactures make
*ings worse. Godwin created a great sensation during the French Revolution
*d entered in its Radical Staff. You also find revolution in England. In
*gland they formed a corresponding society in 1792 and some of them were
*orkmen, like Hardy, etc. Some were writers and they went so far as to attempt
* interpret the theories which developed insurrectionary movement. This led
* a trial in 1794, and trial for treason now filled the papers, and public
*scussions followed, but incidentally there were a number of writers who have
*ver been adequately treated, like Hobbeson, Barlow, who was an educated
*holar, and Jarvin. Of course their influence is seen in the English literature
*nich now followed primarily by Shelly, also Wadsworth, Coleridge, and etc.
*u find this radical movement permeating in all kind of classes from now
*, but on the other hand naturally this whole movement was met by
*nservative movement. This was in the early years of last half of 18th century
* a reaction to radical movement. There are three or four writers in this
*ovement who must be mentioned, because without this we can not
*derstand Ricardo and Malthus.

Burke had written Vindication of Society, a satire on Bradenbrook. Then,
course, when the revolution broke out Burke multiplied his speeches and
*blications, tens of thousands of them were sold in a year. It was Burke that

called forth these writers, as Spence, etc. Burke was followed by Wallace wl
was a preacher in Edinborough. He wrote a dissertation on the numbers
mankind. He took exception to the view of Mandeville and others. He sa
that frugality, patience and contentment are the things that we should stri
for. Little later on he wrote his characteristic of the present political situati
which is a virtually panagery on the existing economic situation.

Archbishop William Paley, who wrote a famous book on normal [sic: mor:
and political philosophy which came to the defense of private property. I
says, private property, indeed perhaps not natural, but has to be justified f
four reasons:

1. It increases wealth
2. It preserves production to its maturity
3. It prevents contest and fights of the producers
4. It implies to the convenience of life.

When the great movement arose in England, he wrote a very famous wor
entitled, Reasons for Contentment, which was addressed to the laboring boar
He also wrote an essay on wealth, this was a most optimistic view of the prese
situation, so that you see there was no lack of defense of opinion
conservatives as over against the radicals.

Now, we come to the many theoretical works in economics that was do
after Adam Smith. Very few people now dared to enter the field. There a.
however, 3 or 4 names that ought to be mentioned in this period of 40 to
years. The very year Adam Smith wrote there was published a book by Pown
The title of the book was, Examination of Adam Smith's doctrine. It is n
worth while going into detail. Pownell was not convinced by Adam Smit]
doctrine of value, free trade, or error of England's treatment of colonies.
is a very interesting book, however, for Americans to read.

The next year another work was published which is interesting from entir
different point of view. These were two volume book of Anderson. (1) Inqu
into the Corn Laws. (2) Observation of the Exciting Spirit of Natural Indust:
This is very interesting because you have here a part of the famous theory
rent, which was afterwards to receive the name of Ricardo. Anderson point
out that rent was a premium paid for cultivating more fertile soil. You do
find the theory of diminishing return, and that Anderson believed in increasi
returns and favored production for this reason for cultivation of inferior s(

A decade or two elapsed without more discussion, until we come to Dug:
Stewart. He succeeded Adam Smith's chair of Moral Philosophy in Glasg(
and he was the first one to give a separate course of lectures on Politi
Oeconomy. His lectures were attended by a whole group of young men w
soon became distinguished economists, as Callow, S. Smith, Dugald Stew:
was also interesting as he collected Adam Smith's papers, wrote the fi

mprehensive life and criticism of Adam Smith. In his lectures which were stroyed by fire, but which were taken and brought together these lectures, ich were afterwards published in two volumes, and his views therefore are portant only in so far as they influenced his theories, who soon themselves gan to write on the subject. He discussed the subject of population [a]ffected means of subsistence and devoted good deal of time and attention to two oblems: (1) Agriculture and industry on the one hand and (2) Relative vantages of large and small farms on the other. Then, when he came to more neral problems of wealth, he discusses the Physiocratic doctrine and Adam nith's criticism and emphasizes especially over against some of the writers, e advantages of machinery. He also has a good deal to say about many cations and poor laws. He was one of the great advocates of the free societies. Stewart therefore gave a very decided impetus to study political economy England and brought together a group of students. One student had one of work and wrote a very remarkable work. This was Lauderdale, who ote in 1804—"Inquiry into the Nature of Public Wealth." And, there he took some of the fundamental points of Adam Smith and developed it, sometimes tical sometimes approving in all cases from original point of view. In the st place he denies that any thing is real measure of value, and takes exception the views of Adam Smith on that point, and in the second place brings up ore forcibly than Adam Smith that value is not a value of commodity, and at it depends upon quantity and demand. He makes a distinction however between public wealth and private wealth. Public wealth, he says comprises everything that man desires, whereas private wealth can be same thing where re is scarcity. In other words he makes a distinction between wealth and hes. Wealth being public, riches more with private connotation. He discusses d criticizes Adam Smith's productive and unproductive theories. He nsiders the capital and profits. Here again he seizes upon Adam Smith's tement that profits are deductions from labor. He says, profits are due to pplement of labor. He does not like to stress on division of labor but brings ew point in his discussion. As regards saving and spending, he thinks there a danger in saving too much. He points out that if you save too much you bound to have glut. He then, discusses the problem of sinking fund which d been adapted by Pitt. He criticizes it and calls it bad but he does not really the fallacy of it. He think it is bad because it is paid back too rapidly. His ws were hotly attacked by some of these young men and he replied with ook, his observation and replies of the inquiry, and he goes more fully into question, as to how to increase capital by additional exertion of industries d savings. Lauderdale must be considered a really independent thinker and s started several points of view to which all subsequent writers return. That haps is sufficient for this man's general theoretical presentation. We might ntion also that in the opening years of 19th century that English writers apted French ideas. The ideas of Physiocrats were outworn in France, but now the Physiocratic movement led to a number of works. At the end of tl century there came John Gray's "Essential Principles of Wealth of Nations what he calls single tribute. He was met by one of the students, Mr. Wakefiel holding that such a theory was absurd, but 10 years later the discussion flar up again by William Spence, who wrote a book which was widely read, "Brita Independent of Commerce." There is nothing in the book which is new, b it is interesting. Also another writer should be mentioned—Torrens, who wro a book, "Economics refuted." This covers all the works with one excepti and that is the writers on currency, and we have only recently worked out I Professor Hollander, Silberling's book. It is important to go into this becau you find among these able men a great deal of what was considered by t work of Ricardo, work of Castle and others.

We will now devote a few minutes to the writers on currency. With t restriction of bank payments towards the end of the century in 1797, in ord to finance the war with Napoleon, it is perfectly explicable that some of t economic problems attract the attention of brighter minds. You find, indee for the following decade a succession of very remarkable works. It is only ve recently that any attempt has been made to discuss these problems—t problems of the issue of irredeemable paper money in England and in oth countries. And, we will therefore call attention to a few of these writers, sor of whom are considered as distinguished writers. Lord Liverpoole whose bo was not published until 1805. His book is interesting not because he discuss convertible paper money but because you find in him the greatest exponent the advantages of the gold standard. England like every other country in Euro had bimetallic system. It so happened that there was more gold in Englar less in France. The consequence was that in England movement began in 19 century in favor of gold standard, whereas France still kept bimetallic standa Lord Liverpoole's book is therefore the classic work on the advantages monometallism, but it does not go into the question of inconvertible par money. That method was taken up by a number of other writers.

Behring wrote in the opening years of the century, "Observation of Ba of England", generally devoted to the issue of these inconvertible bank not Then he was followed by Boyd, and in the following year Pitt wrote on t Stoppage of Gold. He took some problems of foreign trade. Thornton to the matter up more fully and wrote, "An Inquiry to the Nature and Eff of Paper Money." First book was devoted to the subject of paper money. T is interesting because now for the first time Thornton calls attention to t fact that two exceptions might be [a]ffected, not only by the state of currer at home but by all sorts of unusual demands connected with foreign tra He said, there were two sides to the problem, one was money side the otl was trade side. In fact you find in Thornton a statement clear enough of t famous purchasing power parity theory which was described by Profes Castles in the theory that prices change not simply by the absolute issues aper but on the relative purchasing power of the issues in different countries.— 'he famous purchasing power theory. In Thornton you find this theory as pplied to irredeemable paper money, but naturally first time you don't find ny great clear distinction between convertible and inconvertible paper money. The following year, in 1803, E. King took up the matter. He wrote, Thoughts on the Restriction of Payment." He especially devotes himself very argely to the question of depreciation and exchange, as being due to foreign xchange and over-issue of money. In fact people began to think and talk about ais very widely and the problem arose also in Ireland. A special committee 'as appointed which made report on the question. The following year, in 1804, eport circulated that government was taking up all these questions. In fact ae Irish situation now attracted such attention that H. Pownell wrote his Observation on Currency of Ireland", and Exchange between Dublin and ,ondon.

There still remains two theorists, who are perhaps the best. Mr. Foster, also a 1804, wrote his "Essay on the Principles of Commercial Exchange." He goes auch more fully than preceding writers. Being an Irishman he was very much aore interested probably. The other writer, ablest of them all was Wheatley. Ie wrote two large books, one in 1803, "Remarks on Currency and Coin," nd he gives new valuation of purchasing parity theory, more akin to the recent aodifications. He discusses especially the problem of operation by which the quilibrium of money can be obtained. And, finally a few years later he ublished his essay on the "Theory of Money".—Most comprehensive general aeory. He lays down the rule as regards paper money. He says, no one nation an possess greater relative currency than the other. He lays down the rule f the principle of Uniform Gravitation of money to this parity. Practically, e had reference to opposition in England.

But, it is to be seen, however, from this little survey, that you have a galaxy f series of men devoted attention to this difficult subject. I might also mention a conclusion two special works by Lauderdale. He now, devoted greater ttention to these problems. Published in 1810 and 1813, works on depreciation f paper currency and another further considerations. You see therefore, from hat I said in the last lecture that this period from Adam Smith up to the rst decade of 19th century was by no means so utterly arid as is commonly apposed. Most people jump from Adam Smith to Ricardo. As it was in ngland, so also these questions were taken up in Germany. They had not otten over the religious wars; and in France, under Napoleon, and also hysiocratic doctrine, there was not any enthusiasm of any kind. So that the 'hole economic discussions at that time took place elsewhere. We have lexander Hamilton in this country. That brings us therefore now to the ritings of great founders of classical school and we take up:

Section 41. Malthus

This is divided into several parts: His book has almost as much influenc
as Adam Smith's "Wealth of Nations." And, other rather neglected work
largely due to a publication of a few days ago of the newly discovered note
of Ricardo. (Copies are now in the reading room edited by Professe
Hollander.) A very remarkably dealt critical study by Ricardo of Malthus an
his general theory. We will begin, first, with his Principles of Population, an
before we are ready for a critical appraisal of that doctrine to understand i
we will run over his theory of population. First, I will say a few words abou
Malthus himself:

Malthus was born in 1766. His father was a very distinguished thinker an
writer who attracted to his home all the leading men of the time. It was i
the breakfast and dinner table that Malthus met so many of the prominer
political philosophers. He was also a friend of Rousseau. So Malthus from
early years was familiar with all these personalities. He was brought up fo
ministry, took orders in 1789. His book was published in 1798, as he tells u
himself. He laid down the fundamental theory and now started to connect fact
He began to travel through Europe, Russia, and down to Italy, and again late
on to France and other countries. And, as a result he published second editio
in 1803. Five years later he published large work full of great many interestin
facts. This time everybody was talking about his book and he was mad
professor of this budding science.—Professor of a little college where Englis
nobility would train for service in India. Thus East Indian College started, an
Malthus was chosen to discuss the economic problems involved. No soone
he did that, he now became acquainted with Ricardo. In the meantime als
he was interested in these problems. And, from that time on although continue
to perform his duties as clergyman devoted all his time to economic problem
He wrote book after book. Helped to found political economy group in 182
and toward the end of his life he took a prominent part in the discussion an
amendment of poor laws, which was the great question in England at that tim
He died a year or two later, in 1834. In addition to his work regardir
population he has works on the causes of high prices. There was dearth o
food in England, and that led Malthus to consider the question, but it wa
not until a decade later that the question of whether protective system, or cor
laws should be given up, or abandoned.

Everybody began to write about it now. Malthus wrote a number of books-
Observation on the Corn Laws, in 1814. Inquiry to the Nature of Theory o
Rent, in 1815. This led to his great controversy with Ricardo. Then, in abou
1820 he had formulated his general conclusions, and he was ready to writ
In 1820 he published his Principles of Political Economy. Finally 6 or 7 yea
later he published a little summary, entitled Definitions of Political Econom

We now come, to his book on Population. First, the book was published n 1798, ran 6 editions before his death, and the title of the book we ought o remember—"An Essay on Principles of Population as it [A]ffects the Future mprovement of Society." He quotes, especially, you remember, the statement f Paine, "Societies produced by our wants, governments by our wickedness." Ie spoke of political justice and calls attention to the phrase of Godwin: "If ou only let people alone everything will be all right ... suspiciousness would anish, everyone would work in his individual existence in the thought of ommon good, philanthropy would increase, all men would live in the midst f plenty ... envy would disappear from the world ..." Now, Malthus did not elieve that, and it is very interesting that although he was very orthodox neologian, he did not think that God intended men to be happy in this way. Ie thought unhappiness was more or less intended.

We call attention to his economic and social views: His doctrine: (1) Food s necessary to existence. (2) Passion between male and female. From these ollows conclusion that power of population is greater than power to produce ubsistence. Population not checked increases in geometric ratio, subsistence ncreases in arithmetic ratio. That implies a check upon population arising from ifficulty of subsistence. This difficulty must be met and felt by individuals. secause of this difference between geometric and arithmetic ratio that you get nis result among plants and animals. As a result you have among mankind nisery and vice. First is absolutely necessary consequence, and vice is highly robable consequence. That is the foundation of his theory, and passing over o Chapter IV. He makes distinction between prohibitive and positive check. Misery of course is a positive check but you can prevent it to contain extent erhaps by having enough foresight to think of the difficulties in rearing a amily, you may possibly prevent what otherwise would happen will be in favor f misery. Now, beginning of Chapter V. He discusses the positive check. Check onsigned chiefly although not perhaps solely to the lowest orders of society nd it resolves itself as he tells us time and time again, into all manner of misery nd discomfort. On the other hand the upper classes by foresight attempt to neck some of these difficulties by waiting to marry till they can afford to upport a family. And, that these two checks are called prohibitive and positive neck, and to this we may add the vicious customs with respect to women, n great cities. Unreasonable manufactures and luxury, disease, pestilence and var, all these checks can be resolved into two terms, misery and vice and that s why population increases so slowly in Europe. That is the main part of the neoretical structure of his work and he sums up his whole theory in Chapter ine.—Increase of population by means of subsistence, population increasing when means of subsistence increases and superior power of population actually ept down by misery and vice. He says as soon as you have private property nd institution of marriage, inequality of conditions must follow, especially vhen the members of family are too large, and that some human beings should suffer from want. That is the theoretical part of the first situation. Then, he goes on to explain what really are in detail more shortcomings of G. Price and others. Most of this book is devoted to a treatment of what he consider the evolution of these writings.

Malthus traveled all over Europe and when he found what he thought i ample confirmation to his doctrine, he published a second edition.—"An Essa on Principles of Population or a Few of its Past and Present Effects." So tha his whole point of view is different now. The only authors of whom he coul get any help were Hume and Wallace and Adam Smith. He was led t examination of these and says, I find much more advantage than that I hav been aware of. Then, he calls attention to the difference between second editio and first edition. He says regarding the whole of present work: "I have so fa differed in principle as to consider another check to population, which doe not come under the head of either vice or misery and later part I hav endeavored to soften some of the harsher conclusions of the first essay."

What is his new theory? You find that in the beginning of Chapter six, an again he mentions two checks, prohibitive and positive. He develops much mor fully. Says, this is peculiar to man and rises from distinctive superiority in hi reasoning faculty which enables him to calculate the consequences. This is th prohibitive check, what he calls moral restraint. This restraint does not produc vice and it undoubtedly is the less evil that follows the principle of populatio concerned as a restraint inclination, otherwise natural it must be allowed. I produces certain degrees of temporary unhappiness. When this evil produce vice, the evils which follow are small evils. Then, he goes on to discuss thos prohibitive check regulating vice. Rest of his book deals with such things a misery, war, famine and the rest. Rest of his book further deals entirely wit history. But the Book four, Chapter one, is worth mentioning. In the first editio of this essay, he says check must exist. It is better to have this check than t be obliged to support by charity. He discusses in great fullness and detail an little later on when some other people suggested possibly you need to includ what is called in modern times birth control. He says, that he is not in favo of any artificial or unnatural checking population, both on account o immorality and tendency to limit the necessary stimulus to industry. By mora restraint he means late marriage. Rest of it deals with full discussion of poo laws. He says it does more harm than good and destroys practically the Englis population. Malthus lays down the principle that nobody has any right to relie on the hand of public expense. In Book five, he has some interesting thing to say about public charity. Malthus is the father of charity organizatio movement, which did not start until three-quarters of a century after he wrote Fundamentally he objects very much to any prohibition of marriage. He point out the natural consequence to produce illegitimate things. He takes up th whole subject of compulsory insurance for old age. He is very much in favo of voluntary system of savings banks, with that his book comes to an end.

Advantages of the doctrine of Malthus: As explained in the last lecture, you must regard this from the point of view of practical considerations. Malthus, you see pointed out to the people, and tried to fortify them against danger of too early and foolish marriages. He also showed in pointing out some of the evils connected with English poor laws as they were then administered. In a letter to Whitebreast, which was published in 1807, he goes more fully into some of these abstract problems and makes very strong appeal to the sense of personal responsibility of every individual. It is true that certain objections were urged at the time, which he attempted to answer more or less generally with some degree of success. For instance, in the very outset people said, well, one of the dangers of the scheme is that if you restrict population by late marriage, then the market will be understocked with labor, wages will rise and ordinary employer will find that very unfortunate thing to compete abroad. Malthus took up that point and said, it is either child play or hypocrisy, like the city boy who gives away his cage and cried for it, you got to face the situation whatever it is.

Second point he discussed is that the objection that diminution or fall in the number of population, it would ensue that England therefore might have been at disadvantage again compared with rapidly growing capitals. Malthus says, this only will be relative, because as soon as supply of food increases the population will advance with it, therefore stress would be laid again on possibility of increase of food.

Third objection was that the possibility of the quantity of sexual vice would increase. Malthus says that he will be sorry if the cause of virtue will be violated but these are not vices alone, in effect they are worse, and the poverty may be a temptation. Says, he is inclined to think that they are in combination with temptation arising from continual distress and largely correspond to men and women, that he believes there will be very few hopeless poverty without a great moral degradation of character. So that, in each of these points Malthus thinks he is really contributing toward the amelioration of conditions.

The last quotation is from appendix to the 5th edition, in which he points out: "I have always considered the principle of population as a peculiarly suited to state of discipline and private." He says, you will find that the ways of God to man with regards to laws of nature are completely vindicating. He confesses in his first edition that he perhaps went to the extreme, this went too much one way, and says he cannot go too much the other way to correct this. After all, he says, What is my object? To improve condition and to increase happiness of lower classes of men. You may consider the result of doctrine. Next point is, What shall we say about the doctrine itself? Is it true or is it false? And, you must begin considering the differentiation between the first and second edition. In its first form Malthusian argument is conclusive, but is based upon untrue premises, and therefore not conclusive as an argument. What shall we say about that? He introduced in the second edition the principle of moral

restraint, with that his principle is no longer one that would be used as a
argument against perfectibility. Like Wallace and Townsend, Malthu
continued to hold that communism must nevertheless, private property mu:
cause moral restraint, this in his opinion depends upon private property. Sti
in his second edition, says, communism is impossible and perfectibility i
wrong. Virtually however, Malthus loses all interest in others. His interest i
in his doctrine from these ideals toward possibility of taking next step forwar
in social reform.

Now, let us take up some of his points. How about geometric and arithmeti
progression? You remember that is the very basis of his argument, wherea
later on that was abandoned by all the supporters, and you remember ho·
J. S. Mill treated the subject of population. He defines it entirely on law c
diminishing returns, not because of any alleged supposition by the arithmeti
or geometric, but on the law of diminishing returns. In the second edition yo
find just a real statement as to law of diminishing returns, but still based ver
largely upon ratio. In the 8th edition you will find it again, but in an entirel
different way. Page 380. He says, a suffering country after being depopulate·
the remaining inhabitants will be prosperous and get enough food, particularl
on account of the diminishing cost of cultivation, more fertile part of th
territory will be cultivated and not to apply labor to the ungrateful sourc·
If you take up Canon's economic history you will find that that point is take·
up very successfully with the whole basis of the Malthusian doctrine change·
from geometric and arithmetic ratio to the law of diminishing returns. Eve
excepting that, taking modern version of Malthusian law, Is it true or false
Here again we should consider it from three points of view: (1) Biological poin
of view. (2) Economic point of view, and (3) Social point of view.

Let us take the biological argument first. Of course we know the importanc
of that, because you all are aware of the fact that Darwin got the biologic·
point of view from Malthus. And, we know that good deal of work has bee·
done in recent times tending to perhaps on some of the biological implication·
of Malthusian doctrine. You got to make distinction between check to
tendency and the degrees of the tendency. I am considering now the tendenc·
not the check to appropriate itself and possible influences brought by biologic·
facts. Furthermore, not alone the tendency to appropriate, but also tendenc·
to increase. You are probably acquainted by R. Pearl of Johns Hopkins, an·
also the others with their so-called lococentric curve. In his book of biolog·
of population of growth and the influence of the density of population, o·
course you must not exaggerate the importance of that of what they had o·
population. They had a conference at Geneva last year of biologists, chiefl·
on the ascendency. American and English biologists who captured the whol·
convention and the biologists did not call it any more geometric progressio·
that Malthus laid down. Malthus got that from Benjamin Franklin. He too·
the population in the 18th century and it did increase almost in that respec·

t seemed at one time to have some foundation for that statement, so that uestion arises whether the fall of birth rate which is noticeable everywhere . a biological fact. As they themselves conceived at the very end of his book ie problem was far more a biological question.

Now we come to economic argument. His first argument is based upon atios, which is not valid, then again based upon diminishing returns. This law, f course, is perfectly true, but when you deal with the problem as a general roposition, as a war proposition. You must remember that the law is met y other tendencies, which for a long time arose and overturned it. What appened, for instance, immediately after Malthus wrote? It was a period of pening up of the wide fields in the new continent, first in North America, ien afterwards in South America, and had Malthus lived a few more years ie situation would have been a very different one, because instead of opulation based upon the food situation, it would have been the other way round. The surplus of food that was now rapidly produced made possible ideed an increase of population. So that on the one hand you have all hroughout the 19th century state of affairs that Malthus could see. On the ther hand not alone immense tracts of fresh land, but also low-price land vas now added to the world supply. By that improvements in agricultural lines ioved in an accelerated pace, not alone this but new inventions, and pplication of capital to land increased the output of food. Then came not ione increase of population but increase of productive genius of population. Ve might call attention to the new chemistry, experiments even now are being arried on. We haven't begun yet even faintly to visualize the possibilities of ncreased production when we apply all the evidence of modern science, capital, lectricity to that. On the other hand the population is not increasing normously. As you find in France in 19th century the population was at a tand-still. In Australian cities and in this country had it not been for mmigration the birth rate also would be at a stand-still. That explains the act that in certain periods of history the problem has been more of inderpopulation than overpopulation. What was the problem in Rome, and vhat has been in France? Why was it last year that Anglo-Saxon peoples were ined up against France, simply because largely under the influence of Malthus hey have been feeling the dangers of overpopulation and in France they are rying for a century pointing the danger of underpopulation. So that even from conomic point of view you cannot say that Malthus's theory has uniform alidity in all places and in all countries.

Let us take now, the sociological side: In other words, How far increase »f population have been due to the volitional element in control? Remember 3ernard Shaw as he puts the problem. He says, look at London today, you ind dinner without appetite at one place and appetite without dinner at the »ther end of the town. Also, horses and comfort without children at one end »f the town, children without horses and comfort at the other end of the town.

In other words, what is the influence of general standard of life? What is the influence between social classes upon the density of population and increase of birth rate? Now, of course, in modern times in recent years we began to have too many unfortunate facts, one is the whole question of eugenic movement which did not exist at all in the time of Malthus. And, the second is the birth control movement. Very few years ago when lecturing, I was very careful and passed over these as though over a thin ice, so far the problem has changed.

It so happened that when Malthus was read, especially by R. Owen he was very much concerned to improve conditions among workers. Also Franci Place did the same thing. Robert Owen traveled in France and noticed the method that the people in certain section in France employed. They had been practicing this for many years in order to maintain the size of their group that this system of artificial birth control was introduced and Owen was very much impressed by it. The explanation was given in his book, and having done this it created an intense excitement. What was widely done in those days is being practiced today. Even by Judge Lindsey by his recent work on companionate marriage. Catholic church maintains that the ethical danger of that system far outweighs any possible social good, or whether on the other hand to agree with advocates of birth control, the case is that there is no doub that the tendency to which Malthus referred may be checked by rational human effort, whether wise or not I am not discussing. Therefore his whole doctrine of moral restraint has an extension which he never thought of, because with him moral restraint meant late marriage. He would have realized moral evil of late marriage by any means to be despised, but with those additions to these doctrines as originally mentioned, of course, it was that the Malthusian theory is not so dismal as at one time it seemed to be. Of course, from purely economi side of it that argument is not a very convincing one, because although you may have temporary increase of supply as in 19th century, sooner or later law of diminishing returns will make itself felt. Therefore you either have to accep the inevitable results of Malthus' statement or have to explain the method which are largely responsible for the French under-population, partly of cours for other reasons, and partly for biological reasons, perhaps, but very largely for economic and social reasons. The conclusion therefore would have to be that if you accept this doctrine of moral restraint and birth control then the whole Malthusian doctrine is free from great danger, but if you don't accep it there is no way of Malthusian logical conclusion which has developed in later times. The question therefore arises in the third place in the form it wa put as one of the drawbacks or disadvantages of the doctrine. There you mus remember the starting point of Malthus, who was a conservative and who wa a critic of French Revolution and one who maintained absolutely that ther was no right on the part of any human being to demand subsistence from community. Even to the end he remained an individualist of the individualist

the very last edition of his book, he tells us that there are future prospects
sponsible for evils from population which may not be bright, yet they will
vor the laws of the principle of marriage. We shall always have class of
oprietors and class of laborers, but the condition of population may be so
anged that gradually improve the beauty and harmony of all. What is more
iportant, he saw no way out of the evil. Trade unionism for him was very
rational.

Malthus was virtually the creator of the wages-fund doctrine and while he
aintained that his argument was needed in order to increase the principle
responsibility, the fact remained that so far as wealthy was concerned they
n't need it, but so far as the poor were concerned under modern conditions,
dustrial capitalism, large family, will benefit, so far economics is concerned
rge family was pleasing, because after a few years they would have earning
pacity of the family increased. While the richer classes are dying out, but
ey are being replenished continually from the lower classes. He says, if there
as a great deal of truth in the doctrine of heredity then of course the situation
ould be very bad indeed and outlook would be not promising. Fortunately
e know that environment plays much more greater role than does heredity.
he general conclusion then of the whole doctrine of population is a particular
ther than a general one. It applies at certain times in the course of history
it would not apply at other times, that so far as it must be considered as
proximately defensible, what will happen is open to the consideration dealing
ith each human being. That in this case you have a different situation, when
u are breeding animals or bees. Therefore we need not be frightened by the
octrine, that there is no such principle which is bound to keep forever the
ndition of humanity.

Further study of Malthus: What we are concerned here is his views on general
onomic questions. We have to deal with problems which brought him in
imediate contact with Ricardo. It is impossible to get a clear view of the whole
tuation until after we study the Ricardian economics from Ricardian point
view. What we can do now is to call attention to the way in which the
roblems arose—great controversy between Malthus and Ricardo, and
(althus' own point of view. We will leave the general conclusion until next
cture or two. In considering the controversy with Ricardo, we will try to get
ie picture or framework of the whole discussion. What were the problems?
ow did they arise? and, What was the question between the two? In order
understand that, we have to study first quarter of the century.

After the first edition of Principles of Population, if you take that in view,
u find that there were three fundamental occurrences which were connected
set economists thinking about new problems: First, there was the attempt
finance the war with Napoleon. At the end of 18th and beginning of the
)th century which culminated in the issue of inconvertible bank money—
spension of specie payment of Bank of England. Malthus never paid much

attention to that. It is true that he lectured on the subject when he was professor and he intended to write but it was primarily Ricardo who as a retire stockbroker asked, What is responsible for the rise of premium of gold? I the time Malthus was ready to discuss them another problem arose and the was much more important in the intellectual life history of Malthus, and the question was, What should be done with the corn laws? The question aro in 1813-14, just at the end of Napoleonic career. In order to understand the situation in those years you got to know the facts and we will say a few wor about the relation between prices of corn and legislation.

You all remember that in 1688 a bounty was given on the export of the corn to help along the farmer. This law provided that this bounty be continue as long as the home price was not over 48 shillings. When it went over the price, it would not be advisable to give the bounty, because it would on increase the dearness at home. As regards importation England did not impo any wheat at that time and the only object of the very high prohibitive duti on wheat was of course, simply the desire to attract as much capital as possibl It was not until about the middle of 18th century that the beginnings industrial revolution and increase of population changed the condition England from exporting to importing country. England stopped exporti wheat in 1760 and began to import wheat and during the next few decad especially there was a change in price. Towards the end of the century the were high prices, almost a famine. In 1799 to 1801 the price of corn went to 177 sh. and the whole country was full of pamphlets trying to explain th situation. Then situation became normal, and in 1791 a so-called high du was imposed. This was a duty of 2 1/2 shillings which was to be imposed on when the price fell below 50 shillings. If it went above 50 shillings the du was then the normal duty. Now from 1799 to 1802 the price was always abo 50 shillings, and therefore there was no import duty, no tax on the importatio of wheat. That was the situation in the beginning of the century. In 1804 t agricultural interests persuaded the Parliament that when the price of whe should be under 60 shillings they could not import any wheat at all, but whe the price was above that, of course this law did not operate, so there was n much excitement. In 1813 the trouble came up and there was therefore ne movement to raise the limit and in the beginning of the year 1815, after a lor discussion the limit was raised to 80 shillings. That is, whenever price of whe fell below 80 shillings there was a prohibitive duty on the import of corn. I the meantime, of course, the bounty no longer operated, that was realized no and it was done away with as meaning nothing at all.

Now, you have the background of the great discussion up to 1815, and duri those two years that was all they talked as over against "Boni", and a gre committee was appointed—the Lord's Committee, which called a multiplici of witnesses, landlords, farmers, actually everybody interested in land holdir or tillage in England. The discussion in this interesting report ranged over th hole problem of the connection between prices of corn, methods of cultivation d more especially the extension of cultivation, whether more land was ailable. Now, it so happened that in these questions that were put by telligent men all sorts of interesting points were raised that had never been ised before, and it was still more natural that the men who had power of neralization in reading these reports should come to general conclusions. nd, there were no less than four men that at the same time jumped to the me conclusions on reading the testimony of this report. One of the men was hn Rooke, who wrote some essays in 1814. The second was Edward West, ho was a fellow at Oxford, a student of economics. He wrote an essay the llowing year on the application of capital to land. The third was Torrens, ho wrote an essay on external corn trade, and the fourth was Malthus, who rote in 1815 two works: One was on the policy of restricting the importation d the other was inquiry into the nature and progress of rent. Only after all ese were printed that Ricardo wrote his essay on rent.

These four gentlemen, all wrote in complete ignorance of the other. And, called attention in my study of economics to the fact that although the theory ' rent is usually ascribed to Malthus and West that in reality it was also lvanced the same kind and had been advanced a year before by Rooke. Soon became known as Ricardian theory of rent. Now, the Ricardian theory of nt is based upon the law of diminishing returns, and the law of diminishing turns was not indeed new in economic science, although it had never been rmulated by any English writer. However, this was found in Turgot, in his inciples of wealth. The other part of the theory of rent, that rent is a surplus t a part of price, that theory was really had been advocated in England, d we called attention to the work of Anderson in 1777.

What these writers did was to call attention to these two parts of the theory they found it, really practical formula in the testimony of some writers. Now, hen Malthus and Ricardo took the matter up they found they agreed as gards the main points but they differed as to conclusions to be drawn. lalthus coming out in favor of protection and Ricardo coming out in favor ' free trade. But, here was the point at issue—the difference as regard the eory of rent. Now, they got into that theory little more fully. They found at they had to go back to the fundamental law of value and from the very ginning a difference now appeared between Malthusian theory of value and e new Ricardian theory of value. But, it did not really assume a very concrete, ute form until a few years later, when new problem presented itself. In the ar 1819, specie payments were issued and it was done, as it is often done, hat we today call a depletion or superabundance of paper money, as prices w began to fall. During the war prices went up, usually in modern scale, neral level of prices running in a straight line at once ran up. After 1819 ll of prices followed without a mercantile depression, and question arose, 'hat is the cause of all these? Has it anything to do with the money side of

Bank of England's action? Has it anything to do with land, with gener economic condition?

If Ricardo and Malthus lived today they would argue very differently. N one thought of general level of prices. Therefore statistical and other facts we the only things that were open to thinkers. What is the connection betwee all this and general problem of value? What is the cause of value and, wh is the measure of value? Now other problems arose. What is the connectic between national economic progress and changes in prices? and Especial change in prices of food, connected with question of industrial progress, profi of landlords, profits of money, interest. That was the great problem whic [a]ffected everyone and Malthus and Ricardo, who were leading thinkers the day took it up. In the meantime Ricardo had written his Principles, ar Malthus now as versus to Ricardo published his General Principles of Politic Economy, and with Ricardo carried on a very active correspondence. The were published three or four works, one was by McCulloch, another was t H. Crowe, and the other was by Malthus.

We now rediscovered notes of Ricardo on Malthus which throw light c many points. The whole thing turned around: What is the law of value? Wh is measure of value? What is the connection between national prosperity ar changes in prices? So that here we have three occurrences of the first ord which started Ricardo thinking and two of which started Malthus thinkir to the extent of writing about it. These are the points that we will take u Because, it brings home to one that every thinker was preacher at the tim There was no place that these things were discussed, even in France ar Germany this was not discussed. So the whole economic theory are outgrowt of those three great episodes during the first quarter of the 19th century.

Let us take up the problem under three heads: (1) Theory of value (2) Theo of Rent (3) Theory of capital and profits.

Now, Ricardo's fundamental theory was that all prices are fixed by cost ar that therefore the real explanation of value is cost, or labor theory of valu Labor is responsible for its value. Now, says, Malthus, nothing of the kin that is not the important thing. It is not the labor cost theory, it is the labe command theory, rather demand and supply and not cost of production th explains value. Now, in his book you will find that he ran over the whole fie of both demand and supply, and what Ricardo calls the natural price, as v shall see, is replaced in the explanation of Malthus what he calls ordinary average price of commodities—demand and supply. He says Ricardo is wror in thinking that labor cost produces values because there are differe proportions of fixing capital. We may have same amount of labor but differe amount of circulating capital. Ricardo fails, says Malthus, because he thin of only supply part, whereas I, says he, want to emphasize the demand sid

Now, Ricardo as we shall see, objected to Malthus, because he said, tl trouble with Malthus is he thinks of only temporary causes, but Ricardo sai that I am after to discover is the fundamentally permanent things and demand and supply are not permanent things. Here is the issue. And, finally Malthus goes back to, or accepts one of Smith's doctrines. He quotes from Smith, and says, labor which is a commodity will command and therefore the measure of value is not the labor cost theory but the labor command theory. This is the Fundamental point of issue between Malthus and Ricardo. The whole discussion seems little empty to us today, because we transfer it to an entirely different field.

We now come secondly, to the views of Malthus on rent and on protection. In his work on nature and progress of rent Malthus denies Smith's doctrine that rent received by the landlord is due to any monopoly of land-holding. Landlord owns the land and therefore exacts the rent. No says, Malthus, nothing of the kind, rent is due to three reasons: (1) To the fact that soil yields surplus of food—Physiocratic doctrine. (2) Food and materials cause an increase of population—the more food, the more population. (3) Fertile lands are comparatively scarce. Therefore instead of being due to monopoly of men is due to a law of nature. These three things being law of nature.

When Ricardo comes to consider the matter, he says, Malthus is partly right and partly wrong. He was willing to accept only the third explanation. Ricardo said the first two questions had nothing to do with it. No, said Malthus, you are wrong. Both, however, you see accepted the law of diminishing returns. This now becomes the basis of rent. Now comes the far more important point: What causes rent to rise? Malthus gives four causes, and Ricardo with his penetrating generalizations tries to reduce it to one.

Controversy between Malthus and Ricardo: These are not important in themselves. Malthus was not an acute and profound thinker as some of the other men. The cause and influence of Malthus' views upon posterity is relatively slight. They are important only because at the time they led Ricardo to make his statement and bring out his views. What we have tried to see was to try to explain how these problems arose, and as they arose they [a]ffected both Malthus and Ricardo. As few things as Malthus wrote in his book, they are not very good. He did not know very much of money and stock exchange. He really made no contribution at all. On the question of value he emphasizes the influence of demand and supply and on the theory of rent he again tries to explain it in terms of three reasons rather than in terms of a single cause as Ricardo.

We now come to his practical conclusions: Malthus was in favor of maintenance of protective laws, protection of agriculture and in favor of corn laws. He favored the retention of corn laws for the reason that they alone could be in cultivation. The lands which have recently been taken into cultivation, he says, if you do away with the corn laws these recently cultivated lands will revert to waste and that in his opinion would be a check to the progress of the community, because according to him the higher the rents advanced—

which always marked methods interpreted as accompaniment of progress-
the higher the rent of landlord the greater the prosperity of the whole country
Therefore the welfare of community was bound up with rent. In contrast t
this now Ricardo felt differently. He thought rise in rents was unhappy an
he deplored this. Malthus thought Ricardo was against landlords, that is
different question. However, they differed in their practical questions. Now
then, leaving for the moment this particular controversy, let us say a wor
more about the other views, other phases of protection and distribution
Discussion of profits and capital now came to the front.

Profits as we shall see according to Ricardo were all determined by the n
rent land, between the returns to the least and other productive lands, wherea
Malthus differed toto silo in that respect and he maintained that profits-
average rate of profits, were determined by competition between the capitalists
But that also is of interest only as serving to point Ricardian views, wherea
the following point is a contribution of Malthus, because of its validity in th
history for a long time. In his discussion of capital Malthus is largely responsibl
for the theory of gluts. You remember, when I spoke of Lauderdale, I pointe
out that it was Malthus who developed this. The problem arose very practicall
as a result of introduction of machinery in the year 1816. In Nottingham peopl
were thrown out of employment in large numbers by the introduction c
machine, and same thing applies to Yorkshire and led to famous Luddite riots
This was a repetition of movement of previous centuries against introductio
of machinery. This started Malthus and others thinking and it was responsibl
for the Malthusian theory of over-production, and the connection betwee
prosperity and luxury as giving rise to a neutral demand for goods. Now,
so happened that as we shall see in later lectures about that, that the theor
of Say became known in England largely because of correspondence betwee
Say and Ricardo. Say was known due to his theory of debauche, which ca
be put very simply in generalization that supply is always correlated with an
involves demand. As soon as you produce anything you must create on th
other side the purchasing power for consuming that thing. Malthus did not den
that general overproduction was rather difficult idea to grasp and not perhap
valid. What he maintained was that through use of machinery and unlimite
powers in the machine you would have at any time this limit overproduction-
overproduction in particular things as in these machines that put the whol
knitting framework out of business that is responsible for the trouble. So tha
this theory of glut led to an interesting controversy with Ricardo, but als
something to be learned as having made its way in economic literature largel
due to Malthus. Summing all up, you may say that all of these controversie
which were very interesting at the time yet did not gain for Malthus any speci
reputation, except through his relation with Ricardo. And, Malthus continue
to be known and to swing a great degree of notoriety primarily because of th
doctrine of population, which is the Malthusian doctrine by excellence.

Section 42.   The Critics of Malthus

We will say just a few words about critics of Malthus. These were evidenced om the very beginning after the appearance of the first edition of the book hich was written against Godwin. Godwin came back to the attack and came out in a different way. There was a clergyman by the name of Parr, who as very much influenced by Malthusian doctrine. He preached a sermon, and odwin answered Parr by his "A thought on Parr's spittal sermon." He was tterly against Parr, not so much against Malthus. The point I want to raise that it was not this essay that led Malthus to reconsider his doctrine and troduce doctrine of Moral Strength in 1820. Malthus had forgotten all about odwin. But, Godwin wrote a book entitled, "Inquiry Concerning the Power Increase", and here he retracts from the concession he made for Malthus d accused Malthus of all degrees of lack of logic, as well as character. urthermore, maintained the fact that Malthus was really an atheist. A number other writers now took up the cudgeons. Jarroled wrote a book entitled, Dissention on Man", which was written in 1806. He was a physician but a ood theologian and he opposed Malthus and his ideas especially, very hemently. His personal abuses for Godwin was now taken up by Ingraham. his led to famous literature and space. Ingraham says, Malthus as a Protestant inister, as a profound leader, thinks vice and misery are to be encouraged, d teaching to invent disease as a preventive to over population. Other writers ke Savoy, Owen, Spence, went further, objected not simply to his doctrine it also to the man. They said Malthus shows hypocrisy, sensuality and morality. So that he was not a very loved individual. Karl Marx says, Malthus' ork in his first form is nothing more than a school boy's superficial plagiarism preceding writers like, Steuart, Towsent and others. The principle of opulation had been slowly worked out in 18th century, and then in the midst a great social crises. Malthus who was hugely astonished of the success of s book now gave himself up stiff in his book material which was superficial, mpliant, and added to it all sorts of new matter, not discovered but annexed y himself. Malthus, however, he says, in one respect is to be favorably stinguished from the other panegyrists because he had taken the monastic view celibacy as one of the clergy in Cambridge and afterwards he forgot it.

Section 43.   Ricardo

As Ricardo in some respects is most important in history, we have to devote tle more attention to him. We have numerous writings and books on Ricardo one of which is really adequate to name. German books are mostly one-sided. ortunately we have in this country working of his life by Professor Hollander, hich is the greatest contribution to the subject. The study of Ricardo goes nder the same difficulty as Adam Smith. There are all sorts of opinions held

about him. It is held by some that Ricardo was proficient in economics, an
on the other hand the other schools represented by English writers, etc. sa
he who really enjoys Ricardo shows that he only half understands economic
So you can take your choice. There is another interesting thing about Ricard
which is that his most subtle work that ever appeared shows to be the founde
of individualism, whereas Karl Marx is the founder of socialism. They bot
were Jewish and coming from Talmudic teachings.

I will say a few words as to the work of Ricardo. Ricardo was born in 177
in Holland, his family being of Portuguese Jews. In the 18th century howeve
his father immigrated to England and made quite a success in stock exchang
He was honored and loved generally. David the son was brought up by h
father in Jewish faith. When 21 years of age he fell in love with P. Wilkinso
a Christian girl and married her, and as a result there came a rupture in th
family. He went to stock exchange and in five years he amassed a great fortun
in the stock exchange and at that time he was a student of natural scienc
A few years later while in a bathing resort he happened to see in a secon
hand book store "Wealth of Nations" of Adam Smith. When he read it b
was deeply interested because it gave him a theoretical foundation for his wor
on the stock exchange. In 1807, he met for the first time James Mill and bega
to talk certain economic problems. By 1809 his attention was directed to th
question of rise of premium of gold and for the first time he began to wri
out of his knowledge gained in stock exchange. He wrote some letters to th
Chronicle on the price of gold, which immediately was attacked as being th
forerunner of bullion controversy. In 1810, he wrote his famous work entitle
"High Price of Bullion." He wrote another article in Bosonquet. He said
had nothing to do with the issue of convertible bank notes, which Ricard
went over very thoroughly. Only after this that he met Malthus and Bentham
He soon became very intimate with Bentham, getting his political ideas fro
Bentham but giving Bentham some of his economic ideas in return. Two c
three years later rent controversy broke out, then the corn law controvers
and in 1815 Malthus wrote his essay on low prices of corn. In it he elaborate
his theory of rent and pointed out the connection with the whole theory c
distribution that attracted universal attention. In 1816 he met McCulloch, an
became a life-long friend. McCulloch persuaded Ricardo to put his ideas i
a more connected form and through his persuasion that Ricardo wrote h
"Principles of Political Economy" in 1817, and several editions followed. I
the meantime he had bought a country estate in Gatkut Park in Glasgoshir
and while liking the life of a country gentleman he was repeatedly visited nc
alone by Malthus but also by Bentham, McCulloch and others and in 181
he was elected a member of Parliament. This work to him does not mean muc
He became a member of Parliament, where he did not shine, but wheneve
he spoke he spoke with measured excellence with gravity, and they alwa
listened to him. Consequently his opinion was always asked mainly on th

.estion of banks, taxation and so forth, and he made some very interesting
eeches and also wrote pamphlets.
He started his famous economic group which even now exists today. During
e last few years of his life he wrote his essay on Funding System and laid
wn his plan for a National Bank. When Malthus wrote his "Political
onomy," Ricardo wanted to answer it but he did not do it on account of
cCulloch's advice. He died very few years later in 1823. We have mentioned
of his important writings, yet he had written great many things that were
t known. The first famous work was his letters to Malthus, published in
87, by Economic Association. Letters to Trower was published in 1899, then
. letters to McCulloch were published at the same time. This includes
erything that he wrote. And, then those notes on Malthus which were
blished a few days ago. That is his work in his life.
The best way to approach it is take his chief work and learn his opinion
general economic theory. His work on currency, money, public finance and
rious other problems, international trade, etc. But we want to set up our
ention first upon his views on general economic theory. His views on values,
oduction and distribution. We will begin with his work, "Principle of Political
onomy." First six chapters which contained these.—His famous edition
blished by McCulloch. Let us start then with his book, and let me call your
ention to the fact that this book is entitled, "The Principles of Political
onomy and Taxation," and that most of the book deals with the taxation.
apter one, value; Chapter two, Rent; Chapter three, Mines; Chapter four,
tural and Market Prices. Chapter five, Wages; Chapter six, profits. He goes
ht on with main discussion. He takes up in turn with different kinds of taxes,
es on land, profits, wages, houses, etc. I might say here that also here again
treats only one problem. What he is concerned with is economic problems—
osperity. His study of taxation is limited as to how taxes act and it is really
study in the incidents [sic: incidence] of taxation. He goes to the heart of
problem, when he finishes that you have series of miscellaneous chapters
values, economic doctrine of Adam Smith, on rent, value of corn, on the
luence of demand and supply, of prices, on machinery, and Malthus' opinion
land. You see it is a haphazard collection of essays though not systematic
in this little book you have virtually the whole classical theory of economics.
deals with values in the first chapter of his book. He points out in the begin-
g quoting Adam Smith, value in use and value in exchange. Dealing with
utility first, he says, utility is not a measure of exchangeability. Value is
solutely essential, but to which you have to add utility. He says, it depends
on two things: (1) Scarcity, (2) The quantity of labor needed to produce
m. Some values are wholly independent from work, but he says these are
very small quantity in the market. He says, in speaking of commodity we
an always such commodity that can be increased by human exertion, and
o he says we mean such commodities only that can be increased by human

exertion and protection of such commodities from competition, which operai
without limit, also element of scarcity value, and element of monopoly val
must be considered.

The first problem which showed itself at this time was money problem-
the question of premium of gold. Second problem was the matter of co
laws—protective duties. He wrote his essay on low price of corn in 1815. Y
must remember exactly what he was driving at. Malthus, you remember, a
other writers suggested the restriction of importation. Now, Ricardo reasoni
that restriction on importation naturally would raise the price of wheat at hor
and it would raise the price of food, he says, increase of price of food w
bring higher wages. Higher wages according to Ricardo always meant low
profits. And, it was primarily the profits of the farm that would gradually cor
down and also all other profits. He finally wrote his principles. He found
was necessary to prove that the rise in wages would follow the rise of foo
but would not necessarily mean a rise in prices. He says, high wages do
necessarily mean high prices, on the contrary high wages might mean lc
prices. Things that might cause higher prices would be the condition of land
proprietor. You can easily realize therefore, why it was that he got into t
fundamentals. If the only cause of higher prices is greater labor that is embodi
in the commodity that brings them around to the cost theory and that of cour
would bring us to the whole theory of value and therefore the problems wi
which he had to deal before he spoke about incidents of value were: Wh
was necessary of value? What is really the cause of it? What is the influen
of rent upon values, or prices? What is the connection between the wages a
prices? What is the connection between wages and profits? And, it is only aft
he answered those questions that there would emerge his general law
economic progress. So that is the thing that occupied Ricardo's mind fro
1814 to next 5 or 6 years until after Malthus' principles were published. Th
he goes on again to take neutral problems—the problems connected with spe
payments, funding, etc.

We began in the last lecture with his general theory of value and point
out that he calls attention to utility as the basis of value but not, as he sa
the measure, although every thing must have utility. Utility, he says, is n
a measure, although absolutely essential. Then, scarcity and quantity of lab
was considered. He says, scarcity applies to certain commodities, but
eliminates these for not being worthy of much discussion. He says, he m
deal with commodities that are produced every where and also forms of sta
of most business. Then, next point you remember, he again assumes that
is dealing with problems of value only where competition operates witho
restraint. Now, so far we got it. So that, you see the Ricardian theory of va
is based upon certain definite hypothesis. Summary of his hypothesis bei
where scarcity plays only minor part and that where you are dealing w
commodities under the regime of competition. Having eliminated scarcity,

ιits himself only to the other one which is quantity of labor required to obtain
ːm, and then he goes on in the next few pages and pays his respect to Adam
ιith. You remember, Adam Smith's theory of value. He contrasts the
ιmmand theory of labor with the cost theory and as Ricardo puts it in chapter
ːe: "It is the comparative quantity of commodities which laborer produces
ιt determines the relative value and not comparative commodities that are
ːen for exchange of his labor." In other words you get to the cost theory.
Now, in the succeeding sections of this work you will find that there are
ded certain considerations which are to do with the second edition and not
ιh the first edition. They are concessions that are made to criticisms that
ːre made and while Ricardo makes these concessions, he thinks that they
ː comparatively of little importance. For instance, in section two, you find
ιt he calls attention not alone to the amount of labor but to the fact that
ιor of different cost are differently rewarded, and he can see that makes some
ːference. But in comparing the value of same commodity, the consideration
comparative skill and intensity of labor needs scarcity to be attended to,
it applies equally to both theories. It is not important to have to change
theory as to the quantity of labor, as only its cost is of importance. Then
section three, attention is called not alone to labor but also to the capital
ːd. That does not give him very much difficulty because not only the labor
plied immediately to commodity which [a]ffects their value but labor
ments, tools and other belongings with which labor is assisted. At that he
ːes call attention to the fact that sometimes conditions may arise [a]ffecting
ː capital which is employed in producing commodities. You will find that
later edition in section four he says: The quantity of labor regulating the
ative value is considerably modified by the employment of machinery and
ιer fixed or movable commodity. And so again on Section five: Value does
ιy with rise and so the wages are modified also. Unequal durability of capital
d unequal rapidity with which its rent employed. In other words while his
ːory of value is hypothetically true in the main it is true that it may be
ιdified to a lesser degree by some considerations.
Before we go on, however, to try to estimate his theory, let me call your
ɛntion to a few points that you find in the later chapter in the book.
ːluenced somewhat by the comments of French writer, Say, Ricardo tries
distinguish between what he calls value and riches. Wealth from the point
view of value and wealth from the point of view of riches, you find that
Chapter 18. What he is dealing with is wealth from the point of value.—
ιlue and price, and he understands perfectly well as it is shown in a section
Chapter 28. This whole chapter is devoted to discussion of demand and
ɔply. Now, the Ricardian theory may be explained from the very beginning
being a supply theory. It is not that Ricardo does not consider the influence
demand, but that he maintains that it can, of course, but in the long run
[a]ffecting the supply, and therefore the important thing he says is to

consider the supply side. You remember, that comes out in the words I r
to you about utility which is important from the point of view of dema
Had he the modern idea of utility—of marginal utility. He says: Utility
necessary, but important thing is how really in value does the supply wo
out. Because he is not dealing with the question of scarcity where the dem
is important factor, but he is dealing with commodities which can be virtu
increased ad libitum and therefore supply side is important. Therefore
theory resolves itself into a theory of cost which resolves itself into theory
labor.

When we say marginal, we find that Ricardo has a conception of final uti
in our modern sense of marginal utility. In chapter on rent—chapter two,
is speaking of the theory of rent. You find this very suggestive and import
sentence: "The exchangeability value of commodities whether they
manufactured or produce of mines or produce of land, the exchangeabi
value of commodities is always regulated not by the least quantity of la
that will suffice for and produce under circumstances highly favora
conditions and enjoy by the peculiar facilities by better growth ..." "You h
no such facilities for those who produce under most unfavora
circumstances." Now, that is a very important sentence that shows Rica
was perfectly aware of the real theory of cost. His theory of marginal c
when he talks of labor, or he calls being the measure of value. As he s
it is not cost in general but cost of producing under the most unfavora
circumstances. What we would call the theory of maximum cost.

It is very significant that he neglects it and does not think of it any m
because you find that his whole theory is on primarily to land as worst la
When you talk of cost, Ricardo is also responsible for another very great
important theory, e.g., the theory of comparative cost. The theory
comparative cost, now, has played a great role in economic science applica
primarily to international trade—not absolute cost but comparative cost. W
we come to this question of international trade, which is discussed in the si
chapter, Ricardo is under the feeling that it is an exception to the general r
The same rule which regulates value of commodities in one country does
regulate the value of two or more commodities within the country. In inter
trade it is the theory of labor cost, the theory of production, in between
countries it is the theory of comparative cost. Now, then, if it is the gene
What are we going to say about it? It all depends what your attitude is
criticising Ricardo. If you want to call attention to all weak points in a m
reasoning you can find many, as he says: First, my theory is not a gene
theory; second, it is not true of some commodities under same condition, e
under theory of competition; third, it is not true even of some commodi
of theory of competition because it is a theory which is considerably modifi
fourth, it is a theory of value which applies only within a country and not ot
commodities in the international affairs.

'rom that point of view you could make a very great indictment against
ardo, and certain writers, especially Germans, have done this. But, if you
trying to ascertain what he is trying to prove, then you could say that every
n is right to make whatever hypothesis he wants. It depends upon the
mises, and from that point of view there is no doubt that Ricardo is very
rect in his conclusions, if you grant the premises, and what he is concerned
h was an attempt to lay down the rule by and large to govern the transaction
ried on at the time.

Now, this theory of value has played a great role in economic doctrine, and
w for the first time you have a clear statement and it is for that reason that
rl Marx bases himself upon Ricardo, and considers Ricardo a great thinker.
rl Marx merely accepts that. It is also very easy to criticise a man in the
it of what has been accomplished since Ricardo wrote over a century ago.
ardo was the first one to attack these fundamental relations of production
l distribution. It is not to be expected that his theory should be one that
uld have been stood the test at all times. And, if you sum up his point of
w in a more generous attitude and compare it with the present point of value,
:ourse, any man could at once point out where the differences are between
point of view and the modern point of view.

umming up in two or three sentences: First, what Ricardo was interested
vas the supply side, whereas we have the demand side as well. In the second
:e, although Ricardo was right when he tells us that the demand side be
ized, yet we utilize the marginal concept as well as the cost, whereas Ricardo
lied marginal side only to cost and not all of them. In the third place, what
ardo was trying to do was to find out the causes responsible of value of
mmodities between man and man, individual and individual, whereas we
he modern times are not neglecting what has been tried to and what might
called social aspect of the problem. We now know normal prices after all
e influenced by social considerations, although we may still find in certain
ustries such thing as social utility. Contest is rather in words than content.
social utility we mean utility to group as modified by social aspects.
hough it is an individual act, yet from certain point of view it is a social
and social aspect. However, it is true that by value you must mean social
ue. Now, Ricardo was not interested in that. From these three points of
w of demand, marginal element, and social element, if you take Ricardian
ory of comparative cost you will find that it is precisely an element of modern
v, those social things applied to both demand and supply which Ricardo
; keen enough to see, just as well to having all that we have done in the
dern times is to catch up with Ricardian idea. That is enough about his
ory of value. Before we leave the general theory of value, let me tell you
:w words about it. You see, at once, in comparing his theory with the
lthusian theory, what Ricardo looked for was the underlying permanent
ig, but Malthus with his less logical mind was calling attention to temporary

thing. Of course, from temporary point of view demand and supply was more important. Ricardo shows his greatness by going into the heart of the difficult which is the normal value and the market value. So, there is no comparison at all.

Ricardo's theory of rent: Quoting from chapter two, "Rent is that part of land which is paid for the use of original and indestructible power of land" that is rent. "If all land had same property with unlimited quantity and even in quality, no charge could be made, unless possessed peculiar advantage of position ..." I read you this passage for another reason. Any critic of Ricardo later on might say that Ricardo calls attention only to the good and bad land and their fertility. What, they say is equally important as to the situation; and Ricardo entirely neglects the situation. In passage that I just read you, Ricardo is perfectly aware, and he puts advantage in situation side by side with fertility. He discusses all from the point of view of fertility; that is his hypothesis. Again there has been a few criticisms, saying that his theory was wrong because he thinks only of the quality not of its situation. Now, then, he starts out with the sentence that the exchange value of the whole commodities is regulated by the amount of labor under the worst possible circumstances.

The reason why there is progressive rise in value is because more labor employed in the production of last portion produced, and not because a rent is paid to the landlord. Rent is a result and not a cause of high price. High rents are the consequence and not the cause of price. That is his theory of rent and he says, "therefore, any circumstances which make the portion of land last employed in the production of food which means low production, will lower rent and only increased quantity of labor that you got to put into operation that causes the rent to rise." Now, as regards to that point you see the question between him and Malthus was as to whether improvements agriculture would have any such effects upon rents.

Another criticism of Ricardo, which was made first by a German, Hild, was of course that, he said, it is perfectly natural for a man who is a stockbroker as over against Malthus, and naturally Ricardo hated land owner and Malthus hated stockbrokers. Therefore, he said, Ricardo's whole theory is based upon his opposition to landlords, that is why he did not want to have corn laws that is why he wanted to have cheap food to have cheap laborers. Ricardo felt very keenly about this criticism which was proved against them even Malthus, and you find that in his notes—which are never published—he comes time and time again pointing out to Malthus and saying: I am not opposed to landlords. I am trying to explain the situation, and if you have these protective laws you are going to have unfortunate results upon laborer and upon others. Or, again, as regards the improvement of agriculture he says hope I am not going to undervalue the improvements of all sorts to agriculture and landlords. Their immediate effect, he says, is to lower rent, but they give subsistence to population and cultivate poorer lands, which are of immense vantage to landlords. So that here again, all Ricardo was looking for was fundamental, the permanent causes and not mere temporary causes. In the last lecture we began discussing the appraisement of Ricardian doctrine and we spoke of his theory of value. I will add one other word to what I have said in the last lecture. The judgment that we shall reach will largely depend upon the attitude we take—whether sympathetic or unsympathetic; whether consider the point of Ricardo as he expressed at that time, or as what mean today. As Ricardo went on with his discussion and after making the concessions to which we referred in the last lecture, about the end of his life became more and more doubtful as to the exactness and accuracy of his views, and that comes out very strongly in his letters to McCulloch. You will find the statement on page 65, McCulloch. The thing that bothered him was the question of some old wine he had. After a while the wine became valuable, the question of the oak tree which becomes more valuable as it becomes older. Ricardo says: "After the best consideration that I can give, I think there two causes which occupy valuable relative values (1) relative quantity of labor, (2) the relative time that must elapse before such result of labor could brought to market." On page 132, you find this passage: "I am not satisfied with the explanation that I have given of the principles which regulate value." And, finally, on page 71—"I sometimes think whatever to write if I had to write the chapter of value over again. I should acknowledge that relative value is regulated by two causes, instead of one, e.g., by the relative quantity of labor necessary to produce the commodity, and second, by the rate of profit." You see, as he went on he began to be a little uncertain as to the accuracy his views. Had he lived a few more decades he would have come much closer our present point of view. He seems to be a very conscientious thinker, and how unjust it is for us to have an unsympathetic point of view. Of course if you apply absolute quantities you see, that Ricardian theory of value in his own opinion is not a final thing. Now we will discuss it from the following three points of view:

1. Historical point of view. You remember that some writers have thought that they were victoriously dealing with Ricardian theory because they pointed out not the question of fertility but the question of situation of land, and we alluded to that in the last lecture and pointed out what Ricardo said. But, furthermore, other writers, and our own American writers, Carey, and Bastable he later on, criticized Ricardo. We shall try to decide who was original thinker. Both of them said Ricardo is wrong historically because instead of going from the bad lands to the worst lands, he went just the other way and went from bad lands to the good lands. A great deal has been made out of that, as if that had anything to do with the case. That is to say, the historical development of cultivation is one thing and the case we have on hand is another thing. And, both Bastable and Carey are wrong because there is no

generalization of that kind. Some countries are on top of hills and some tov
are below. Now, historically we don't know every thing that happened, i
that has nothing to do with the case, because what Ricardo really meant
his theory was that, he had reference to the marginal increment and not
the last increment. In time, this does not make any difference, because at a
time you have some lands which are under the circumstances worse lands. Th
you can conceive that Ricardo is wrong in the history.

2. Static Theory. What interested Ricardo was, you see, the differe
between land and capital that in the case of other factors of production y
don't seem to have any such result of most expensive kind, but that the l
of diminishing returns applies to land and land alone. Now, as to the man
that static theory applies to land is beyond all question, when you think
the thing as a kind of successive dose of labor and capital applied to la
Of course you cannot impugn that statement, and that therefore rent i
residual income, which of course is also perfectly true. So far so good. A
also, again rent being a residual income is not however a cause of price, l
is a result of price. His static theory is perfectly true with this exception t
it assumes, you see, a no-rent quantity and quality of land. Marginal lan
the land which fixes the price of produce and therefore it does not enter in
the price. From Ricardian point of view that is true. But, land is also u
for different purposes, and a piece of land is no-rent land for one kind
produce may be rent bearing for another kind of produce. A land may be a
rent land for wheat, but that same land may be useful for potatoes, and e
house. So that, when you are dealing with static theory of land you m
remember that what is no-rent land for one purpose may not be no-rent la
for another purpose. But, apart from that the theory, of course, is perfec
true, and yet in its implications it is subject to a good deal of criticism
the reason that you are dealing now with the difference between land and
other factors of production. Now, you remember, I did call your attention
Ricardo's incidental passage in which he makes perfectly clear that the margi
cost applies not only to land but also to all factors of production, yet he forg
about it, for all intents and purposes land for him entirely differs from ot
things. Now, from our modern point of view, of course, we have gotten beyc
the Ricardian position. We realize this, especially since the work of an Austr
and John Clark. We realize that theory of diminishing returns is not limi
to land and from certain point of view you can look upon interest in the sa
way as upon land, as a kind of residual. From another point of view you c
conceive of what is paid for land as entering upon the price paid for cap
interest. Those who are familiar with Clark will at once see this. Now,
consequence of that we will see when we come to the third aspect.

3. Dynamic theory of rent. Now, Ricardo, you remember, in claiming t
improvements would not [a]ffect rent, concedes later on to Malthus that
meant in the long run but not of short run. But, when Ricardo compares

sition of land owner in general over a long period of time with the position capitalist his theory is perfectly true, if you allow the assumption which he ide with the hypothesis, which was at the bottom of his theory. His sumption was that during the period of time there would be no changes or turbances of the differences between those successive units and between ductive powers of successive units of capital and therefore, it is easy to see w logically follows from Ricardian Dynamic theory the theory of John S. ill in his unearned increment as applied to land. It does not apply to capitalist. does not apply to capitalist and that the land owner has interest which is the long run opposed to the interest of capitalist. We shall see this in a ment when we come to the general theory of profits.

When profits go down rent would go up. That is why Henry George when veloping his doctrine of single tax based himself on Ricardo. And, it is the jical conclusion. When Francis Walker wrote, he did not limit the residual ory to rent but also applied it to wages. The point I want to make clear re is that if you accept Ricardian theory of rent you have to say that while m the historical point of view it is wrong, but it does not make any difference, from the statical point of view it is entirely correct, but not distinctive, and m the dynamic point of view it is incomplete. Therefore, of course, your neral conclusion is that the theory of rent played so immense a part in history economic doctrine which it does not deserve primarily the importance that s been assigned to it. However, with all that Ricardo was a pathfinder. So t, here again, you see, the theory of value has made an advance forward t it did not go far enough. That is true of the theory of rent, it is also true the theory of wages. In the first place Ricardo was virtually formulator of n law, or brazen law of wages. In Chapter five he says: "Labor like other ngs that are purchased or sold, may be increased and decreased in quantity its natural and its market price." Now, then, the natural price which is formed the cost of rearing human beings as laborers, that is the cost of production, d the market price of labor, is of course, the wages that are given in the irket from time to time and would oscillate around this normal or natural ice. Now, when he elaborated that idea in his first edition, a writer to whom : shall refer later, objected. This writer was C. Torrens, who called attention the influence of standard of life and that led Ricardo to make some ncessions and in his later editions you will find this statement: otwithstanding the tendency of wages to conform to their natural rate which minimum cost of subsistence, and market rate, may in an improved society r an indefinite period of time be constantly above it, and even then", says , "it is not to be understood that natural price of wages estimated in food d necessity is absolutely fixed, and varies at different times in various untries. It depends on habits and customs of the people." So that, we see re that he oscillates and does not seem to know what it is.

Here, says, Ricardo, you may have market price which remains permanent above the natural price and never goes below at all: Well, although he mak those concessions, yet pursuing his usual practice of having allowed for certa contingencies he goes on to argue as if the fundamental theory of the natur price of wages were the one and the most important of all, and he tells for instance, that the supply and demand of laborers is only of incident consequence. He brings out, however, a point which ever since his time h been an acquisition to economic science which is the distinction between mon wages and real wages. You see, demand and supply are really only an incident consequence. He says: "Diminish the cost of production of hats, and their pri ultimately will fall to the new natural price; diminish the cost of subsisten of human beings by diminishing the natural price of food and clothing th wages will ultimately fall ..." It is the supply side of the question, he says, th after all is important.

There was a great controversy in 19th century as regards the movement wages fund theory. And, the question arose, Did Ricardo originate or did set the wages fund theory? The theory was that wages are paid of capital a that there is always a definitely restricted amount of capital which is availab for the payment of wages. Therefore, you can easily get the result by dividi this fund by the number of laborers. Now, Ricardo does indeed believe a says that wages are paid out of capital. He frequently uses the term funds f the maintenance of labor, but Does he hold the doctrine of unelastic a predetermined wages fund?

If you take Professor Taussig on wages and capital, Taussig says yes, Ricar believes in predetermined wage, and he gives a quotation from Ricardo. Bu if you look at that quotation that he gives on pages 93-97, you will find th the explanation is an incidental one and susceptible of different interpretatio Taussig himself says in his book: "It would be a mistake to infer too mu from these passages", and I think too much has been inferred from the passages, and I think it will be hard to prove that Ricardo is the originat of this doctrine. There is no doubt, however, that when the theory came be more precisely defined a little later on that the founders of the theory d base themselves upon the theory of cost, and Ricardian theory of wages a profits. You can say that what Ricardo definitely states is that wages vary wi capital, but he does not say that wages vary especially with predetermin amount of capital. Even though he does not definitely advance that theor he works toward it and in that general direction. So that, his theory of lab really can be mentioned as in harmony with the labor doctrines that have bee derived.

Before we pass any final judgment, we have to say something about his theo of profits. Now, in the first place, you remember that one of the main poin in the whole Ricardian statement was to attempt to prove that the high wag don't necessarily mean high prices. That was the main point, but he does n course, maintain that high wages mean low profits, and wages and profits y inversely with each other. When you go to the conception of profit Ricardo epts much the same view that you also find the distinction between profits d interest in Smith and others. But, just as there is a natural rate of interest according to Ricardo there is a natural rate of profit (we can now say normal fits). Now, the price of anything, especially in agricultural production is surplus over the produce of no rent land. Therefore, price depends upon t, but since prices are made up of profits and wages and not rent, therefore fits vary inversely as wages, since they are the only two constituent parts price, and profits will depend upon money wages because profits are money fits utterly irrespective from the point of view of laborer. You have to tell difference between money wages and real wages. Then, you come in that y to his final conclusion, the theory of economic profits which makes him damentally different from Malthus.

Here, we have high prices, that means new accumulation of capital as a result high prices, that means greater demand for labor, that means increase in pulation, that means cultivation of poorer lands, that means higher cost of d, that means higher money wage, that means lower profits, that means her rents. You see, it is a very different sequence from what Malthus had. ages will remain about stationary and rents will rise and in the course of e profits will fall to the minimum. So that, you can easily see why those o are unsympathetic to Ricardo will say, here you have the stockbroker ain his class would derive the benefit and land owner will suffer.

Ricardo deprecated the idea that he was in any way opposed to the landlords. cardo said, he was a landlord himself. But, this was so as a necessary result his general theory. Now, that being in a general way the Ricardian theory distribution, it had immense influence upon everybody that followed him, ether they favored the land owner or whether they favored the capitalist, ply because of his clear cut, almost inevitable thought, which he put his nclusions so far as the natural laws of economics, natural law of value, tural law of wages, natural law of prices and the theory of rent and profits re concerned. You see, therefore that Ricardo was always after all after the damental and general things.

Before we come to a final conclusion as to what it all means, we now have say something about his theory of distribution. This has two parts: Money ory and his fiscal theory. Because in practice he was a man interested in money theory and also in fiscal theory. Now, we take up his theory of ney, on which quite a little light has been shed in the last few years. Ricardian ory of money is expounded in several works. In 1809, the prices in general d began to rise, in 1808 people had began to worry about this, and asked to what did it all mean? Why should the prices rise? In 1809, there was greater eculation in coin and money, in 1810 Ricardo wrote his first pamphlet on, hy fall in price of bullion is a proof of depreciation of bank note? Following

year he replied to Bosanquet and 15 years later he wrote on problems of insecur
economic currency. Ricardo tries to show that redundancy and deficit are onl
relative terms. He says that if the coin covers the situation, the value can ris
above that in other countries only by the cost of importation, but that if yo
have inconvertible bank notes which of course cannot be exported then whe
exchange goes below the mint price, it shows that there is too much, of i
that is his fundamental theory. That led to bullionist comments of 1810 an
tried to bring about resumption.

Ricardo's views on Banking and currency: He advanced two doctrines: Firs
the quantity theory of money and that of course is based partly upon his gener;
theory of value and tells us that gold and silver and all other commodities a
valuable only in proportion of quantity of labor necessary to produce then
Then, he goes on to tell us that supply may be so that it will overflow. C
course, it must be remembered that what Ricardo interested in was primari
the situation with reference to inconvertible bank money and his whole theor
of the relations between money and price was predominated very largely b
that situation. It goes without saying that it is true in extent as to quanti
theory but it is not true of inconvertible paper money more than anything els
we saw this in Germany during the last war and also in Europe on genera
Then, more especially his seigniorage theory, that when a government issu
paper money, the cost is virtually nothing. The difference between the valu
of the cost of production of gold and the cost of production of paper represen
the quantity which the government is able to get for itself, and this he ca
the seigniorage. He says when the state alone coins there is no limit to tl
charge by seigniorage. If you convert the metal bullion into coin, why the
coin will have the same value as the bullion because the value of productic
is same. But, if state charges seigniorage for coinage then the value will exce
by the amount of seigniorage. Now, by limiting the quantity of the coin
the money you can raise this for any conceivable value and therefore, say
Ricardo, it is on this principle that the whole charge on the paper money m;
be considered seigniorage, although it has no intrinsic value yet by limiti
the quantity its value may be as great as equal amount of coin. The effec
which will follow from the limitation of quantity is more important than iss
of paper money. So that, his whole discussion of situation is based upon tw
theories; first, limitation of quantity of the money, and second, the fact th
by issuing paper money instead of coin you have 100% seigniorage charg

The result of that whole theory is, and it is perfectly true so far as the situatic
was concerned that if there is a premium on gold as over against the bank no
that supplied them that premium is virtually due to the depreciation of tl
inconvertible paper money. You see, when you get to inconvertible bank mon
it amounts to the same thing as irredeemable paper money. It does not ma
any difference, whether there is promise to pay or not. Promise to pay dc
not add anything to the value of paper in either case because if you can n

ay, promise is broken, if you can pay the irredeemable paper money will
ecome redeemable. Therefore, Ricardo is perfectly right in making analysis
etween bank of England notes and ordinary issue of paper money at that time.
he practical conclusion from his theory was therefore the only way to bring
he notes to par and to start gold payments again by limiting the quantity and
hus reduce seigniorage. That was his whole theory. Now, those two points,
think, have become part and parcel of modern economic theory.

When we talk about the theory of money today, we think of quantity of
oney in general. The other side of question is one which is more subtle and
ifficult and there has been little more disposition to call attention to some
f the prohibition of Ricardo, that is to the relation between the money supply
t home and the international situation—the exchange situation. Now, certain
oints of course Ricardo brought out very clearly and since then they have
een applied to economic theories. The basis of his whole theory is that gold
ill be exported under normal conditions only, and also if it is relatively
edundant as compared to other countries. This theory has since been accepted.
t the second place, however, Ricardo advanced the doctrine that export of
old is always the cause, and influences the effect of an unfavorable balance
trade. Now, it was this point, you remember, that not alone Malthus accepted
ut that Thornton had already taken a different view. This is dealt by one of
ur most distinguished economists, Professor Viner of the University of
hicago in a fine book, entitled "Balance of International Indebtedness." You
ok under chapter nine of that book, you will find a very beautiful appreciation
what Ricardo did and what he didn't do. Of course, you can also find a
eat deal in Professor Angel's book. But Viner's book brings it more clearly.

Another point that Ricardo stated in his earlier works was that a crop failure
things of that kind, or granting of a subsidy to a foreign country which
uld lead to gold exports does not create a redundancy in currency. If,
wever, you will take up Ricardo's letters to Malthus, he points out later on
at perhaps, he says, other factors may come in to bring about the export
coin, while he mentions the chief points, and that he admits that perhaps
is wrong about that. In fact, as we shall see in the next few lectures, that
S. Mill, as well as Cook rather sided with the later views—concessions of
cardo rather than with his original idea. In his theories of value and wages
d other theories you have to consider what Ricardo is trying to point out
y are the fundamental explanations, the final explanation, the long-run
planation. He was not so much concerned with the temporary causes or
ignificant cause. There is no doubt that fundamentally Ricardo is right, and
t he is correct in his fundamental explanation of the causes of variation
xchanges. Yet, some of these minor points are not very exact. Here again,
ou take a sympathetic view of Ricardo you will find in Ricardo a good
l of purchasing power parity that has been developed by Castles, Wheetley
other writers. Without going into detail it may be said that on the whole

perhaps the most enduring power of the Ricardian theory, not absolutely final not absolutely correct in its detail but is in its fundamentals. It is found that every one must go back to Ricardo in an attempt to explain these theories So, you have there a great contribution of Ricardo.

Now, I will call attention to the third class of contribution of Ricardo, which was overlooked on account of being over-shadowed by his more important works. I refer now to his views in public finance. He was interested in those during later part of his life. He thought much about the relative merits and debts and taxes. There are two things to be noted: First, in his theory of taxation the attempt is again always to give the fundamental explanation. As a practical stock-broker he, of course, more than anybody else was aware of the influence of fractional and influence of market changes, because the conclusion depends upon those temporary causes. But, in his book he neglects all that, he pays no attention to that. He tries to get the underlying principles and therefor for practical purposes it is not so valuable as it is the treatment of his money question. In his treatment of incidence of taxation he was more concerned i trying to test his general theory of distribution, that is the reason why public finance received less advantage. It is pretty hard to fit in with conditions actuall existing. It is difficult to make hypotheses and assumptions which will perhap not enter in actual life and yet it will grant his theory of distribution. The mai reason perhaps why his fundamental theory of incidence is no longer accepte because we no longer accept his theory of distribution. You see, in moder days the theory of profits as a residual takes possession of almost who Ricardian theory of rent. However, the facts about the whole Ricardia statement are that he considered very carefully two points which had bee pounding up very much for the last ten years. First, was how to conduct th war. You see this was aftermath of the war, and Ricardo considers ve carefully the three ways of paying for war:

1. By taxation of property
2. By borrowing every year
3. By borrowing, but at the same time to tax to set up a sinking fund get rid of the whole debt.

Now, without going into detail it must be said that Ricardian theory is great in favor of taxation, as over against either of the two others. Of course, sor of us think he went too far, but when he enunciated them the war was ov But, on account of last war we rather appreciated that more, and the rise prices during the war was of course due to the dislocation. There are certa limits of raising this sum by taxation. We spent about 30 billions of dolla in one year, which we might be able to afford, but nothing would be left consumption. Ricardian theory is sound, and most countries of course pre the easier way of borrowing. The other point was like the one in England political question. What to do with the debt which was left on account of the war? We find argument in favor of capital levy in Ricardo, which nowadays it is only favored by socialists. Ricardo did not go into all the details of the arguments such as we find in recent years in England and on the Continent. It is interesting to notice that Ricardo brings it out and that in the long run he says, it is better to get rid of your debt by capital levy. England has made practically no progress. England leaves this as perpetual debt same as we do in the case of railroad bonds, and debts. Now, Ricardo did not think that some day we would return to his views with greater interest. Of course, this is not necessary for this country, as we could meet our debts. But, what is true for this country is unfortunately not true or possible for Europe. Summing all up, you find that almost in every economic theory you go back to the wonderful mind of Ricardo. And, if you ask why it was that we go back to Ricardo, the answer would be that it was Ricardo's really able fiscal mind that attempted to analyze our modern economic life. Adam Smith, you remember, was the theorist of the domestic system—the first stage of capitalism which had developed. You find new and old theories in Adam Smith, whereas by the time of Ricardo manufacture was not being worked by the hand. Ricardo is the first man to analyze modern factory system as developed by capitalism, and is for that reason that all of our modern views always go back to Ricardo—what that great theorist said. And, we see, therefore that if you give a sympathetic approach to Ricardo, you will see how one-sided are the criticisms which came generation or two ago. Part of those were largely influenced by the conclusions of the Ricardian school rather than Ricardo himself. Ricardo like Malthus was one of the kindest men that ever lived. Again, we see the fallacy of calling Ricardo a Napoleon of the landed interest, which Malthus was fond of doing, calling him representative of capitalists or stock-broker class. But, Ricardo is about the finest example of scientists who attempted to analyze the situation according to the lights that are given, and if his conclusions are no longer accepted in some respects we must not talk of his foolish upbringing, etc. Ricardo then, really starts a new train of thought in England and soon all over the world. We will now run hurriedly over this situation and describe the rise of what is known as political economy and development of Ricardian school.

Section 44. The Rise of Political Economy

Just as in this country we find two separate phases in the development of economic thought, one after the war of 1812, where factories began and second after the civil war in the 70's, when the modern problems were ushered upon us. In the first period we find beginnings of chairs of political economy in United States and in the second stage large movements. Also in England there was the practical problems of this new factory system, the labor question

that developed and started people thinking and that made them take the
matter of investigation of these new topics. Now Malthus' chair, you
remember was established to prepare noblemen for India but in 1816, Mr.
Pryme was made lecturer in Cambridge University for the first time, "to
facilitate study of science hitherto inaccessible." A few year Books published
articles about this now science. The Encyclopedia Britanica, in 1810 devoted
first article on Political Economy. Edinborough Review started at that time
also devoted a few articles.

First book was written by Boileau, entitled, Introduction of Science of
Political Economy, which was published in 1811. Then a German writer took
up some of the problems. The interesting point about Boileau is that he now
divided the book into several parts: (1) Theory of increase, (2) Theory of
international circulation, (3) Theory of consumption, and he, for the first time
uses the word undertaker—entrepreneur. A few years later Mrs. Marcet, who
had won great popularity by her work on "Conversation on Chemistry", now
wrote a "Conversation on Political Economy." This book is simply to
popularize the Malthusian doctrine. Next one was Buchanan, born in 1779.
He published a critical study of Wealth of Nations, also later on he wrote
something in taxation. He was very much opposed to the Physiocrats. He also
in certain minor points gave both Malthus and Ricardo some points.

The only other writer at the time to be mentioned is Simon Gray, died 1859
wrote on the Happiness of State. This was an attack on Malthus and Adam
Smith. In his book he finds fault with Adam Smith for neglecting the theory
of consumption. So far so good, but Gray was an erratic heterodox on the
doctrine of money and thought high taxes would enrich a nation. So, he never
had any influence on the progress of science. Quite different was Thomas
Tooke, who approached the subject from the point of view of price—history
of price with a result. As regards the theory of money we shall come back
little later. In 1821 the Political Economy started and from that time on the
had monthly meetings and Political Economy began to be heard of and
doctrines were formulated. But before we can explain what really was chief
tendency of Ricardian School, we have to take up Section 45.

Section 45.   Ricardian School

We shall devote little time to the discussion of individual utilitarianism, and
we take up Jeremy Bentham, who died in 1832. He was a son of a lawyer and
was educated in public school. He studied law in Oxford, tried to practice law
but failed in the first case and was very much disappointed. He preferred
live a life of a student and studied all the different sciences, what we today
call social science, not alone jurisprudence but also ethics, and above all
penology and economic legislation. His most important works were not
economic works. One of his works on government was a bold attack of

Blackstone in 1780. "Introduction to the Principles of Legislation", is perhaps his best known work, yet no one read it in England until 1802, when a Frenchman Dumont published two volume edition of this book. His fame then began to increase and later on he became well known. In 1787, he wrote his Defense of Usury and his Political Economy in 1798, which has now become famous. A few years later he met J.S. Mill.

Bentham was originally of a Tory family, and Mill, was of course a Whig. Through Mill he became acquainted with Ricardo, Francis Place and Taylor and others. You see, they represented two different thoughts. Mill with his insistence upon economic democracy and Bentham was trying to invent a kind of government which would make everybody happy. Bentham, therefore, represented political democracy to its very extreme limits. He wanted to do away with king and House of Lords, etc. Bentham died a very old man. He left his body to one of the scientific societies. His idea of showing himself to posterity was to sit in a chair, as an old gentleman, a big hat in his hand ... The best book on him is in French, by Halevy—(I think it is translated into English).

Bentham was a leader of philosopher radicals. He was a utilitarian, but the reason why Bentham made his mark was while other writers were utilitarians, he tried to put it on scientific basis. The way he did that was to take the foundation of utilitarianism and endeavor to measure the utility. He does that in his Moral Arithmetic. He also calls, you remember, Philosophic Calculus, and his measurement of course is based upon this attempt to deal with two sides of problem—pleasures and pains. He deals more fully, especially in his great book with his system of reward and punishment. He tries to measure pains and pleasures. He starts out with considering different attributes of these qualities. He measures the intensity of pleasure and pain, the duration, the certainty, the personality what he calls fecundity. And, when he discusses fecundity of pleasure and pains he divides them in different ways, for instance, he says, you cannot measure either pleasure or pain according to its movement the chances of that idea being followed or the sensation of similar kind which would arise. He says all those things are fecundity of pleasure and pain. In the next place he discusses the purity of pleasure and pain. He says, if it is impure it would be followed by revulsion, and then finally he discusses the extent of the pleasure and pain. Now then, as soon as he begins to discuss the points of view, he realizes that he needs a yard stick with which to measure these different aspects of utility. As soon as he does that he faces three fundamental difficulties:

1. Is the pleasure equal in intensity with different individuals?—You and I hearing Kriesler playing his violin.
2. Are pleasures and pains really commensurable? Not alone the qualities but also the quantities.

3. How far is a man's pleasure or pain is [a]ffected by riches or poverty?
    Although same man has different reaction according to his economic
    conditions.

Of course, these are philosophical problems and Bentham deals with them.
For instance in his Principle, in Chapter six, he mentions no less than 32 points
according to which sensitiveness will differ. It is a very interesting study but
he thinks in any way there are several ways you can get over the difficulty.
The Legislator dealing with problems has to look after the large classes and
certain points he conceives in pleasure and pain that you could not use such
item. He admits however the postulate of addability for scientific analysis, that
you could be able to add one thing to another. Second difficulty is more serious.
This was due to the difference between simple and complex. He gives us 14
simple pleasures and 12 simple pains. To what extent can those simple pleasure
and pains enter into the ultimates and chemical constituents? This involves very
serious logical difficulties. Bentham recognizes the existence of the problem
and rules and the proportion between offences and punishments. He reduce
everything to a common denominator and tries to convert the pleasures or
pains into a money equivalent. You have therefore a utility to measure. As
regards the third point he does bring out the doctrine of diminishing utility
in his constitutional code, but you see he did not think it was true, otherwise
he would have reached the modern concept of utility. If you add money to
your existing stock, then you have there certain amount of addability. His
doctrine, he says, is always true for small addition. There, you see, he tried
to work out all the refinements of this doctrine of pleasure and pain. The
interesting part is that he applies this to those sciences where he had least
chance. He says if it is applicable to other things, it is applicable to economics.
And, yet he refrains from emphasizing it. He does not emphasize the peculiar
side of pleasure and pain so much. Of course, if he were primarily economist
he would have called attention to the consumption side and cost of production
but he did not do that. What he was interested in was to develop a political
and juridical theory which would end up with his realization.

Priestley [sic: Bentham] in one of his publications—Panopticon, works out
his five criteria: He starts out with (1) Human nature. He says human nature
is hedonistic, or pain avoiding. (2) Men are rational and will use their plan
to secure greatest happiness with least possible pain. (3) Society is passive rather
than active. (4) All human weaknesses are due to differences of intelligence
and understanding in character. (5) Education is the one aim to solve the
different problems.

Now of course, we have to deal with government. He says government was
instituted for really four purposes: First and foremost is subsistence; second
to provide abundance, because the more wealth you have higher things of life
you can have; third security against the foe both internal and external; fourth

equality. Those were the only four functions of the government, but when government does those it has done everything. He elaborates what he calls ideal system—the quiet system. He says that the request that the individual has to make from government must be just as much as Diogenes made: "Stand out of my life, get out." That is the way, he says, in which politics and economics can be brought together. Well, when you ask what were some of his more specific economic doctrines, you find very little in him. He always said: "Although I have been teacher of Ricardo in politics, Ricardo has been my teacher in economics." Therefore you find that all he concludes is that progress depends upon the increase of capital. He lays stress upon direct taxes and opposes the indirect taxes. At the same time he shows great sympathy with the poor. He advocates the formation of a national charity organization which would provide industry and give bonus for the deserving poor. Bentham was also originator of savings bank idea. He calls them "Frugality Banks."

But taking it all in all his social doctrine can be summed up as follows: That the interests of the individual are the really important things. They are the only real interests. He says, take care of the individual, don't molest him, and never have him be molested. That is the argument running all through his book. So that, Bentham is not so much of a utilitarian but he is a founder of individual utilitarianism. Everything is based according to him upon this "Philosophic Calculus." In modern times we have gotten away from this. In jurisprudence, penology and ethics he was a pathfinder. When, however, people were more interested with social rather than individual problems it is not a wonder that they disagreed with him. He was at the other end with Karl Marx. He refers to Bentham as, "that incipient reticent article of ordinary parentage." Bentham, he says, among philosophers only born and manufactured in England, and no count[ry] has struck about in so self-satisfied work. Bentham simply introduces in his favor what they set in 18th century to know what is useful for a dog sense. Bentham makes it look all of this dried, and dullest. He takes the role of a shop keeper especially English shopkeeper with such a lot of reputation ..." Now, you can take your choice, but with all that, Bentham was a mighty mind and it is worth while reading Bentham even today—all of his analyses of pleasures and pains. Between the two, Ricardo on one hand and Bentham on the other you have the beginnings of a group and this was added to by the others.

James Mill was one of the first Orthodox writers (1773-1836). He was the leader of utilitarians. The driest and sternest, most rigorous of all logicians. He was a son of a shoemaker brought up as a preacher and afterwards went entirely out of it and got interested in economics. We shall see little later on what influence he had upon his boy John Stuart, wrote one or two books on policy of corn laws, and a few years later in 1807, he wrote against physiocrats, and that brought him to the attention of Ricardo and he met Ricardo then. They soon became very good friends and before long he became friends also with Francis Place. It was he who tried to make Ricardo publish his book. In the meantime son John was born. He gave him lessons in logic and political economy. He published elements of political economy. This has some very interesting points. In the first place the arrangement now being followed for a century you see, it is logical. He divided it, what he calls political economy, into production, distribution, what he calls interchange and consumption. There was nothing new but everything was written with clearness, just as though he was dealing with a science—the absolute immutable laws, and so in his whole theory of value and cost he takes from Ricardo without any modification. His theory of population from Malthus without any concessions, so that his general outlook is a dismal one. He says great problem of humanity is how to deal with birth rate. Artificial prevention was unthinkable. All you have in him was a man of rigorous formulator of laws of economics. He was soon followed by J. R. McCulloch (1789-1864).

McCulloch is referred to as a genial whiskey loving Scotchman. He wrote an essay on public debt in 1818. That brought about his acquaintance with Ricardo and the next 20 years he remained chief economist of Edinborough University and he started classes of political economy. He became a member of political economy group and in 1825 published his Principles. In 1826, he wrote an essay on subsistence of wages. He formulated the whole wages fund doctrine. He wrote his big book on Free Trade. He published great many other books. In 1845 he published first book on taxation in England. One of his best books is published in 1845. This is his Literature of Political Economy. He also issued most popular editions both of Adam Smith and Ricardo. They are excellent editions, especially the one on Ricardo. You have to be, however, on your guard in reading him, because he was so extreme. When he takes up the cost theory of Ricardo he goes to the extreme, as most people would get into this. Of course, in some other ways a little injustice is done to him.

The practical consequences of this Orthodox theory which led to a good many unfortunate and undesirable aspects, yet in reality you shall find that those things are due to second and third rate mouth pieces of Orthodox classical school and rather at later times. You take for instance, book by Rae. His book on contemporary socialism, Chapter eleven, 2nd edition, which brings out the fact that Malthus was by no means so cynically opposed to labor as is often thought. We have talked about Mill and Malthus. We have now to deal with two other men, although these men are not independent thinkers.

Whateley taught economics at Oxford for a few years, and in 1831 he was made Archbishop in Dublin. He devoted his time to a new chair of Political Economy in Ireland, also founded statistical society. He published a few books. He proposed a name for political economy—Catallactics, meaning science of transfer and exchange. He afterwards was quite mixed up in two great questions: (1) Poor laws, and (2) Railroads and transportation. But in reality he did not add much to the science.

Very different thing might be said about Senior. He had most original mind. He has never yet received all he deserves. One of our students went over to England and came back with an immense mass of literature on economics that have never been published. He has in mind to publish a big book. Of course, Senior has himself published a book. Senior was a famous lawyer but a great advisor of the government and being one of the leading thinkers in Europe he met all the great men, statesman and the scientists. He has a four to six volume work on travels. This is important because it contains conversation with most distinguished men of the day. He was a professor at Oxford in the early period of his life, and then again later on wrote outlines of Political Economy and other questions including some of the Irish problems he dealt with. Now, in the first place he took the position that political economy is a science. He said, the business of political economy is neither to recommend nor to dissuade any question, but its only purpose is to state the general principles. He was interested in theory. I have here in my hand the little book called Political Economy, last edition, 1872. It is his most interesting work and quite a few passages are noteworthy. He says, political economy can be summed up in four heads: (1) Everybody tries to get as much with as little work as possible, (2) Work is limited by moral and fiscal evils, (3) Powers of labor can be indefinitely increased, (4) This point is the statement of the law of diminishing returns. In agriculture, he says, additional labor in general does not yield proportional return.

Coming now to his real contribution, we will first take his theory of value. He says, value is not due to cost of production. Any other cause which tends to limit supply is just as important as cost of production, therefore he says, it is a great mistake to build up your theory on Ricardian concept. Furthermore, his concept of cost is entirely different from Ricardian concept because he introduces the subjective idea rather than objective idea, and he speaks not alone of utility of labor but also disutility of labor. When he thinks of cost he is thinking of subjective sacrifice undergone by the individual and this subjective idea runs through his whole treatment. So, there you would say that in his theory of value he introduces subjective idea, because our modern idea is different. Then, he enters into discussion of Malthus and Ricardo.

Senior was such an original caste of mind that in some respects he should be differentiated from other economic writers. He was a very distinguished lawyer and an expert on government matters. He wrote a great many smaller works. Now, we shall first study his general views on economic theory and then his special views. He was not much of a business man or a practical economist. He looks upon economics as an entirely theoretical science. In his theory of value the point he emphasizes is his insistence upon the subjective side. Ricardo talks about cost—labor cost. Senior opposes to the whole labor theory and he emphasizes the sacrifice of the individual in doing labor and further stresses the fact that any other factor which limits the supply is just as important in having its influence upon value. He was the first one to call attention to the disutility of labor, and when you apply that conception to capital, the idea of abstinence. He says, just as sacrifice is important to human beings so abstinence is important when dealing with capital. So his whole theory of interest consists in the idea of abstinence from consuming. Then, of course, he says, one should get something through the abstinence which he practices. That he went to the extreme with it, and finally brought about wrath, for advocating saving to get interest. Now these are not so important as other phases of Senior's views, where he struck out into something new, somewhat newer paths. It was Senior that for the first time called attention to the connection and the similarity between profits and rent and he says in his 6th edition, page 130: Profit is the reward of abstinence. Profits he considers reward of abstinence, just as wages is reward of labor and rent is spontaneous reward of nature. He says in certain ways you can look upon rents and profits as same thing. Doctrine of wages, you find, is his chief contribution. He takes the doctrines, such as he found them and regulates them, what is now definitely known into the wages fund doctrine. It is an important proposition to Senior. This appears to him so self-evident that if political science was a new science it would be accepted without any controversy, that wages are paid out of capital and the capital is predetermined, therefore the less the number of laborers the higher the wages will be and vice versa. It was Senior above all that made wages fund theory, but it led also to a very remarkable practical result. Although his conception was not a practical kind, it led him also to some extreme conclusions.

When the government was very much concerned about the Trade Unionism Act, they called upon Senior for careful investigation. Senior made out his report and it came out against Trade Unionism, because of his emphasis upon the theory of wages. And, it was not alone his opposition to trade unionism which helped to secure for this new science prominence but also it was for the same reason—his opposition for the factory acts. And, it was in this connection that he wrote. He tried to show that the profits in the cotton factories of that day were all made in the last hour. This was written in opposition of 10 hour day. The question was, Shall there be a reduction? No, said Senior. His rigid economic theory brought him to the conclusion that profits were made in the 12th hour and any reduction would undermine all England's prosperity. And he did not succeed quite well in this. I mention these things because it was despite of his statement to the contrary, the practical results were different. In other respects he did better work. He first called attention to economic consequence of absenteeism, especially in Ireland, and he has some very interesting thing to say about it. So that, if you sum it all up, you will find in Senior a very original mind in some respects, because through him it was introduced to economics the subjective conception in the sense that Jevons took it, and only later on that J. S. Mill brought in new point.

We will now say a few words of what was known as Independent writers. Men like Mill, McCulloch, Senior, were prominent and their views to such an extent sympathetic to dominant interest in England that this was known here and any where else, but until very recently we did not even know that there were different writers. That period from 1820 up to the year 1848-50 were considered "dark ages" in English political economy. There were great many writers, however, very able men, who discussed all sorts of problems which arose and many of them advanced ideas which remained unknown until very recently. I would say that you would find in these writers from 1820 to 1850, almost everything that we had to rediscover and redevelop in the last generation. Some of these writers I dealt with two or three decades ago and I wrote about them in my essay, but I don't pretend to exhaust the universe. But, only the other day that Professor Viner told me that he discovered in one of these men the most remarkable of the problems of international trade and on currency—things that we have been finding for the last 15 years.

I have no doubt that further study of these minor English writers at this time will bring out a great deal more. I will, in this lecture try to sum up what you will find in the article I wrote. It is very significant that nothing was mentioned in Palgrave's Dictionary of any of these men. Let us now take a few of these men:

Torrens, was a Colonel, and wrote a good deal on economic topics. He devoted his attention to a good many of the problems of the day and wrote a number of books on corn trade, production, wealth and etc. His contribution can be summed up as follows: He was rediscoverer of the law of comparative cost, which is generally ascribed to Ricardo. That statement of mine led to a discussion with my friend Professor Hollander, who knows more about Ricardo than any one else. He thinks that perhaps I have misinterpreted. I am sure, I still believe Torrens ought to be ascribed to this. As regards the other points there is no doubt, that he independently discovered the law of rent and wrote before Ricardo or Malthus. That of course was a simple matter of priority. Third point was the theory of wages, which differed considerably from the subsistence theory of Ricardo and based itself upon the conception of standard of life, which afterwards seriously modified Ricardo's views. That was a contribution of Torrens. In the fourth place his theory of profits differed also from the Ricardian theory in that he for the first time stated that profits were really a surplus and not as Ricardo thought a cost. Torrens tells us that is a surplus. Torrens was not of course as great a mind as Ricardo. He said some very crude things. He opposed to the conclusion of the theory of population. He says all endeavors to improve the condition would be idle. He had no sympathy with that point at all. He has finally another great point: Torrens of course did not believe in machinery throwing out the laborers out of work. But, he did not deny that in the short run there would be a great harm done. He was the first man to point out that while having economic equilibrium the burden of this transition was put upon the laborers themselves. He says, humanity and justice demand that those who suffer from public good should be relieved in the expense of public. Whenever, he says, a new application of mechanical power throws out of work great many people, a national fund should be provided to aid them while adjusting themselves to the new conditions. Now you see that is a new idea. It has not been realized yet, but some day that would be considered as important thing in social legislation. When that comes, it will be known that Torrens was responsible for this idea.

Now we come to Craig, who wrote a three volume work on Political Science. He among other things objects to the whole doctrine of Smith with reference to productive and unproductive doctrine of labor. Craig's contribution may be summed up under three heads: (1) He called attention (although not in our modern way) to the relation between utility and value. (2) He objects to the Ricardian doctrine of necessary opposition between wages and profits. That was important point. (3) He declares that he would make the analogy of the return of capital and rent and land. He makes this much less rigid than Ricardo did. But it was not long when you got away from these theoretical problems and came to its practical applications.

The first of English writers who cast little doubt was Ravenstone. He calls his book "A few Doubts as to the Clearness of Expression on the Subject of Political Economy"—1821. He was the one who first contrasted the rights of labor and rights of profits. Of course this then was quite new. He was also the first one to intimidate [sic: intimate] that there was something in this doctrine which was important. He puts it this way: whole rent arises from the surplus produce of labor. Rent shares directly, profit shares indirectly. He does not work it out in detail but you find fundamental conceptions in Ravenstone. It was mainly over to the influence of his discussion of Ricardo and Malthus during the remaining of 20's that most writers now talked about the theory of value. We now come therefore to a whole series of writers on what you might call the theory of value.

Among these Boileau was most important. He wrote a critical dissertation on the value and he goes very much fully into the doctrine. You can sum up his contribution as follows: (1) He criticizes the labor theory of Ricardo. (2) He emphasizes the element of time and by that he brings the question of Ricardian wine. (3) He also tends in the direction of broadening the rent concept. (4) He gives a criticism of the doctrine that rent never enters into price. (5) He lays stress upon the idea of productivity and value and that values largely are influenced by productivity. Boileau, however, in most of his discussion does not get to the bottom of the things. You have to pick out his gold from good deal of grass. The idea that was developed by Boileau was taken up by De Quincey in his Dialogue of Three Templars. He wrote a book on the logic of Political Economy. He was never a profound economist. I only mention him in passing because he at the time had great influence.

W. F. Lloyd was a professor in Oxford and who in several lectures first explained the relation between utility and value, as we today do—an explanation which is generally ascribed to Austrian and German schools, but it is found very clearly in Lloyd. Clark uses the term and what he calls specific utility. Lloyd uses the same thing, and he calls it special utility. He also wrote some other things but they are of very slight importance compared with these fundamental points which were step forward and which cleared up in modern times our whole discussion which at the time no one noticed although some people read it. So that we now come to the writers who really made a little more of stir and those are the ones that are mentioned in the syllabus.

We now take up S. Read, who wrote a book on the Rights of Property. He is interesting. He says we should discuss the problems not only from the point of view of what is, but also what it should be. But apart from that fact he was very acute critic. There are three of four points in which he made a distinct advance. He was the first one to point out the connection between Ricardian theory and what we now call socialist theory. In the second place his theory of profits is very interesting, because he for the first time advanced the idea of risk,—as profits are paid for the risk involved. Thirdly he broadens the concept of capital, and finally he emphasizes the fact that capitalists in industry have duties as well as rights. He refers to doctrines of Malthus and Ricardo as elaborate nuisances.

Ramsey wrote an essay on Distribution of Wealth. He was not perhaps as important as Read, but he discusses a great many interesting things and he responsible for great many advances made in economic theory. For instance, in many modern books distinction is made of value—time value, place value and which is generally traced back to Knies (my own teacher), these are found in Ramsey. He tried to introduce in English the term entrepreneur instead of undertaker, not with great success. One passage from Ramsey, which is especially interesting and that is the idea that England's industrial prosperity which now was becoming very large, is bound to be short-lived as compared with this country. He called attention to the fact that England's position was not permanent.

S. M. Longfield, Professor in Ireland, lectured in 1884. I may say that just you find in Lloyd, so you find in this book of Longfield the whole theory the original discussion of profits of wages and interest. In other words the theory of marginal productivity which is the basis of the whole Austrian school. worked its way, and it is found not indeed fully and in a detailed way, but for all intents and purposes it is so clear that it ought to have produced greater interest. One of the Irishmen, Mr. Butt, wrote a few articles about it, he was just about a half century until recently. That gives you a little survey of what was going on in England at this time.

We will now discuss a few of minor writers in addition to the independent authors. At first we shall take up Scrope, who became quite well known in the last few years in economics. He was a member of Parliament then too a geologist. He wrote his "Principles of Economics" in the 30's. He discussed natural law of social welfare. He is especially noteworthy for being opponent of Malthus. He was an optimist rather than pessimist. He developed the whole idea of index number and he seems to be the originator of this, although Joseph Lowe had presented it, but it was really Scrope who first presented in a clear form, and discussed it in connection with his doctrine of currency problems and bank of England. It may be said that he was the originator of the whole idea of standard of value as related to index numbers.

The next name mentioned on the syllabus under the Philanthropists is Thomas Chalmers. Although at one time he was very much read, but not now. His work on Christian and civic economy of large towns is published in 20's, and also a book on economics published in 30's, and who is often quoted. He is a difficult man to read, he is very declamatory, and has a great fondness of rash generalization, but he was a great friend of poor and did quite a little charity work. He outdid Malthusians by his striking pacifistic attitude. He was exponent of the poor laws. He treats doctrine of overpopulation in connection with the theory of over production—glut of capital. But what perhaps most striking about Chalmers is that he might be characterized as a feudal conservative. He really wanted to see good old times—the middle ages back again and who was the last Englishman who shared with the physiocrats. He makes certain contributions: For the first time he uses the name of marginal population and then his contribution in practical social economics. He is also to be remembered because of his social conception. He had quite a little influence at this time. Next point we come to is his currency and banking doctrines. The doctrines as they developed in 30's and 40's. Now it is quite noted that in England at this time you find in this respect two movements in a period of social unrest, especially in the early periods. You always find some thinkers who associated the evils and abuses with the currency conditions, and who seek to find a panacea for social and economic evils in the form of money. Of course this is also very common in this country. But in England when this social reaction took place one side of this was represented by an endeavor to find a remedy in currency form.

The chief representative was Thomas Atwood, the founder of Birmingham School. By which we mean the currency agitation. Atwood began to write in the 20's. Whole remedy that he advocated was as follows: Higher wages, higher price; higher price, more money; and increase of money would solve the problems. That of course is a very primitive idea. This represented one side of a great movement, the other side of course was represented by businessmen and which was an attempt to utilize money and currency as medium of credit as a method of improving business conditions and the development of the factory system,—immense growth of industry during this time, from the time of Ricardo on brought with it this attempt to reliven this whole idea of improvement of credit. This was a period during which the idea of cred leveloped in England, just as at the present time, what is beginning to develop vith reference to consumption. This period marks this development and great ›ank act of 1844. And, again, we have nothing good at all—no literature in :ngland, dealing with this problem. A German wrote a good book about this. "here were two great schools in economics: The currency school and the ›anking school, which I will bring to your attention.

This all turned around the quantity theory of money. You remember that Ricardo applied the quantity theory to the situation as he found it, which was 1convertible bank notes. Now, gold payments having been resumed in 30's nd 40's, controversy arose that the quantity theory was applicable convertible ank notes, what related to banking system. That was the problem which was eing worked out. Now the currency school took from Ricardo the doctrine f possible redundancy of inconvertible notes and they applied to convertible otes also. The name itself is due to Mr. G. W. Norman, who began writing ι early 40's. The principles of the school may be summed up as follows:

1. Prices vary with changes in the amount of money in circulation.
2. Banks have in their power to increase the amount of currency.
3. The import and the export of gold must therefore be regulated by regulating bank issues.

Norman was soon followed by S. J. Lloyd. He became so important that ₂ assumed a name of Lord. Also associated with them was Colonel Torrens ho were responsible for the bank act of 1844. On the other hand opposed › the advocates of banking principles that quantity theory applies only for convertible paper. They said it is a mistake to apply to convertible bank notes ιd foundation of that theory is the idea that the currency school overlooks ιe possible effects of deposits and that bank deposits are just as important bank notes in [a]ffecting prices. This was made familiar for the first time. he view of this school is that bank notes are credit increments, like checks, c., and now they attracted the majority of better writers, starting with Thomas ›oke. Because of the history of price, he was forced to go over to the other hool. In other words he thought the rise of prices was due to a great many her considerations and not simply due to changes of money conditions lffecting the commodities themselves and affecting also the state of exchange. The chief opposition is represented by Fullerton, Wilson, etc. and economists ₂wmarch and Gilbert—a fine array of thinkers. And the controversy between ₂m culminated in bank act of 1844 and this has been discussed. Now, I pass ' these because it is a side issue, and what we are trying to develop is economic ₂ory. We come now to so-called Manchester school, as over against the rmingham school. It is very easy now to pass judgment on these since we ve a few wonderful books on Cobden, and we can now have a clearer picture.

After all when we speak of Cobden, it is the movement that we are interested in. He was a powerful man and had great influence. Of course, we have now gone far off from his views. But Cobden was a practical man. He called political economy the highest exercise of the human mind. He emphasized of course the industrial and commercial characteristics and he was too, a great friend of United States. All of his views culminated in his doctrine of trade. He was primarily the representative of manufacturers, but he also was farmers' friend and he pointed out that what England needed at that time was free trade. He said England could dominate the world only by free trade. Free trade therefore with him is the international law of the Almighty and eternal fruit. He was the first to call war an immoral and damnable trade, a brutalizer of humanity. He says the best way to get rid of war is to abolish the nationalism. Although he was not a pacifist but he carried his views so far that anything which interfered with his cherished idea he opposed strongly. About buying the cheapest way and selling the dearest way he says of course this is not alone unequal but also immoral and therefore trade unionist so far as internal trade was concerned was opposed to that. He referred to the factory laws and trade unions as constituting a brutal tyranny. He refers to socialism as being the doctrines of fools behind them. His whole attitude was complete acceptance of principles of the school and opposed to any one interfering with that and he says, doctrine of population is nonsense. Carlyle spoke of Cobden's activities as "calico millennium." He says many other things should be done beside free trade. At all events the practical work done was immense because there is no doubt that high protective laws were bad economically as well as socially. Exporting machinery was absolutely prohibited. You remember, the design of the first machine in this country was brought in the head of the builder. They believed in absolute efficacy of these extreme nationalistic protective tariff which also applied to corn laws. Cobden had a great sympathy with this movement and felt that he was really an agent of God in helping along the situation. And with the beginning of the abolition of corn laws which was of course right, but unfortunately it went into effect without the acceptance of the whole economic criticism of classical school, and it meant the assumption of complete adequacy of free competition in its extreme form. They did not recognize any difference between service and commodities. The Manchester school opposed laws against drugs, opposed legislation against women and children working all their lives underground in the mines, they opposed factory laws even for infants. They opposed governmental regulation entering into trade, opposed trade unionist to do anything to elevate their class. Of course that movement is a mistake and that the corn law regulation was made possible for large manufacturer who ostensibly advocated cheaper bread for workmen. Mr. Rae in his book on socialism says: "Manchester school is nothing but a stage convention, a device for the marking off of a particular extreme theoretical attitude regarding the task of state, the state of laissez-faire has never been any more than it is now..

There is no doubt the followers went much further than the founders. The reason that political economy was popular at this time with the capitalist interest and all land owners, because the doctrines that were reached happened to fall in with their particular interest. Every man of course runs away from the danger. Then, again, you were rated either a socialist or a capitalist. That was true in his, as we now know, that at that time political economy was the political economy of the capitalist class, it was political economy of laissez-faire and it was for the prosperous. From that point of view, the Nemesis soon came in a double way. With the growing prosperity, of course these doctrines soon became to be criticized, instead of being God-given science now it became a dismal science and developed the whole theory of socialism. Then, of course, here came a movement of intellectuals, as Karl Marx and etc. Then, fortunately came at this time a great mind whose effort served as a kind of bridge and that is the work of J. S. Mill, who was brought up in the Manchester school, but assumed a different part and started entirely a new side of looking at things, practically at all events. Bright, of course, was really primarily a mouth-piece of Cobden, but he was a more imposing human being. He had all the good points of Cobden together with his weaknesses. Now, leaving them, and those other great men who were primarily statesmen, we come to John Stuart Mill, representing the social standpoint.

John Stuart Mill is the most important figure in English economics between Ricardo and Marshall. Marshall says he produced upon me the saddest impression because his opinions were all of them formed for him and he was brought up in the most intellectual strait-jacket of extreme Benthamites and his whole biography presents to me an example of noble nature confined at the strongest intellectual fetters and these fetters which were forced upon him did their best in all his life to revit [sic] upon himself, and then at the end he tried to get rid of them, but never succeeded, and there was a continual fight. You all know how he was educated by his father. He was trained in the midst of discussions of economics.—That was his relaxation. He really had been taught through the whole subject when he was 18 or 19 years old. He wrote in 1829. He wrote that remarkable work: "Essays on Some Unsettled questions", which he wrote when he was only 23. There are two things in that remarkable work: in the first place his whole conception of political economy resumes from assumed premises—premises which might be thought without foundation and fact and which did lead to conclusions which are absolutely true just as geometric or algebraic science. Secondly, he tells us that he is dealing with a science which has already reached complete truth.

I called attention in the course of the last lecture to his training and to his first work on international trade. He finally completed his general treatise on principles of Political Economy a few decades later which as a clear and systematized resume of accepted principles at once took the first place in British thought and opinion, and retained that position over a generation. So that, when people spoke of Political Economy in England they always thought of Mill. If you take up the book you find that in the first edition in the beginning he was feeling these clumsy forebodings by his training under his father, that in successive editions, which were many, changes were introduced, and those changes were almost entirely due to his wife who he married during the later times of his life. She was a remarkable woman and did exert some humanizing influence upon him. This change was however not entirely due to his wife. He began to read French, and then too, he got acquainted with Kant. He tells us that Kant was largely responsible for his being opened for the limited and temporary value of the whole political economy.

The next step is marked under 60's, when a lawyer, Thornton wrote that remarkable criticism—Assault upon Wages-fund Theory, and Mill with his open-mindedness and generosity now accepted and abandoned completely his whole wages-fund theory. So that in his book on socialism, his essay on socialism which he now wrote, although they did not appear until after his death, he went considerable step-forward. In the meantime he had taken a very advanced position on private property on land and had become President of Lantama Reform Association. Mill developed the doctrine of earned and unearned increment and he was largely responsible for disposal of Australian public domain, that land ought to be kept rather than be sold. In his autobiography you find a statement which gives his final views. This was around the end of his life. He always spoke of his wife, as well as of himself.

John Stuart Mill marks the close of the old and the beginning of the new school, and despite his gradual changes he remained the accepted leader of all the English Public Opinion largely because in his book as such the main line were in accord with those of the Orthodox class of school. After all concession he made at the end of his life he was no longer in agreement with the work but never changed his work. We therefore have to spend a few minutes to discuss the fundamental points in the book, especially the new points. In ordinar edition of two volumes, in the first volume we will first take up production and exchange and in the second volume, value and distribution. The most importan part in the first is the point brought out as demand of capital for labor. In his discussions of population there is nothing new. He takes the attitude as trade unions conversion of workmen. He took strong position in his views in the late edition of his second book, where he deals with his distribution and where h still remains an individualist. You find that in later editions he make concessions. Another point might be mentioned is that in his discussion of land question he was very much influenced by Jones and there he gives about the only evidence of his attachment to the whole interest in the historical method in economics, only in connection with land that he goes into problems connected with large and small farmers. His views on some questions like that of women and children are exceedingly liberal, this is ascribed to his wife. His views on money and credit were exceedingly interesting, because he adds there to the accepted doctrine, and especially his chapter on credit where he makes application of quantity theory to the convertible paper. This chapter is one of the very best. Chapter on cost of production is also interesting and Mill was responsible for the theory of joint cost. That was his contribution. In his doctrine of foreign trade Mill although not original but was the greater exponent of the doctrine of comparative cost. Ricardo did not put it so beautiful as Mill puts it. In his doctrine of speculation we note another addition. He calls attention to two sides, the stabilizing and unsettling function of speculation. He also brings out very clearly the influence and differentiation between increase and decrease of goods [a]ffecting value. In all those points he really marks additions and everywhere he clarifies. As regards his outlook upon the future of capitalism, it is very interesting to observe that Mill stands between the old and the new schools.

Section 46.   Opposition to the Orthodox School

This went on during Mill's time, beginning early in the 20's, it acquired increased momentum every year. We start therefore with those whose influences in the abstract economics and then discuss the effects on practical life, and also men whose influences are felt in recent times.

In Historical school there is only one independent development. This was due to Mr. Jones (1790-1855). He was a professor at the Kings College and he wrote not alone an essay on Wealth, but also a series of essays which were later on published under the head of Literary Remains. Now, he did not reach Mill's position. He attempts to explain the cause of distribution of wealth. He discusses industrial paradoxes. He speaks of Ricardo as a man of talent, of Mill he spoke as being most delusionary. He says the whole trouble comes from the wrong method that these so-called leaders have followed. You have to remember that things are what they are, because they have been and they explain things in the light of their development, he says. And, he started out his printed work with the attempt to explain the development of private property in land, which had a great influence on John Stuart Mill. But, while he lectured on the other topics—on the history of wages, of which we have the syllabus, also on taxation which was never published—he got interested in practical works. He never published any books, never developed his ideas on the other parts of economics, his works therefore became entirely terse. He made good beginning but he did not finish it. Some of his essays were very interesting. He was the first Englishman to point out the unfairness of Adam Smith to mercantilists. He called attention to bullionists as over against mercantilists. Had he gone far enough with his work he would have done much to change not one public opinion but also the attitude of economists.

There were two other writers: Banfield and Jennings. Banfield published in 's, before Mill, his "Four Lectures on Industry." He studied in Germany and brought back with him to England many ideas. He was especially influenced by Hermann, who was the German Ricardo. Perhaps his most interesting theoretical contribution was his graduated scale of Industry, where he points out industry increases in graduated scale according to human wants. These are primary and secondary wants, and which apply all the way through the industry. He was a follower of Jones, and also after all he was largely influenced by his times—trade unionists; and so forth. He, however, only made a beginning.

A more original writer who only later came to front was R. Jennings. In his "Natural Elements of Political Economy" in 1855, Jennings was the first Englishman who cleared the way to appreciation of the nature and importance of the law of utility because other writers on this topic had not much influence In other words he bases his economics upon psychology and physiology. He called attention to static and dynamic value, and he makes a very interesting analysis of the sensations which are at the bottom of utilization—special sensations, etc. He points out that the idea of value depends entirely upon the idea of probability of future utilities. It was Jennings who clearly pointed out long before continental writers the contrast between present and future satisfactions. He denies entirely Mill's statement that demand for commodities is not a demand for labor. He said it is demand for labor. He goes on especially to emphasize social consideration in wealth. He even declares that mathematics must be counted upon more in the future to do a great deal in the laws of economics. He calls them numerical laws. I may say that Jennings was really forerunner of Jones who had represented that phase of intellectual economic enquiry. There is scarcely any side of economic questions of the time that were not represented during these decades in England.

Now we come to Socialists. There are several stages in the history of socialistic doctrines in the 19th century in England:

1. You have the early labor period which lasted up to 1825-30, when you find also the beginnings of labor periodicals. (Here there is material for half-a-dozen dissertations). Good many of later ideas are found to be developed in early writers.
2. R. Owen.
3. A group of writers who were known by the name of Ricardian socialist

It was during the period 1825-40, that we find the great efflorescence of the labor literature, a dozen or two dozen of remarkable labor periodicals. The beginnings of Socialists, etc. All these are summed up in the Chartist Movement which was primarily a political movement, but also economic movement. So this movement had become important, most of the literature on this movement has not yet been worked out.

Let us say a few words about these writers: As to Owen, I can be short as we have excellent work on Owen by Mr. Cohn. You remember that Owen wi always live in the history of economics for two reasons: First, as a practical manufacturer he was the first one to spin cotton on rollers and second, the first one who tried to introduce modern and humane methods in his factory. He refused to take in his factory workers under 10. He started schools and tried to improve the morality of his workmen. His practical efforts were also successful. He found that philanthropy paid, then he drew from that his theoretical conclusions. He began in 1814-15 and continued in his attempt to do away what he calls, white slavery. His fundamental idea, as you know, is that people's opinions are formed for them and not by them, and that heredity is of a very little consequence, as compared with environment and therefore the education which you can give to people, general and industrial, alone is calculated to bring about progress, and as a result of that he developed his idea of social cooperative villages, what he calls mutual cooperative communities, and these cooperative communities are people who lived together which formed these communistic group and his followers were called communists, later on changed to socialist and communist. Now in books after books and periodicals after periodicals he builded the foundations of a new science—new science of society and tried to put into operation during the 20's and started communistic movement in Scotland and Ireland and then he came over to this country. His mutual factory attracted attention of leading statesmen of England, and every other important people. At that time he was exceedingly popular, but when he unfortunately for him ventured to oppose the factory owners by being responsible for disturbance among their help along the great factory of 1818, he got into trouble and also opposed the basis of Christianity. He held that real religion was social religion, and this now became bugbear, and yet this was during the period when he was so much sought after. He came to this country and his influence was so great that the House and Senate stopped to listen to him. He started in this country his great communistic movement in this city and everywhere else. When he left, everything broke up. At one time he made a great attempt, spending money lavishly and made agreement with Mexico to carry on his plans there. There are several interesting books on that.

When he returned to England in 1830, in came this sudden outburst of trade unionist development. In England he traveled up and down and started the remarkable periodical the Crises, and then carried on some practical experiments, such as labor banks, etc. He soon got into trouble with the people religious views. He was the most gentle person to meet. In his debates with clergymen he was very strong but when it came to anything dealing with economic and social problems he never resorted to violence and he cooperated with people. That of course did not happen to coincide with labor movement England. He retired and lost all the millions that he had acquired, yet he retained to the end his belief in human nature and belief in the efficacy of cooperation. Toward the end of his life he became a senile and from that time he was converted to spiritualism. He lived to be a very old man, and last few years of his life are marked by those remarkable passages on the future state of mankind. So towards the end of his life, he was looked upon as a good but utterly impracticable visionary person. John Stuart Mill remarked that two things were left out of him: First is the beginnings of cooperative consumption or consumption cooperation and the second point was of course the beginnings of the idea of socialism as a theoretical and not a scientific movement, which might be put in place of competition. Owen however, had very little influence after a time upon people's opinion.

Now we come to that group of writers who also were not recognized at the time and who contributed to the working out of Karl Marx's qualities a scientific socialist, as over against Owen and French writers. The book of Mr Menger was first to call attention to the precursors of this whole movement The first man to doubt all the advantages of capitalism was Charles Hill. He wrote a book entitled, "The Effect of Civilisation on the Peoples of Europe. His position was a double one. That according to him manufacturing industry marked a step backwards and not forwards. You might call him the Gandhi as he has very much the same idea as Gandhi. His second point was that the labor does not get the whole profits of its product. It was he that called attention to that.

The next writer that I want to discuss is an Irishman William Thompson who may be called the founder of scientific socialism. He was brought up in the Owenite doctrines. He wrote a book entitled, "Mankind and the Possession and Distribution of Wealth." He wrote another book, "Labor Rewarded." H was influenced very much not alone by Owen, but also by Bentham. He says all wealth is produced by labor, that profits represent just as Marx puts it, the surplus of labor that has filched from other laborer, in fact the very word used by Marx. Labor, he says, confers an additional value, material and machiner cannot add anything, and the additional value is given only by labor. The surplus value constitutes the profits of capitalism and it really all belongs t laborer. There is no doubt that you find the fundamental idea of Marx in Thompson.

We spoke in the course of last lecture of efforts of Owen and the beginning of so-called Ricardian Socialists. Now I will say a word or two more of these so-called Ricardian Socialists: John Gray who became very much interested in Owen, [and] he is noteworthy as he primarily was of aggressive branch of [school] of incipient socialist. He traveled in the United States and [had] great influence in this country, however, his influence was not a permanent one. He after a while changed his ideas and gradually devoted more time to the monetar side of the problem, and was almost completely taken by monetary scheme of so-called Birmingham school. Nevertheless, one lecture of his gives a ver noteworthy example, and that is the one lecture in this country on the human happiness, and he followed that with a large work on the social system. His theory is that human society is divided into the productive and unproductiv

ses, and that real social income is created by the class of manual workers
that rents, profits, interest, are simply represented by series of things that
are taken away from the results of legitimate production of labor. As a
sequence all the methods of modern society, he says, are rigidly unfit for
purpose for which they are intended. He says the object of government is
increase the happiness of people but its real effects have been to perpetuate
ery and struggle, in the social system. He goes little further and finds the
secret to lie in the system of exchange and the way out of the difficulty
puts in this sentence: "I believe the day will come when the entire business
every nation will be conducted upon the basis of national capital." Natural
thods means, he says, virtually no rent and no interest attainable by any one.
he virtually outlines a socialistic community. Gray did not have much
uence at the time. He was rather only swelled up in the whole over-night
vement.

Little more fortunate was the work of Thomas Hodgskin. He was an
icated man and a journalist and who was very much interested and a great
nd of Place, the man who drew attention of statesmen, and Hodgskin was
eatedly quoted by Karl Marx. Hodgskin says, labor is definitely against
claims of capital (1825), that was something new. He tried to maintain
osition to the views of Ricardo and others. He says trade unions can do
reat deal to promote the interest of workmen. Two or three years later he
lished his Political Economy in which he seeks to analyze the foundation
private property. He points out that distress at present existing in England
not caused by nature as Malthus and others mention but by the social
titutions which prevent laborer from getting the whole profits. He published
or three years later, his "Natural and Artificial Rights of Property
ntrasted." In which he develops very much the same idea. Hodgskin
vever, later on got away from latter movement.

We come finally to Bray, perhaps in some ways most important of all these
ters. He was a German printer, and who was quoted even more frequently
Marx than any others mentioned. Bray wrote in the 30's after the Chartists
vement. His book is entitled "Labor's Wrongs and Labor's Remedies", and
mentions pretty much the same idea that every social and governmental
ing existed today always was due to rights of the institutions to private
perty and that entire mass is growing in the accumulated load of evils. He
intained that it was impossible that the present economic situation could
on without killing all the germs of democracy. He pointed out that in the
g run you cannot have political democracy unless you have social
nocracy. He laid down four fundamentals, all of which amount to this that
italists, the private owners, fasten themselves upon the productive classes
suck out all their earnings. So, there you have a group of writers in whom
find in a nut shell pretty much whole of later scientific socialists.

Now when it came to translate these into politics, the political side of movement was culminated in the Chartists' agitation which was ostensi primarily political. Of course, at the bottom there was the economic distre Their point was that the only way to prepare changes in the econor institutions was through giving the working class more of the voice in government. Now, Chartists writers, the Chartist readers, were mai politically inclined but they all wrote more or less on economic topics. L William Levitte, who was a workman, Helmington, the compositor, O'Connor, B. Bryant, all of them and some of whom we became familiar the beginnings our study were Chartists. The movement itself has been scarc touched. Two or three of our own students here did work on this moveme Then in England a boy worked on this also. No one as yet utilized the imme literature of that time. With the abolition of corn laws the heart of Chart movement was taken out in the middle of 40's, although there was certain fl up in 1848, it subsided as the standard of life had changed in England a the agitation stopped like magic. Following few decades after 1848 you f practically nothing. This was the reaction among the working people and public opinion was very slightly affected by the so-called labor classes. T change was due to entirely different set of ideas, which was primarily due Carlyle, and to certain extent to Ruskin and others.

We will say a few words about Carlyle. Although not economist, yet exert quite a large influence on economic thought, more than anybody else outsi of economic field. We now have a few good books on Carlyle. The best bo is in German by Rae, entitled, "Social Philosophy of Carlyle." The best bo is still untranslated, a book by Schultza, some of you had the opportunity listening to this remarkable man, now about 60's or 70's. His first book is Doctor's Dissertation—a little book on "Social Peace", part of which translated, which gives on the whole the best account of the situation as exist in England at that time. Carlyle's books on Social Philosophy and his bo on Chartism, and Sarto Resartus, was published in the 30's and in many his works he refers to social ideas. Of course, Carlyle was a Romanticist remarkable man and was brought up in an atmosphere of complete oppositi to utilitarianism, in opposition to Bentham. Bentham was to him his bugbe representing everything in opposition of truth. He starts out with visions altruism. His "loyalty" shows itself in Hero Worship. Every man, he says, an ideal state of society has got to be susceptible to self-sacrifice. He calls t self-sacrifice a man's enthusiasm. He says, you need religion but not religi of the current kind. Religion of Carlyle is one's relation to his family, relation to his fellow beings. Carlyle says, you got to have creed. He wo these out in his famous spiritual optics and there again his influence of Germ training is seen. He tries to develop historically the idea of self-activity. No he says, in former times when people had such ideas and ideals then you co speak of a positive civilization, positive times with common beliefs. Individu mposing society believes in these common notions, then, he says, you get e cooperation, you get loyalty, and kinship. He says, then these positive vantages are succeeded by the later stages, unbelief comes along, you don't ieve as your father and we find creed reaches to maturity and is bound to :ay and as it decays you could see the abuse and bigotry of religion, and at is worse, bigotry materializes. Now, he says, we are in that stage fortunately, and instead of positive stage, we enter into negative stage. Jesus, says, represents positive stage and Bentham the negative stage. He explains y and how social ethics decays. The utilitarianism and indifference come and social conditions begin to approach to pre-social condition, when he 's, every man is content with other beings. He speaks of social dyspepsia, :ieties as prepared by Bentham. He says combination of isolated needs tends irreligion and all social forms become lies and they are no more real beliefs. says what we get is revolution and what still worse is democracy. He says, y are all destructive forces. He says, we want to build up and what we want o get the positive stage. He points out the contrast, the disparity between : inner force and outer forms. He says the outer forms are the materialistic, : utilitarianism and political economy. He says, he wants something positive tead of laissez-faire, as characterized by hypocritical middle class and litical economists. Of course Carlyle took all his philosophy from Faust. was an enthusiast of labor questions and he was opposed to the ordinary ory of economics. Capital of Industry was Carlyle's idea, but in reality it ant to him something else beside making money. He says, man is not only de of a stomach but also of soul. He preached doctrine of inner reform. w, of course, you see Carlyle was not a logical man, and not a scientist. had certain ideas which brought him in absolute conflict with the prevalent nomic and social philosophy.

What Carlyle tried to do was carried on by still less logical individual who resented the sentimentalists, or emotional side. This was Ruskin. Last few :ades in his life he was far more interested in economical questions than , and to the end of his life he refused to travel in railroad train. If you roach Ruskin from scientific point of view his discussions are nonsense. his discussion of John Stuart Mill he had no idea to amount to anything, at the bottom there was something sane and sound in his opposition. His ole concept of wealth, his weal, the idea is taken from Goethe—The idea t witnessed the sun, the capacity of drinking the sun, etc. Ruskin speaks he enjoyment of wealth, says, you have to consider not the production but sumption side also, and he says wealth cannot be a noble thing unless it njoyed. That side of it he continually harps on, and which has brought about uch more tolerant attitude to appreciation of Ruskin.

The final movement at that time which had more success in practical life s Christian Socialists. We now have good book on that. There were two n; one was Kingsley and the other Maurice. Kingsley suddenly got interested

after the revolution of 1848, in the situation of sweat shops in England.
his cheap clothes he electrified all England by his wonderful statement of t
situation. And the difference between this group and the enthusiastic you
men who came together was the cooperation side. These young men came
the side of Owenites and attacked the consumption cooperation, wh
Christian Socialists used the idea of productive cooperation—cooperation
production—to work together. They differed very much from Carlyle in th
readiness to accept the science of economics as such. They did not agree w
some of the economic ideas but they said it could be done through scien
Kingsley did not agree with Carlyle's idea of political economy. He says Jo
Stuart Mill speaks nothing of the doctrine of laissez-faire, and took econom
as being a complete science, he says their reason and their religion must
poopooed down. So, that was the way in which week after week discussi
was carried on and it helped to create a public opinion in England and gradua
threw open this hard sub-soil of indifference, and what he did start out w
great enthusiasm got well-meaning aristocrats on his side, but within 12 mon
the whole thing went into pieces. We had similar condition here in the beginn
of 80's, in order to get rid of sweat shop and soon enough whole th
disappeared in the same year, but there were still something left, and the pul
continued it for a while.

The other side of it was represented by Ashley, this was the working la
This remarkable individual was a combination of broadest humanitariani
and the most narrow bigotry. Socially, however, he was very broad. He fina
succeeded doing two things: The philosophy of factory laws was never m
really discussed and that from that time on the justification and necessity
trade unionism was never again discussed. England in this respect reached h
or three-quarters of a century ago a position which we have not reached
yet, and we ascribe this progress to the works of men as Ashley, Kingsley a
Carlyle. So that by the beginning of 50's the whole classical school, and
classical economics of Ricardo and of Malthus was very largely confined
the ranks of ordinary businessmen who adapted economics as the science
business and that on the other hand there grew up in the community at la
the influence of the conception that economics was anti-social discipline, t
it was a damnable science and its doctrines were pessimistic doctrines.

Section 47.   Development in France

After the physiocrats and after the revolution, so far as economic progr
was concerned its influence virtually disappeared. In France as elsewh
during the period of Napoleon there was very little inducement for study
economic problems, because there were no economic questions. Those eve
connected with Napoleonic wars and the problems were on the expenses
subject peoples. Nothing of the kind happened in England. When howe

apoleon's career came to an end and the monarchy was reestablished, the roblems were simply minor problems, as how to deal with budget, and debt. Debts were comparatively small. The newer problems were those that resulted om the gradual introduction of factory system, factory system now coming in France as it was in England. There now came to the front the thinker at took up these newer problems. This was J. B. Say, who is generally called y the French their Adam Smith, but who does not possess at all anything omparable to that name. Say was born in 1767 and died 1832. He was the n of a merchant. In 1803 he wrote his treatise on Political Economy in an deavor to popularize many ideas of Adam Smith, and it was after the ownfall of Napoleon that he published his complete course of Political conomy. He was also noted of possessing the characteristics of a common nse man. He carried on a very active correspondence with Malthus and icardo. He became great friend of them both. He accepted the Malthusian octrines and in part Ricardian theories, although he opposed of what he called etaphysics of Ricardo. There are, however, three points in his work that are orth mentioning, because they mark step forward in advance:

1. His theory of debauche, which can be put in a nut shell, that all nsumption is limited by production and that things are not sold because other oducts are scarce. In other words the two things, production and nsumption are correlated and there can never be any such thing as a general ut of commodities as Malthus pointed out, because he says, supply of one ing implies the supply of something else. Prosperity of producer and nsumer is mutual. That he applied this to internal trade and then to foreign ade. That brought him into acceptance of physiocratic and Smith's doctrine free trade as opposed to the system of protection or prohibition. In other ords there was just as much correlation in international as in internal demand d supply. That is perhaps the doctrine that made him known.
2. He never accepted the mercantilist doctrine and disagreed with Smith the doctrine of productivity of labor. He emphasizes the existence of material products. Adam Smith limited his wealth to physical production, ereas Say was in favor of immaterial production.
3. His theory of distribution marks a distinct advance forward. He did not cept Ricardian law of distribution and instead of that, he says, the doctrine profits as the return for the entrepreneur, and it was he that put forth the ea of earnings of management.

He makes distinction, although it must be said it is not completely correct, t gives the beginning of a distinction which is not found in Adam Smith Ricardo. In the main however Say accepts mostly the idea of the English 100l. He emphasizes especially his opposition to mercantilism, the doctrines mercantilism and protectionism, and when he carries that distinction over

to the domain of money, he says, instead of money being sign of wealth, th
less money there is in a country the better. As over against the doctrine o
the net produce as emphasized by the physiocrats he puts the doctrine o
national revenue as a gross profit. Dupont, you remember, was one of th
followers of physiocrats, who edited Tooke's work and carried on a ver
considerable controversy with Say during all this time Dupont still claimin
the soundness of his physiocratic doctrine. But in general summing it all up
it may be said that Say was an advocate of the things as they existed. He believe
not alone in absolute freedom but in complete competition and the unlimite
growth and efficacy of private capital. So that, even though Say does not agre
with some of the theories of distribution of Ricardo, nevertheless he was th
founder of classical school in France and as time went on this movement soo
became considerably greater. Say had great difficulty in starting any cours
in political economy in France because of political questions. Government wa
now very careful in political changes. From that time on however, politic
economy became very popular, especially under the influence of what is no
called eclectics.

The period from 1820 to 1850 was marked in France by rapid introductio
of factory system and industrial revolution and by the growing social unre
culminating in 1830 and 1848. It was in opposition to the movement from th
lower class of people that the writers, not most of them, took up these doctrin
of Say and English School, and carried them to the extreme. The chief writer
Garner and Rossier, an Italian, who spent most of his life in Italy and Austri
There were great many others. They founded the Journal of Economics in th
40's—first periodical on economics in the world. They founded a publishin
house devoted entirely publishing of such books and they controlled all th
officials of the city in the institution. There were two great ideas in the min
of these writers. Napoleon had given to France two great things: One was Cod
de Napoleon, the other was the system of administrative centralization. Cod
Napoleon worked very well but over-centralization of France which made th
whole French system very notable, and that together with this social moveme
which I spoke of led to the natural protective development as a result of strugg
of England and attempt to keep the French goods for France rather for Englis
factories. This brought two great movements: The movement of protection o
one hand and the movement of socialism. And, the characteristics of this scho
were implicably the opposition to over-centralization, more of English idea
freedom, opposition to protection and especially opposed to socialism. Th
means in a nut shell the acceptance of social philosophy of English classic
school. Now this school came to be called in France Liberal School. It wa
liberal only in the sense in demanding liberty and they meant by it the liber
of individual as over against government, liberty in the sense of free trade. Th
school was known as liberal school as over against governmental school, b
in practice they were nothing [sic] but liberal. They allowed no opposition, th

not allow anything against them. A man could not get his book published, ald not get a position if he were against them. Consequently that the school quired more and more importance and by 1850 it had reached to a position ll near commanding influence—monopolists' influence, and remained so m that time on for a generation or two. So that when I speak of French ters all through 19th century, with a few exceptions, I refer to these common se liberal minded classical writers who were in complete harmony with siness and more especially with big railroads that developed during the 30's 1 40's. And, then, of course came a reaction and the reaction was a double d, just as we find in England. There was a reaction from social point of view 1 also a reaction in theory. Now, in England, you remember the socialist vement had very little practical influence. In France for particular reasons y had for a time larger influence. In England the theoretical reaction was rcely heard of, in France there was much more important reaction and oretical in part among certain French writers and also in other countries, 1 only in recent times that we realize what has been done.

In the beginning of the century one thing which had considerable influence on thinkers, although it had nothing to do with any particular idea that was ook published in 1802, published by Connard, and that book is interesting m this point of view that it for the first time compares the body economic the human body—biological point of view, and speaks of circulation of alth and of the importance of money in the circulation. The practical plication that can now be made out of this was introduction of a medicine o the veins of human beings. Just as the blood in the human body takes ything inserted in the body and carries it to the other parts so also taxation es the same thing. So that, he now founded the theory of diffusion of taxation d pretty much all modern doctrines go back to Connard in this respect. I t mention this in passing.

Now, coming back to the reaction we find two writers: One of them is a y well known man, the other is very little known who had something new d interesting to say about the factory system, and introduction of machinery France. First of these writers was Sismondi, who was an aristocrat, came m Geneva (1773). He wrote a book on commerce "La Richesse mmercial", when he was 25 or 26. After having made careful study of factory tem as it was then found in England, he published his new Principles of litical Economy in 1819. In the first place he criticizes the views of English iters, those who were cultivating the capitalist system. He defines the object economics as being the physical welfare of man, so far as influenced by vernment. He says the goal is not the accumulation of wealth, but as he ts it, "it is the participation of the whole human beings in the convenience wealth." He was the first who called it the orthodox school. The school, ys he, forgets the means, they sacrifice the end for the means. Sismondi is ry careful in pointing out how he uses the word communism. He says, a world without pain would be a world without virtue, a world without war would be a world without ends. His idea is by no means comparative sacrifice but his idea is comparative contentment of human beings. Then, he goes on to criticize and makes historical approach to social and economic problems. He objects to the English theory of laissez-faire. Government, says he, must be regarded as the protector of the weak, as the defender of those who cannot defend themselves. The government he says, must be conceived of as the representative to promote the gain and interest of all as over against the temporary and passionate interest of each. Political economy he says, is an ethical science and it is tantamount to science of human welfare. He discusses for the first time the doctrines of self-interest and competition.

Sismondi was not an extremist. He saw the advantages of division of labor as Adam Smith did. He saw the advantages of factory system and machinery. He was not blind to the evils of Middle Ages, yet he had no such idea as Carlyle. He says, unless we look out the capitalism is going to produce proletarianism. He was the first who used this word, and advanced great many other ideas. He spoke of capitalism as introducing new feudalism, quite as bad as Mediæval feudalism, only it was a feudalism in land, and it was Sismondi who pointed out the existence and the growth of this schism between the two classes. He did not agree with the English writers in any thing. He did not agree with Malthusian doctrine of over-population. Under the existing theory, says he, every new invention which inevitably leads to more population will be a calamity. He thinks real trouble with all modern 19th century economics is that it follows false gods—the economic gods, the aim being greatest possible production and lowest of prices. That he says would lead nowhere. You see, that the criticism was very powerful. For the first time these ideas were advanced and they were recognized as being forerunner of historical school and forerunner of ethical school by three quarters of a century. When you come to his positive construction there he was very weak. He ethically developed but did not have very great subtle logic power. He really does not know what to make of it all, and he is lost somewhat of the complexity. He is in certain sense conservative and not radical. He believes in private property, believed in profits and so forth, but he made a very interesting positive suggestion, some of which have taken root: First, he said some way or other laborer must not be divorced from his tools and materials, and that therefore the ideal scheme is industrial profit-sharing scheme. It was Sismondi who was responsible for that, and Beveridge used this idea a decade later. Second, he thought that marriage ought in some way to be put off little later and advocated compulsory prohibition of too early marriages. Third, he advocated compulsory insurance as a social phenomena. He was in favor to make some recommendation to cure all the evils caused by the inventions and by the machines. So Sismondi remains an important figure, and in course of time he becomes more and more important rather than the opposite. The importance lies in his critical attitude

The other writer who is only just beginning to got what he deserves and
*h*o started out in life in his connection with some of these socialistic projects
*h*o soon developed more importance, and that is C. Perqueur, born in 1801.
l 1838 he published a very interesting book, which got the prize of French
*c*ademy for the best treatises on the influence of factory system upon the
*w*orld. He wrote "On the Interest, Trade and Industry under the System of
*St*eam Engine." He followed it by one or two other books, especially by his
*N*ew Theory of Political Economy." And, putting it in a nut shell, it may be
*sa*id that Perqueur represented rather the social aspect of economics, and the
*n*ed of considering every economic problem from the angle of ethics as well.
It is a very interesting study in marking any decided step forward in economic
*q*uestions, by emphasizing the school of optimism from the critical point of
*vi*ew. In recent years he has been studied with very much more interest. He
*ha*d great influence on Karl Marx, and had great influence upon List. But,
*wi*thout going into detail, I might say that there was going on in France quite
*a l*ittle reaction and we find also some other interesting writers as Fourier, who
*di*scussed some of the labor questions. The other side of the reaction was
*m*arked by the socialists, and here we have of course three or four very
*pr*ominent names.

First is St. Simon—a nobleman, born in 1760, died 1825, and who may be
*ca*lled in certain sense the father of both of socialism and positivism. He was
*th*e first one to turn his attention to the mischievous evils of industrialism and
to take much more decided stand against it than Sismondi. His appeal however
is entirely to intellectuals and he approaches the subject from the point of view
of history. He advocates the abolition of all distinction between the bees and
*dr*ones. He finds as over against liberal school, what he terms economic
*or*ganization and that implies the transformation of the idea of absolute private
*pr*operty. He is not very extreme than his followers and he had most unusual
*su*ccess in associating with himself the enthusiastic young men from every walk
of life in France and industry and politics. For the time being they were all
*att*racted by this new religion. This religion was not theology, but only religion
of economics—very much like in Russia today. His attempts combined with
his followers, especially with an important one, culminated in two doctrines:
*th*e criticism of private property and putting stop to exploitation, and, the
*ab*olition of inheritance. And, the philosophy of the history was a very
*int*eresting one culminating in the contest, as he puts it, between economics
*an*d anarchy, present situation as over against collectivism. Of course, many
of his followers were eccentric men and developed all kinds of formulae and
*re*ally St. Simon had always great influence upon the intellectuals and quite
*a li*ttle on Karl Marx.

*T*he other French writer had perhaps a stronger mind, and that was Fourier,
*wh*o was even less practical and who limited his efforts to all kinds of schemes.
He worked out his very theory into a shape what he calls cooperative

community and he calls it the theory of integral cooperations, production an
consumption as well, and he thought that only in that way could you mak
labor really attractive and bring about participation of labor in the profits
capital. He develops that idea further in his work, and an important part
his plan was his insistence of family life and contribution of women to soci
economic problems. In France itself his chief follower was V. Considera
who was also a Humanist writer and who contributed toward the rath
difficult and subtle doctrine of Fourier.

While St. Simon and Fourier were at the front of these writers there is o
who contributed largely and this was Louis Blanc, whose famous work
translated. His contributions lie rather in the efforts to contrast work wi
competition. He calls competition the anarchy side of modern life and by wo
he means virtually productive cooperation. You see what was being done
England at that time under Owenite influence cooperation applied excessive
to consumption and no one tried out in practice this conception of producti
cooperation without entrepreneur—without the captain of industry. An
when revolution broke out, the famous national work shops started in par
of Paris, in 1848 and all of which came to an end for obvious reasons. Bla
continued his doctrine and ascribed difficulties to political and other defec

The other two are men who figure very largely in French thought and
that time did quite a little work also in practical accomplishment. First w
Leroux. He was not very able but still was a man of considerable prominen
and who developed the theory of solidarity. Same idea but different nam
and the work he calls the Humanity. It is a very interesting work and
characterized by the inveterates of ethical and religious ideas and the soci
problems. Finally there came that fascinating and charming personality a
that was Cabot, who first wrote his Utopia and his travels in Icaria, but w
whereupon at the end of 40's went to Texas and established his various Icari
societies. Cabot was frankly a communist.—Communism in consumption
well as in production and many of our states as you know were distinguish
by these Icarian communities.

The last of the names, considerably much better thinker than these
mentioned is Proudhon, who started out in the early 40's with his remarkab
work on private property. He asked, What is private property, and the answ
was, theft. That was the foundation of private property, and he was the or
perhaps who more than anybody else who developed in France the idea
unearned increment and then in 1846 he published his famous econom
contradictions and started out on a career of very widespread literary activi
Proudhon, however, would be misunderstood if he were interpreted of bei
a socialist or a communist in the sense of other writers that I have mentione
On the contrary he defines communism as being a religion of misery. He sa
communism has to break down, and what he was after was freedom. He ca
his theory, mutualism, but mutualism of Proudhon is simply another na

f philosophical anarchism. He was the founder of philosophical anarchism, nly he carried that idea into economic field and mingled with it very crude leas on exchange and money. You remember I spoke of Owen calling attention) labor bank and labor money. Now, Proudhon started also toward the end , Paris, and labor in exchange was based upon the very same idea. So that, roudhon's contribution is not so much in the economic field. It lies in the eld of political philosophy and in the whole religion of anarchism. I mentioned ily first leading thinkers in France. There were in France series of critics of ipitalist system and especially dominant school, and yet they had nothing at temporary influence. Of course, the conservatives were satisfied more than er before, and the economic discussions went on as if none of these writers ad existed. The practical movement died out and even in theory it was more aimportant than those in other countries. And, thus we come back to the rthodox Liberal School.

We come to the first representative, in some respect, and in other respects e optimist. After all the leading embodiment of the idea of laissez-faire, he d more influence in this country than any other Frenchman, and who played great role for many decades in this country as he advocated free trade and is is F. Bastiat. He died in his 50th. His theoretical views deserve some tention, because of the very great reputation and influence he exerted upon e thinkers as well as upon public opinion. Bastiat was really a businessman d retired to his estate, and for a long time, like most of Frenchmen he felt spicious of the attitude of English. He referred as "perfidious Albion", but the 40's he tried to aid the anti-corn law regulation and that started him nking and writing and in the course of 5 years he poured out big torrent work, wonderfully written and compelling the attention of everyone. He ote a book on Economic Sophisms, and also a book on Free Trade. He pularized the petition of candle makers—protection against sunlight, and inted out as a result of protection increase of tallow, sheep breeding, ricultural progress, resuscitation of whale, fishery, pointed out what an mense profit would ensue from these. That was one side. The other side the activity was that he now became a great protagonist of laissez-faire, epting the doctrine of English school by opposition of theoretical points Malthus and Ricardo. He developed this idea in his famous work in onomic Harmony. There are four or five chief points in these books. In his ory of value he starts out with wants of human beings and satisfaction, and es into detail, as to what he calls the utilities of things. He makes distinction ween free and gratuitous utilities, and what he calls ownerless utilities. He s, they are the things that require some labor. Such things have value only en there is some effort. On the other hand, he says, What are you going do with a piece of land or a pearl? Where is labor there? After thinking r the matter, he says, what we need is moral judgment, and he finds the ation in the term service. He says because it means two different things.

Service means personal exertion for somebody else, and also you may do man a service really without indulging a labor on your part. Now, he says the one is really equivalent of the other. He defines value: "value is the relatio between two services that are exchanged." Then, he says, if you say, well, thi thing has no value because it has not required labor. Well, says he, if a ma is giving you a land or pearl, he is doing you a service. His theory of privat property is that he takes the same attitude as Proudhon. He says property i just and he defines property as, "a legitimate mutuality of voluntary service. He says, when a man gives his service and indulges his efforts, then you hav labor theory, but if you deal with property there again it is legitimate. Bastia says, he attacks Ricardian theory of unvulnerable part, and he denies the are such things as indestructible power of soil, and therefore he says Ricard is wrong. He says value of land is determined by the service necessary t cultivate, such as taking out the stone, etc. Bastiat says service and value a not necessarily proportional to labor cost, and therefore there are the elements in land which depend upon human beings, and by all events Ricardia theory is wrong. His fourth doctrine is the doctrine of Harmonies. He say everybody tries to get the equal of service that he performs. In other word he says, profits continually are falling, wages are continually rising, re increasing positively but decreasing relatively, and therefore that being his la of distribution it is very different from Ricardian law. Fifth, this being the be of all possible, therefore the doctrine of laissez-faire follows. Now, you see wh influence he had upon businessmen, upon free traders. And, from 1850 on t to Civil War when they spoke of free trade they always meant Bastiat, ar for the time being Bastiat had great influence.

Now we spoke of the reaction to the English School, but we have n mentioned the name of one who laid the basis for much more importa reaction, e.g., reaction of the theory. That was a great thinker, who becau of the dominance of Liberal School in France found no opportunity to wri or publish. This is Cournot. Even in French Dictionary that was publish in 1895 you do not see his name, in spite of the fact that he was a great leadi thinker. In 1895 [sic], he published his first study of mathematical princip of economics. Here for the first time he attempted to bring mathematics the aid of economics. No one spoke of him in Switzerland. He then decid to write a book on Principles of Science of Wealth, and he published anoth book. Marshall called attention to his work. He says Cournot was importa as he was the first to represent by equations and by grooves the relatio between prices and quantities of commodities. It was the first attempt to analy this relation between supply and demand, and he was especially interesti also for the first time to apply all these theories to public finance. He represent the quantity of demand by d, and small p is the price, now then the law demand he puts in the form of equation $d = F(p)$, and that enables him go on with much further and contrast doctrine of cost of production of a mmodity is a function of commodity produced and the relation of cost to oduce is $p = F(D)$, when you are dealing with the function of D, which made ssible to determine the law of increasing and diminishing returns, that is ere the interesting point comes in. It goes more and more elaborate ogression and he comes to very interesting results. Now you remember, from r modern point of view there is nothing about utilities. This is simply the estion of relation of price and demand. And, after he worked all this out the theory of monopoly then he goes on and introduces competition, until u get the modern system. Mathematicians tell us that his formula is very gant and very true. Great importance is ascribed from a new point of view. hen reading the preface of this little work that started Jevons on his great rk. Cournot was highest class of mind, far superior to any one writing on onomic and social topics, yet he died in obscurity.

The idea of utility was independently developed by Dupuit. He was an gineer and was very much interested in the reform of the roads and especially lroads, and what the principle charge ought to be, how to fix the tolls on roads and highways. So he started out with an article on, how to measure utility of public works, and another one on the influence of tolls on the lity of railways. Putting it again very shortly, it may be said that you find him the first full and accurate statement of the entire law of marginal utility, ch as made familiar to us in recent years, yet it was a work not by an onomist, but by an engineer. Perhaps another reason why Dupuit was so tle heard of because it might have been that the whole discussion was bedded a little work that he wrote on free trade, and who practically sided with dominant school of Liberte Commerciale. Only two or three statements his work that becomes more important. So that France in the first half of th century represented interesting theory of economic thought.

Section 48. Developments in Germany

Germany was in a pretty bad way in 18th century, and they had not gotten er the bad results of wars of 17th century, and Germany was still very ckward economically. Now, Germany was in back waters, just as England d been few centuries earlier. Therefore economic writings of Germany was ited to Cameralists. When Adam Smith brought in a new attitude, German iters were second class writers and had no influence upon the prevalent ought. The only two writers that need be mentioned among them that took Smith and tried to develop are Jakob, and Rau. Rau was a professor of idelberg. He wrote a text book first in two volumes, afterwards developed to 6 volumes. He adapted the theory of English school.

There was one writer of real original merits and who is sometimes called rman Ricardo. This is F. B. Hermann. He published his Economic Essays 1832, and he makes his work exceedingly interesting. His contribution to

economic theory is that he emphasizes the psychological aspects, plus theo
and classification of wants and then goes on with a much more interesting ar
detailed analysis of capital concept. He was the first one to discuss the differen
between productive capital and consumption capital—enjoyment capital. An
then he has a very elaborate and fine analysis for the first time of the conce
of income as over against capital, and until recently the whole idea of incon
which developed income tax laws in Germany is traced back to Hermann
analysis. Above all he opposed the wages fund theory of English writers. H
says, the real fund is the social income and he made very valuable contributio
to the various elements and cost and the relation of cost and price. In all tho
valuations he had little influence upon John Stuart Mill through Banfield. H
was a strong and original writer.

Thunen (died 1850), was an agriculturist in his ancestral estate in Northea
Germany, and was interested in working out some of the importance of theori
underlying agricultural prosperity, and began writing in 1826. His first volun
was "Isolated State", another volume appeared quarter of a century later. Wh
he did was to make economic explanations as to the best system of cultivatio
and he worked it out on the theory of relative distance from the market. The
he tried to elaborate his conclusions on the bases of certain hypothesis a
later on applied to practice. This led him first to a law of rent, which virtual
identical with the Ricardian law, but with an emphasis of the second of tl
two elements mentioned by the emphasis by Ricardo. Ricardo emphasizes tl
fertility of the soil, Thunen assumes that all the lands are equally fertile b
vary according to the distance from the market. Both amount to the same thin
Now, then, he elaborates the whole law of diminishing returns, diminishi
according to the distance and that law he goes on to apply to the other si
of distribution. That is his great contribution. Now, applying this law to tl
other share of distribution he comes first to his theory of interest and he defin
for the first time interest as being use of capital last applied increment of capit
the final increment of capital. And, the utility, so that part of capital whi
has been last applied. He says, use regulates the rate of interest and then,
goes on to apply this marginal increment idea, shows how it works out, poir
out the utilities of machinery, and then he goes still further and applies to
the law of wages. You find in Thunen virtually the whole of the law
substitution, which was elaborated by Marshall. Marshall ascribes l
indebtedness to Thunen.—The law of substitution as effected between margin
efficiency of production and his theory of wages, also a marginal theory.

Professor Moore wrote for his Doctor's Dissertation many years ago a wo
on law of wages, who first got his reputation as being a subtle thinker, a
Moore points out the three contributions which are simply ascribed to Thune

1.   The classical economics tending to regard labor as commodity, where
Thunen points out that labor after all is a function of man, and that wag

must be looked at only from the point of view of something that will satisfy human wants. He brings human idea rather than this mechanical concept.

2.   The Orthodox school regards labor primarily the operation of natural law. Thunen goes further and this is also the equity of the case. The matter of wages according to him exists in this isolated state, shut off from all other states. He says natural wages will exist when the laborer receives the same income for his surplus that would be received by the surplus of interest that would be received by the employer if he puts his capital in marginal firm. There is equality of marginal increment in the shape of wages and marginal increment of every other source.

3.   The most important classical economists regard the requirements, the needs of laborer as limited by his surroundings, cost of production, standard of life, and etc. Whereas Thunen emphasizes primarily the productive side, not what laborer needs but what he does. Wages in other words depend upon marginal product, and therefore Thunen worked out a mathematical explanation:

If A represents the cost of the necessities of life and P represents the product then the amount of product, rather of wages then is [square root of AP]. He thought so highly of this formula that he had it on his tombstone. Some American students some time ago went over to see this tombstone. Thunen is rightly regarded as the originator of the whole theory of marginal productivity which formed the very basis of the independently discovered theory of our colleague, John B. Clark, in his book of Distribution of Wealth.

You will find this beautiful passage on page 321 of Mr. Clark's book. Thunen apart from his agronomic conclusions is interesting also in that this formula of AP, led naturally to the whole theory of practice in industrial profit sharing. And, it is only in recent years that various young scientists have taken up the work of Thunen and went further in some of his experiments. Thunen's archives are devoted entirely to the research of these fields, so that he must be considered man of very importance. Thunen came into recognition only very much later.

We come now to consider F. List, who is perhaps nowadays considered most important German economist. He was born in 1789, died at age of 46. He was professor at Turin, and going over to France he happened to meet Lafayette who was then returning to United States. Lafayette became very much interested and fond of List and he was so much impressed by this country that List became citizen and he settled at Penna. near Harrisburg. At this time two important things were being developed: The one was the movement consummated in the first railroad in 1878 [sic], and the second was the utilization of black diamond—coal, especially hard coal. List soon learned English, edited country paper and got interested in the new coal mines, made out of money, but what was more important now he worked out a theory which soon acquired importance. While coming to this country he was impressed with

the immense market that was afforded by free trade of all states, at the sam
time he was still more impressed by the work of Henry Clay, and adaptio
of American system. He now therefore became a convert to these two ideas
free trade within the limits of the country and high protection in order t
develop its industry, and he began to write editorials. These were very we
done, so much that when complaint of 1827 came the bill of abolition of th
tariff wall, Ingersol got List to write. He wrote series of letters which becam
platform of the political party in power, and List more than anybody else wa
responsible for these and became the mouthpiece of protection party. Tha
brought him great prominence and Jackson sent him back to Germany a
American Council. When he got to Germany the whole influence reasserte
themselves. He decided to spend the rest of his life introducing American idea
to Germany, and List therefore was responsible for the introduction of railroad
in Germany in 1835. In the second place he was responsible for the Germa
Customs union, trying to introduce in Germany the same principles that w
have in United States, and then finally he worked out his theory and towar
the end of his life he wrote in French for a prize offered by Paris Governmen
He wrote it in a few weeks, a work in which he tried to embody these principle
of nationalism, which he had learned from Henry Clay in this country. In 184
he gave a German version of it under the title of National Principles o
Economics. This work has been considered the most important work of 19t
century, because in it you find fullest and most elaborate plan of protectiv
system, also you find the fullest defense of nationalism as over against Adar
Smith's internationalism, and many people ascribe the cause of the last wa
to this. At the bottom of his ideas were really the whole national competitio
which led to war. His reputation is growing from day to day. A great Lis
society which is now publishing all of his works, first volume is out, there wi
be ten or twenty more volumes, and his works have been collected and soo
be published with professor Natzen's editorials—between 1823 and 1833, i
this country. So that the next few years will bring him to greater attentior

I will give you the substance of his theory: First, his theory of nationality
The title page of this book "La Patrie et L'Humanite"—My country as we
as world. He was not a mercantilist. He was opposed to mercantilists, but h
was still more opposed to Adam Smith, and all of his conclusions stood fo
free trade. My theory, says List is a national cosmopolite theory. He finds tha
national theory is also needed, but that the one must lead to the other an
that you can get to the international point of view only through the nationa
point of view. He works that out through two doctrines which he calls th
theory of protective forces. He begins, especially with Adam Smith and wit
the whole classical school of England. He calls them the school representin
the theory of value and as over against brings the school or the theory o
protective forces which he says he belongs. And it was List who firs
popularized this opposition to the doctrine of production in Smith—

production or wealth, tangible, physical commodities. He says according to Adam Smith, man who produces swine is productive, man who produces bagpipe is productive and the great artist who uses a great violin is unproductive. He says since the real thing is labor embodied in service, since productivity of labor lies at the bases of wealth anything that develops these productivities and productive forces is to be wanted and only that. He says if you look over the history, you can classify history into five phases (you have here first analysis of the world): First is the agricultural stage, second is the agricultural, commercial stage; third when industry added to it, etc. Now, says he, in order to develop from one stage to another you need certain conditions, in order to get from the agricultural stage to the commercial stage you need free trade which is most conducive. And also free trade is needed certainly in the final stage again in the industrialism. But in the third and fourth stages where you are trying to develop your industrial life and the factory system, you need protection in order to help along your productive forces. This is really putting into another form of argument which later on was accepted in part by John Stuart Mill under the name of young industries. You find that in List. He was not mercantilist because his ideal was cosmopolitanism. Now when you ask, how far List was original there is a great controversy which has sprung up. There had developed in this country a writer who had accepted the views of Clay and that was Raymond. He put in scientific form the views that are found in Alexander Hamilton in report of manufactures where we have the system of protection. It is claimed that List really did not but plagiarize from Raymond. Also in his French essay completely or great deal took the ideas of Perqueur. I don't want to pass judgment now, because you shall soon have proof one way or another, but of course List was a great genius and he could put the ideas in a form that no one else could put. From present point of view his history was very unscientific, very defective, childish, but if you will judge the man by the influence that he exerted it may be said that he exerted perhaps with the exception of Adam Smith, no man had greater influence upon economic thought. He was very inferior to Smith and even Ricardo as a theorist. The free traders themselves recognize that the greatest opponent they have to meet is List. So that you have another German who ought to be mentioned. This is the one man in mathematical school.

Gossen, who died in 1858. He wrote a few years before his death the "Development of Laws of Human Intercourse." Gossen had pretty good opinion of himself. He called himself Copernicus of economics. He was a professor and for many years he worked to bring out his two contributions: (1) You find the first application of the whole utilitarian philosophy to economics in a very narrow and pedantic way. (2) A very interesting statement and elaboration of the law of marginal utility. He begins for instance with what he calls the law of diminishing utilities and its relation to what he calls satiety or satisfaction. He says man can always reach his greatest happiness by so arranging his enjoyment and satisfactions that the magnitude of each enjoyment at the price movement, enjoyment remains the same. In other words when he uses the whole theory conception of marginal utility and he use grooves and equations to show how this comes about through the process of time, now he says in order to work out the complete theory you have to work out not alone laws of outer world, but also still the laws of inner man, laws of pleasure and satisfaction. He divides the outer to two classes: Articles, media leading for consumption and over against that, articles or goods. He says second class of materials have to be worked out before they enter this stage and finally he has articles of the third class, raw materials, as land, oil and things of that kind, and he applies the law of diminishing utilities for each one of these in a beautiful mathematical form. He then discusses the law of cost in order to secure maximum enjoyment. He says, you must so arrange things that the worth of last increment equals the pain of last movement of exertion. Marginal utility must be equal to marginal cost. He gives a very exhaustive account of the theory of economic equilibrium. Marshall recognize that his theory is contained in Gossen. These theories are in full elaborated in Gossen more than any other man. No where the find the psychology of the thing is worked out so much. His practical conclusions are not equal to his theoretical. As to his theory of exchange and others it is not necessary to go into detail. His whole doctrine results in a state of complete harmony of interest. Like Bastiat he came to a conclusion that interest was due to nationalization of lands. Like Henry George he believed that all the soil ought to be nationalized. He also had peculiar doctrine of credit. But above all his practical views was complete laissez-faire—leave alone. You remember that Jevons in the second edition in his work says that Gossen has completely anticipated everything that Jevons conceived and that Jevons had rediscovered. So that in German thinkers now you have very substantial contribution. The other man to be mentioned is Mangoldt, who lived a decade or two later and he is interesting from our present point of view. He advocated, first, the separation completely of profit from interest, excepting the marginal productivity theory of interest, and second, he generalizes the whole doctrine of rent, and he speaks therefore not alone land rent also speaks of others, as rent of capital and rent of wages. Mangoldt in this respect was a modern thinker.

Section 49.   Development in America

This is familiar to you. Of course, in a primitive community during the colonial life the only chief problem was the money problem. Really first scientific literature revolved about the question of banks and government papers. The first individuals who really attempted to deal with the problems of public wealth in a larger way were statesmen; Benjamin Franklin, who was in some way a leading economist. He also made his modest inquiry into this paper money in 1789. Whereas all the experience in the land bank were not successful, and land as a basis of currency is not very good as compared with gold and silver. We must remember, however, that the currency was based upon land in Penna. and which was successful because it was very well managed. People generally forget that the paper money issued in Penna. was the one that never depreciated. The reason is because it was very well managed by Franklin and other trustees. And, in his essay he tells us very naively that his fellow countrymen gave him the job for printing paper money ... That is a chapter which has never been worked out. The right method works out well, whatever your basis is. In his enquiry, Franklin goes into the question of value and shows that really that is labor. Then in later essays that were published he recommends the limitation of American paper money (1764). As regards to the increase of mankind he foreshadows many of the conclusions of Malthus, and furthermore he has some very interesting things to say about immigration of Germans—Penna. Dutch, into Penna. Expresses the feeling that at one time the language might entirely be German.

Those of course are minor points. Far more important is his views on Colonial system of England. He wrote: "The Interest of Great Britain Considered in 1760." There he lays down foundations which afterwards became his opposition for economic reasons also to the whole of the British domination. In his work on the price of corn and management of the poor he discloses the useless perspicacity by pointing out in opposition to the views of English writers as regards to wages. "The best thing to do good to the poor is not to make easy in poverty, but by leading or driving them out of it." Before he went to France he came to the conclusion that agriculture was really the source of wealth, and he takes a position which seems to be essentially similar to that of physiocrats. He was probably influenced by physiocrats. In 1768 you remember, just a few years, held that manufacturers really make transfer but don't create any new wealth. He also took a very strong position in favor of free trade. You remember he wrote before industry had been developed in this country, when agriculture was our virtually sole source of enterprise, and it is interesting to observe that he agrees here that the early stages of community ought to have free trade and more production. He wrote in 1789 when certain tariff bills and laws were passed. He wrote a book entitled "The Way for Broadening Manufactures." It is full of humor, and demanded that protective duties should be taken out, everything except on manufactures. In his economic views however in general as in his political and social views he never stopped his advice for thrift, sobriety and saving. If you take his works altogether you find that he discusses good many of general problems of economic life as he saw them. Now when the revolution broke out the great economic problem became the question of war finance, as during the last war, and to make any headway against British there was nothing else left except issue of paper money.

One writer now developed some very interesting theory of the irredeemable paper money, and pointed out that it was best to prevent Congress from issuing this flood of continentals. This was Pelatiah Webster, who may be considered one of our leading money theorists and his works were collected in which he for the first time points out the necessity of lessening the issue and emphasized the danger of inflation. When you refuse to tax and finally you make your loan in shape of tax which is called paper money. The only other writer comparable was Gale, who wrote a three volume work on public debt and for the first time tried to apply mathematics to economics. He wrote in South Carolina.

Now when we come to our statesmen you come to two or three men who were at that time great economists. Alexander Hamilton, who created public credit of United States who laid the basis of fiscal prosperity by our industrial prosperity and has his great report and treatises on economics, reports of public credit and report on manufacture. And the report of credit and the theory rest very largely upon the work of Pitt. Whereas his report of manufacture is far more original, and really lays down the basis of the whole theory of List. In other words, protection of infant industry. We have to pass also with mere mention, except saying that Hamilton shows really more broad economic views and intimate with physiocratic writings. He does not accept the conclusion of physiocrats. The other writer was one whose economic contribution laid rather in the detail than in great principles, that was Albert Gallatin. The man who introduced so many things into public finance. He was primarily interested in public finance, although later on interested in private finance, banking. He wrote a good work on the theory of credit. Just as Hamilton founded the theory of protection, so Gallatin's report the free trade, which was written several decades later. The other statesman we can pass without even mentioning.

Then we come to those who were more interested in the practical application of the theory. As you all know the economic problems arose in this country after the war with England. It is only when factory system began to be introduced in New England that you have the first development of capitalism. Panic of 1817 and the problems now associated with the development of capital and especially also with the accompaniment of credit, the banking system to make possible the new protective system and therefore we now find lecture in economics beginning here suddenly all over the country. First chair was in this institution. John McVickar after whom my chair was named. He was responsible for two things: He first outlined the new banking system which afterwards became the basis of the local system. Second in his outlines of Political Economy, simply followed what was being done in England. First books were reprinted with some addition, especially with opposition to socialistic movement and so these early books now placed emphasis on this new capitalism and this new industry which was going to emancipate United States from England.

He was followed by others. But, in the South the conditions were different and they were left in between industrial system and agricultural system. Another end was the plantations and slave system of the South, which now became greater and greater. There were two writers who represented that. The one was Cardozo, who was not alone great opponent of McVickar but also for that reason great opponent of the theory of Ricardo. He was indeed a free trader, but he disagreed entirely with the economic conclusions so far as Ricardo's theory of distribution was concerned, but most optimistic living man, he was, in new country. Then, too, he was in politics.

However, there now arose a writer who nowadays figures most important man and that was a man who attempted to follow in line with the prevalent political movement of the day. This was Daniel Raymond. In his practical work he was first protagonist writer in this country and without mentioning Hamilton he virtually repeats the whole Hamiltonian art, and it was he that was read by List. The second was his views of bank. He was a great upholder of the advantages of capital and all industry by seeing the kind of banks they had in those days. He thought banking was a poor speculative enterprise, and that banking credit was illegitimate, just as today still in certain parts of the world you have this opposition in consumption credit. You find precisely the same argument a century ago advanced by Rae on production credit. But, Raymond thought he was in favor of production, was very doubtful as to whether the attempts of the new capitalism did really benefit the world, unless it was very carefully regulated. He took issue with Adam Smith of the whole fundamental principles of the ideas of individual freedom and took issue with the government taking charge of everything. The theory of individualism had not begun with in this country, therefore, he is the theorist of economic situation as it was developing in the United States.

Passing over the other minor writers, especially text book writers, there are perhaps only two names that are worthy of more careful study. In the University of West Virginia, there was a very remarkable man, this was Professor Tucker. He wrote a book on the laws of wages, profits and rent, in which he perhaps shows greatest opposition to the criticism of Ricardian doctrine of distribution, especially as inapplicable to the condition of this country. The other writer is one who in recent years attracted much more attention. This was Canadian Rae, and Rae in his important book, which has been recently reprinted under the name of Sociological Theory of Capital, although it was not the original title, the original title was "Statement of Some New Principles of Political Economy", he seeks to bring together entirely a new foundation of the theory of protection. His objection to free trade of English schools differs from most of other writers and he gives a very elaborate account of the nature of stock or of capital. He introduced into economic language the terms instruments, and also the phrase, the effective desire of accumulation, which later on taken by John Stuart Mill. He develops his theory from the workings out of the

capital. Virtually identical views also a century later was developed by Austria
writer Bubarbier, in his Wealth. About production it was Rae who pointe
out the whole productive capacity, anything [a]ffecting the durability an
efficiency of the instrument of production and he goes very fully into the whol
problem, and how you can accumulate capital. He has very interestin
theoretical discussions of the relation between the present and futur
Furthermore he introduced into economics discussion the whole problem c
invention, invention as a means of economic progress in society and it
connection with the development of luxury. He draws the conclusion fror
these theories of capital, which is that the legislator has a great function t
perform in influencing the accumulation of this stock, and that the productio
is as much a legitimate part of modern economic practice as anything els
He says there must be no exemption for presumption of legislative interference
The object is to presume that nature gave man brains in order that man migh
discover laws to control nature. Like United States and also Canada, one o
the chief objects is to transplant by good methods as far as possible that hav
been accomplished in other parts of the world. We find in him not alone thi
interesting new basis of production also quite a little of what was later o
developed in Austrian school on the relation of capital and interest. Th
movement beginning in this country and with it the beginning of what yo
might call the economic Utopias and theories, what was not yet called socialism
The book of Skidmore which is about 400 pages is written about the righ
of property. He denies the right of man to private property.

Francis Wright took up the cudgels for women's rights and for negro, an
also went still further in his equalization idea to general communism—a ver
great but short-lived movement. A decade later came the influence of France
This was not much, but Fourier had great influence through certain youn
Americans that went abroad to study and under their influence, we had a larg
number of communistic experiments in the 40's and 50's, and other men wh
were interested in the theoretical phase of it made their independent effort t
repeat here the philosophy of the anarchists. This movement was headed b
J. Warren and Andrew. Warren with his book on commerce, and Andrew witl
his Exchange Bank, etc. But all these movements, terrifying greatly the ne
system, had nothing but local and temporary influence.

Quite different was H. Carey, who was to acquire international reputation
because Carey was a great embodiment of the new optimistic spirit of th
American enterprise, and because he had a philosophical mind attempting t
go deep beneath the surface. He started school not alone in this country, bu
had followers in Italy, in Austria and pretty much everywhere, except i
England. H. Carey (1793-1879), was the son of Matthew Carey. He was
printer and got interested with social questions. He must have written a fe
hundred books, all of which turn around production. He was a big pamphle
writer. His son brought up as a printer's devil, never received education. H

rst book was written at the age of 42, and he had started by reading and
wallowing and believing pretty much all the doctrines of English school. In
rder to understand Carey you have to divide his work into certain number
f theories. His theory of value he defined as the measure of resistance to be
ndergone in obtaining commodities. Value, therefore he says, means power
ver nature, as over against this you must put utility which is nature's power
ver man. His law of progress is that utilities tend to increase value tends to
ecrease, and the way this is done is by association. Virtually the same doctrine
s we discussed when speaking of Bastiat. He thinks he is making improvement
pon Ricardo. He says value is the cost of reproduction as over against
roduction. Of course, nowadays, we realize this is not a distinction at all,
ecause it meant continuous protection.

Carey makes a very interesting analysis of production. He says production
eally involves changes in nature and these changes are either changes of place,
r changes in form, and changes in form may again be subdivided into
mechanical and chemical, and on the other hand vital change in form. Now,
ow does he develop that idea? Take up first, changes in the matter of place,
hat can be brought about by either trade or commerce. He makes distinction
etween the two. Trade, he says, is the exchange of one commodity for another.
Commerce is exchange of one commodity or several commodities with each
ther. That is to say, commerce is the object to be attained while trade is the
nstrument. Now, he says, commerce leads ultimately to freedom of
ocalization, whereas trade leads to centralization and death, and has to be
educed to minimum. In fact most wars, he says, are the result of trade. The
eal object is to bring producer and consumer together, where they can
xchange one thing for another. He pays very little attention to the doctrine
f international division of labor. All that with him is of very little consequence.
When you come to the changes in nature, in form, he thinks that progress
lways means a cheapening of the industrial products and a rise in price of
aw material is not desirable. Finally, in the third place the most important
hing in any country's protection is the basis, which is agriculture, because upon
his broad basis of agricultural protection rest the conversion in form, and then
inally the question of transportation of things, until you get into the hands
f ultimate consumers. He devotes three volumes to that analysis. It follows
hat we must have production, because in that way you bring consumer and
roducer much more closer, and that you get rid of the tax in transportation
which is involved in all trade. And, while his doctrine of production rests
rimarily upon this philosophical analysis of production, it must be said that
here is another feature, a revision whole doctrine of balance of trade, he still
elieves in favorable balance of trade and excess of export over import. Now
f you compare Carey in this respect to List the doctrine seems to be more
hilosophical, yet in reality it is List so much in extreme. He insists upon
gricultural protection as well as industry. Whereas List devotes more attention

to industrial protection and in the second place, Carey's doctrine of productic holds good for all times, whereas List's only for intermediate stage—countri developing from agricultural to industry.

We come in the next place to his theory of distribution. He objects vei much to the whole Ricardian theory of rent, but he puts upon the historic objection his emphasis, that the development of American Agriculture was development from bad soils to good soil and not as Ricardo stated the opposit Furthermore, also brings into play here his theory of rent, doctrine of valu which was not the cost of production but cost of reproduction. When we con to the doctrine of population and compare by facts of the American life, h could see nothing at all in the gloomy foreboding of Malthus. His doctri of wages and general theory of general distribution which is most interestir must hold exposition. Here again he opposes to the whole English school. H arrives to generalization just opposite of that of Ricardo. He says, wages a continually rising (of course that has been a fact in this country). Interest, h says, will fall, (that also is true); and rent is bound to fall. So, that the resu of the whole economic progress of society is thought [sic: brought] into harmony of interest, which comes out exactly where Bastiat pointed ou Sometimes he was accused of borrowing this from Bastiat. Of course, you wi observe that Carey with all his abilities was not very logical. He says, ever progress tends toward the harmony of interest. Why then you need governmei interference in shape of protection? Why not start off the doctrine of laisse faire? On the law of his book the doctrine of laissez-faire is true—doctrine i government, freedom of trade, freedom of action. But still it remains that h final law of progress is in contradiction with his theory of production. It simp shows the influence of his surroundings. Finally we must add his later view on money and banking. When he became an old man he turned into a advocate not alone of free banking, also during the Civil War he broke o of fiat money—greenbacks. He used to have meeting in his house like Quesna in Paris where foreigners would go to his house. He became advisor of Preside Lincoln and Chase, in certain way pretty much to their misfortune. So th Carey with all his remarkable qualities of self-taught philosopher had immen influence, and his policy of protection was adapted by the dominant party f the 100 percent Americanism. Today Carey was, so to say, the economist our Golden Age—the middle period of century when everything w prosperous. So that Carey really stood out as the one great philosoph American economist. Yet, in the light of our present attitude he deserves pret much the forgetfulness that has been caused. Today, in Penna. he still has th institution which must always be devoted to protection and the emphasis that in Penna. it must be Carey's followers who would hold chair of economic Passing by then first half of the century we go on to the recent past. It wi take a great many lectures to cover this, but as time is limited, I will just ca attention to high spots.

BOOK VII. RECENT DEVELOPMENT

Section 50. The Founders of the Historical School

The historical school started out in Germany, although Sismondi had the
*undation. It was an independent movement in Germany and the beginning
industrial revolution—after 200 years of faithful work and just getting over
*e 50 years' war. This nation now began to develop economically and younger
*en were face to face with problems that had developed in Germany in the
*st half of the century.—Historical bank, historical school of law, so also in
*e other forms of social sciences. So the time was ripe for its application to
*onomics. There were three men who really need only be mentioned.

Hildebrand wrote about the middle of the century, and he was a deep student
*d contrasted Adam Smith and Kant. He was the first one to emphasize the
*ct that man is always a child of civilization and product of history and he
*jected to the atomistic view which was prevalent in the English school and
*nong French writers. He said Adam Smith was characterized by commercial
*ntract, social contract and economic contract, and both Rousseau and Adam
*mith did not recognize the organic character of relationships. First volume
*his book is a critical exposition of the economic doctrines. He expected to
*o on with his work on economics for the present and future but he never
*d go on with it.

Roscher was a young student of history who was deeply concerned in Greek
*d Roman history. He got interested in the economics. In 40's he published
*tline in economics. He gave a course of lectures on economics. He soon
*veloped his ideas more fully saying that economics is the science of the
*velopment of society. That was his idea of economics—a branch of
*vilization. He divides it as historical and physiological method. He calls it
*alistic method, sometimes he called it inductive method. He did not differ
*fundamentally from Ricardo or from English school in his theory of
*roduction and distribution. What he emphasized was rather the need of
*ading of everything comparatively and especially from the historical point
*view, and his book is valuable, today. From the origin of economic doctrines
*became exceedingly popular. He had been in no man's class.

Knies, who was teacher of Professor Clark and myself was a remarkable
*inker. He wrote a book on economics from the point of view of historical
*ethod. This book was not translated. A sentence is sometimes a page or two
*ng. In his introduction he was the first to emphasize that political economy
*really a social science and has to be brought in closer relation to sociology.
*e emphasized the fact that economics is a moral and ethical science and being
*hical it is a historical science. His views are new. Knies's national economics
*in some respect to be pointed out. The characteristic differences that are

found in economic facts says he, are: (a) With reference to territory and (b) with reference to nationality.

As regards territory Knies first lays great stress upon facts of geography of agriculture, chemistry, climate and of the standard of life; and as regard nationality, he emphasizes the influence of ethnography, great importance o heredity—blue blood. He goes on to discuss the influence of them, how sam community in course of time becomes entirely a different economic community He gives great many interesting examples. Next he discusses the influence o religion upon economics and connection between the two, the positive influenc of church upon economic life, especially in the early period and finally abov all it was Knies who first called attention to the character of economics o one hand and law and custom on the other. He points out the interaction o law and economics. Having finished that phase of that subject he goes on t talk of fundamental assumption of accepted classical theory and he finds t constitute of two facts: (1) Ideas of absolute private property and (2) Idea of self-interest. He gives first very admirable discussion as over against privat property. Property, he says is historical evolution, and then as regards sel interest he discusses the difference between selfishness and self-interest, an he points out the connection between altruism and egoism. The last of thes fundamental ideas is the idea of natural law, and we find here in Knies discussion of difference between physical laws as applied to natural scienc and social laws and laws which apply to the social science and then as a resu of the whole analysis he gives conclusion that economics ceases to be an edific to take the whole world. He says like the condition of economic life itself th theory of political economy are production of historical conditions. He say you cannot understand what is unless you know what has been. His great thre volume book on money and credit goes into detail of history, primarily. H discusses rent and discusses inductively. He has influence on the young me who he turns out and who develop these ideas. In the meantime before thes historical school showed fullest products the other side of English scho developed and that is socialistic movement.

Section 51.   Scientific Socialism

Of course, in Germany at least socialism went through several phases. began in the 30's with Karl Marx. Afterwards it was called sentimenta socialism, the idealist, the communists. But it was not long before th introduction of industrial revolution and especially acquainted with condition in France and England where factory system was making much more progres that later German writers based upon economic analysis as over again sentimental socialism, which was at first the socialism in France and German

Among scientific socialists we have K. Marlo. This is his nom de plum His real name is Linkenblut. He got interested when traveling in Norway i ertain chemical used in agriculture. That led him to devote more and more me to economic questions. In 1885 he published his book, called, Organization of Economic World." In a word his doctrine may be summed p as opposing to the idea of monopoly, which he thought was inevitable. He pposed the idea of what he calls "paupoly (?)", which is to express the universal ssociation of all mental and physical forces in economic life. In other words ve must in order to give the world full benefit be arranged in a federative ystem. The next is Rodbertus. He was a lawyer and had a large estate on vhich he worked out good many experiments. He became a deep student of conomics, especially of Ricardo. Like Ricardian socialists he developed Ricardian theory into its opposite. He published great many books and his iews may be summed up in a nut shell as follows: Especially in the book on he theory of value and theory of labor, under present condition the standard f life of laborer, he says, does not rise with the increase of productivity of ıbor and economic forces. He says wages depend upon cost of labor, and ıust be, as Ricardo thought, in the minimum of subsistence, no matter what appens. The consequence is this that there is a relative diminution in the mount of wages, relatively to the growth of wealth rather than keeping even. t is interesting that he finds in this fact that laborers don't get enough money n account of crises, and his theory of prices gives rise to an immense literature. Ie says you can only get rid of commercial crises by spending more. Rodbertus hought when buying more luxuries in the long run you have to depend upon vages. He says, in the third place, you could not accomplish this without having normal working day. He fought for a normal working day with restriction f long hours. He thought in all those things government has to virtually nanage the whole question, just as the case as is in Russia today. He had quite nfluence upon thought, especially upon the theories of labor. The following eneration accepted good many of his points. He was soon thrown away.

Afterwards came Karl Marx. His work now becomes bible of socialists. All can do here is to sum up, acknowledging the advantages of the leading ideas n which he elaborated his system. He was the first economist who used English lue books and used in connection with his analyses. His first doctrine is conomic interpretation of history. I shall pass all this with mere mention. I ave already published a book on this. There is a book published by Professor arookian [sic: Sorokin], a Russian, on Sociology. He speaks by saying that ou find great deal economic interpretation before Karl Marx. He quite forgets hat the originality of a man is not to get the idea but he was the first one o appreciate what ideas mean and put together to interest people. Until Karl Marx no one ever thought, certainly no one ever said that civilization is to e interpreted primarily in terms of economics. So that, Marx is rightly onsidered to be the founder of that theory and the only point about him is hat there are different version of economic interpretation and his own version as been also it has been under good deal of criticism. Second; his idea of class struggle, which consummated with the famous manifesto of 1848. That you will have struggle in economic life always, contest becomes subject interest of the group and only with combination that you will have progress. Third Doctrine of value, and again building upon Ricardo. He comes out with the still more common element in the element of all things is the social labor, the evaluation of social labor requiring to produce a commodity and building upon this he represents his whole explanation of modern capitalism through th fourth doctrine which is surplus value, which is that of profit. This exploitation of laborer through this evaluation of social labor, and then he gives an interesting interpretation of capital and what capitalism really is.

He looked upon capital as a social relation existing in the process of production and the interesting thing from his point of view was to consider capital as an historical development as an institution. Of course, he brought that through close relation with his whole theory of economic development doctrine of surplus value with which you are familiar. Now, his three practical conclusions of his way of looking at economic development are summed up in his so-called, Concentration theory of the law of what he calls a historical tendency of capital accumulation. He was writing at a time when capital was still not used in the enterprise, although Adam Smith had pointed out certain combination of certain forms of industry. Marx considered it to be an inevitabl process of all capitalist development and that is the movement, what we call integration and concentration. Side by side with this he emphasized the so called impoverishment theory, which was not based upon the wages fund doctrine but which rested upon the iron law of wages, and his view was that as a necessary result of this capitalist concentration rich get richer on the one hand and poor get poorer absolutely and relatively. The one necessarily went in hand with the other. That capitalism necessarily spell proletarianism. Then finally his doctrine centered in the cataclysm theory. He wrote his book very much under the influence of great crises of 37 which was followed by that of 57. He himself lived through both of those crises, and the facts seem to share out his analysis of his whole theory of crises and possible depression. His doctrine was that with every new change the pendulum would swing more and more to each extreme that each crisis was becoming more and more vivid and finally as a result we would have cataclysm—final breaking up of the whole system. So that, you see his analysis of economic principles went hand in hand with his historical views of industrial development, and fortunately for him at the time when his book appeared everything seemed to be going his way and his book attained more importance. Had he lived half a century longer the situation would be different. The commercial and industrial situations were becoming less and less rather than more and more extreme. Crisis of 73 was not as big as '57, that of '84 was less than '93, and so forth. So that instead of having the increasing side it was actually decreasing in temper. Of course later followers of Marx made great change, which led to the reform of socialism

But if you take Marxian doctrine as a whole you will find it a well, neat and most interesting analysis which started out from the premises you grant. They did lead to the conclusions to which he drew at and it served to be the basis of a great world movement. It is of course very easy to criticise than it is sympathetically appreciate and it all depends upon your point of view. If you sympathize with his doctrine, of course you consider him as they do in Russia, one great economist. If on the other hand you will not sympathize with those views, although he was a man of mighty mental power, yet line him into by-paths. He was one of the first to call attention to 18th and 19th century writers. His views were exceedingly interesting. An adequate discussion of Marx would call a very detailed lecture, and that is given in another part of this University. We just mention that he was one of the leading minds and both from critical and constructive points of view he is certainly a great man, even nowadays, the ure scientific socialism which he was supposed to have originated.

The other great German writer was Lassalle. He also was a great mind, an engaging personality. He had much greater influence at the time than Marx, and he had almost one over Bismarck. From the theoretical point of view Lassalle started out a great philosophical work. Savigne called him the ablest man of law of 19th century. Yet when he turned his attention to economic topics he made himself responsible for some very remarkable new ideas. In the first place it was he who first developed so-called the iron or brazen law of wages. In the second place it was he that in that famous speech called the attention of the whole world to the relation between labor movement and public finance, and his work, "Working Class and Indirect Taxation" is famous. He pointed out that democracy ultimately means the shrinking of the field of indirect taxation and development of income and direct taxation. In his great book on the Labor, he outlined much of what is now came to pass in the succeeding three-quarters of a century. He also like Marx was a Hegelian, and bases his conclusions upon the three-fold stage. In the history of labor, the ancient and feudal soldier, without freedom, development of capital and growth of middle class since French Revolution, and finally the third movement is the modern movement which is the new era, which tends to reconcile the two ideas of freedom and solidarity through association. He approaches from technical point of view of analysis of value, laws of distribution, and for instance, philosophical conception of the historical development of society, and for the time being he carried everything for him. But his influence was short-lived compared with Marx. Now we said enough. We called attention to reactions against the economic doctrines; historical school and socialistic school. Now we come to the third form of reaction, which is the Austrian school.

Section 52.   Earlier English Writers

They centered around the great work of Jevons. He was trained in the college and universities. He got interested in the coal question and sources of modern wealth, and published in 1871 his extremely original work on the theory of Political Economy. Little later on, you notice more particularly the two current of thought that always characterizes Jevons. The one was the mathematical streak which he used in currency and finance, who originates the modern treatment of mathematics, and the second was his growing interest in the practical and especially social relations of economics. And, his books now multiply. "Methods of Social Reform", another book, "State in Relation to Labor", and many works of that kind, which showed that both in his approach and conclusions he differed very fundamentally from the prevalent school.

If we consider his theory for a moment you can realize exactly how he got to the point as he did. The older he grew more and more he felt that the Ricardian school was working on the long [sic: wrong] lines of walk [sic: work]. He was very extreme and full of enthusiasm. As you all know his fundamental view was that you must start out with the idea of utility, and that the ratio of exchange and value is always the reciprocal of the ratio of the final utilities (page 103, Book on the Theory of Economics, you find that summed up), and then his law which is found on page 129, where he tries to determine the influence between cost and value. He says, cost of production determine supply only, supply determines the final degree of utility and final degree of utility determines value. In other words he makes basis of this whole treatment what he calls the final degree of utility, and that all economic problems depend upon what he calls final equivalents and labor utility. He worked out that doctrine absolutely alone and applied it to his theory of capital, his theory of interest, and his theory of wages. And he reserved for a future volume—the second volume—which he expected to show the application of this fundamental theory of what he calls final utility to all the different phases of distribution. He did not live to do that. He died untimely. This would have been a great work but now it is terse, very incomplete work. He realized that this doctrine of final utility was of great importance and the newer edifice would have to be based upon the doctrine of consumption. He never lived to do that. But he did create quite a stir at the time, early in 70's, in laying down a foundation which was complete at variance with the accepted doctrines of the school. So that Jevons without trying to work out the details by calculus, he attempted to define utilitarian economics in a new sense of utility. Now when Jevons published his book, he made great stir and that led abler defenders of the school to come to defend and of these writers most important was Cairnes.

Cairnes published two or three years later an essay on Political Economy its theory and principles. In his criticism of Jevons he did not quite grasp what Jevons was after, his criticism therefore is not valuable from that point of view. What he did do however, was to try to put the whole concept of value and production in psychological terms, and that he made familiar to the economic world the doctrine of sacrifice as well as cost. His treatment is different from Senior. He brought up together in closer relation. That is to say the sacrifice f labor is to be brought into relation to the sacrifice of the capitalist, and erefore abstinence as well as risk are to be recognized side by side with labor. ost of production which he retained as basis or value is to be resolved into bstinence and effort and the practical conclusion he drew from that was a ontribution, which was doctrine of non-competing industrial group. Cairnes omes to the defense of wages fund doctrine of John Stuart Mill. His real dditions to economic theory is to be found however in another field, which ows his great capacity. (He was in continual bad health.) His doctrine of ternational trade is very important. He developed the doctrine of comparative ost and brought it into very close relation with his doctrine of reciprocal emand of international trade. And, he was the first writer who clearly istinguished between balance of trade doctrine and what he calls equilibrium f commerce. That equilibrium of commerce takes into account all these oncealed and superficial factors in the problem of international relations. This e chief constructive contribution of Cairnes.

What Jevons attempted to do was being accomplished in another part of e world. It is remarkable in the history that when scientific conditions become pe, then human beings have same ideas, same inventions spring up from tirely different parts of the world. Same thing is true in the matter of lephone, telegraph, airplane, etc. These doctrines were developed by Jevons England, by Menger in Germany and by Walras in France and Switzerland.

Menger whose book has never yet really been translated, which was a book n the Foundation on economic theory and little later wrote a book of a very itical kind on the efforts of historical school. In his book he like Jevons speaks f the older doctrines from this newer point of view. He starts out with onomic goods, economic life. He divides the goods into first, second and ird order, or as he calls them also immediate goods, complementary goods, id instrumental goods—capital being an instrumental good. And, that brings m to his fundamental distinction between subjective and objective value and is curious that although he does not use the term marginal utility, he expresses e idea very clearly. Goods says he, have a value only when the condition satisfaction, and his definition of value is the following one: Value says he the important change of the goods acquiring for us through the realization f our dependence on utilizing them in the satisfaction of our wants. As soon you get that idea you see the whole conception of margin is applied. Then, ou see, if he says that is value, the question will be, how to determine value. his leads him to analyze all these different kinds of wants, and that of exchange n which values are based means giving goods of less power of utilization for oods of great power. That brings him to his analysis of market and prices. tarting out with his subjective idea of satisfaction of wants he gets to the two des of competition; starts out with isolated partner he comes to monopoly id he gets to market of the idea of two sided competition. Finally, he says at the theory of prices can be extended to cover also the factors of

distribution, and that the theory of value involves the theory of price. Of th
factors of distribution by that particular thing that he reached and his follower
especially his son-in-law, Wieser accomplished it. He died only a few yea
ago. He has two great books on the origin and laws of economic value. Wies
is responsible for working out and carrying out this theory and adding som
very remarkable parts. It was Wieser who worked the so-called paradoxes
value,, the difference between increasing utility and marginal utility. It wa
Wieser that gave the name marginal utility. It was Wieser who worked ot
the theory of imputation, e. g., that the value of productive goods is to b
derived from the value of their products. That the value of the ground on whic
potatoes grow is due to the value of potatoes. Then, he applies that to his la
of cost and in every phase of distribution, pointing out that the Ricardian theor
of land is only one side of looking what is possible to be in a much more gener
phase, and that the marginal law holds true of all productive goods and
all productive ages, and it was this theory of Wieser that started the thinkir
of the whole subsequent generation. It was taken up by two first class mind
also in Austria. In Germany no work was being done.

Bohm-Bawerk gave a very beautiful description, more beautiful than Wies
had done and attempted to give a very remarkable explanation of capital
involving the rent, about system of production, railroad, about system
production and the conception of interest as resting upon the difference in ov
valuation of present and future goods. Of course, he pointed out in his histo
of doctrine that preceding writers had caught glimpse. And, therefore the who
doctrine of marginal productivity can be applied to these problems of tin
as well as space and what Bohm-Bawerk did in his great Capital and Intere
was attempted by another Austrian, Sax in the endeavor to show the who
application of public finance. Sax in his book, the Real Essence and the Objec
of Political Economy and especially in his book on the basis of the Theoretic
Economics attempted to really apply this doctrine of marginal productivit
something that was difficult to apply, because whole doctrine of margin
productivity rests upon the theory of competition and the theory
substitution, both of which are at present in the theory of fiscal science. S
that it may be said without going any further that the net result of this thre
fold objection to the whole classical school was not long before it made t
historical attitude, the socialistic attitude the marginal utility value attitud
And, it was now reserved for the subsequent writers to try to build up rath
than to destroy, as in the last half of the 19th century what we call anarch
economic doctrines where people were beginning to lose confidence everywhe
and every thing was beginning to go 6's and 7's.

Walras was born in Switzerland in 1834. He published his book
economics in 1870, while he was professor at Lausanne. He makes a ve
interesting approach and comes to the same conclusion from very differe
point of view. He works out elaborate algebraic and mathematical formul

applied to economics. And from that his work is very interesting. He takes
: organized market with free competition, and the hypotheses he builds
rtain effective demand and supply and it is his task to discover the conditions
der which market would be in equilibrium with the effective demand and
ective supply. In the course of his investigation into the composite demand
ledule, he develops the idea of utility. He differs from Jevons, who you
member laid great stress upon the doctrine of pleasure and pain, and with
n, he takes simply the fact that every individual must possess a standard
th which to measure these phenomena. As the utility of any given satisfaction
ninishes you reach the conception what he calls rarete,—we would translate
scarcity. So that he bases his whole theory upon this scarcity. He works his
nclusion that in state of market equilibrium prices are always equal to the
tio of the phenomenal or marginal decrease of utility of the process to carry
. trade.

Now you see, difference between Walras and Jevons is that Walras starts
om the concept of price and then and enquires into the psychology behind
for instance his well known doctrine that the maximum utility can only come
om this equilibrium of prices. Now he gives us three kinds of tests in this
oblem of price. There is a three-fold front to his theory of general equilibrium:
l You have the market for the finished products, products that are ready
r consumer. You look upon the purchaser and consumer representing all
e members of the community. (2) You conceive of the market where you
ve the sale of the productive service, where the buyers are not consumers,
iere the sellers are the people who have labor or land or capital. (3) You
ve the market which is the market where savings are capitalized, where the
iyers are represented by the entrepreneur, where the sellers are represented
 the savers. So that you see his approach is little different, but virtually the
me conclusion as Jevons or Wieser. But his approach is interesting and
iginal and really introduction into economic science this whole doctrine of
e equilibrium between forces. His practical conclusions are perhaps not so
teresting, but it is worth perhaps telling you that one of the reasons he did
t have so much influence is that like Gossen he believes in the nationalization
 land—forerunner of Henry George, as practical means of social reform.
condly he was considered rather heretic in the matter of currency problem,
d he developed his doctrine of gold and silver currency. He also worked
t some very interesting results in Public Finance, especially in taxation which
ve rather been overlooked. Walras was a man of exceedingly original mind
d he made us familiar of newer concept of equilibrium.

We come then to what we might call a new point of view in modern
onomics, although the situation has differed in different countries, yet in a
oad way the influence has been pretty much the same. You can divide that
riod for its proper discussion into two periods: up to the end of the last
ntury and then the quarter of the century. Taking the period covering the

last half of 19th century in England, you find there two great names, e
Marshall and Edgeworth. You are all familiar with these. Marshall got h
inspiration from Garnier and Thunen. He was not in favor of the extreme ide
of Jevons. He did not have any sympathy with Jevons, but having bee
threatened with mathematical science and under the influence of Sidgwick,
became very interested in the science of human behavior. His whole intere
you remember centers around the idea of money and prices, that is really t
center around which everything economic clusters. His idea was to attem
to secure a measure of these opposing forces. But he tried to get beyond t
market price, what really lies beyond the price in the market, and that led hi
to discussion of real forces of economic life. He started out as few Engli
economists with desires and satisfactions and disposition to labor and wi
the idea of weighting [sic: waiting]. He was not at first acquainted with t
work of Walras. He worked out his whole theory of equilibrium betwee
demand and supply, attempted to analyze supply schedule and demar
schedule. He introduced some very interesting conceptions, for instance t
doctrine of surplus. Of course certain cases of surplus was similar, more
less, ever since the time of classical economics, but now Marshall works o
the theories of consumer,—the subjective side as well as objective side. Li
later writers, he introduced the idea of quasi-rent, so in his theory of capit
and interest it was Marshall to make distinction between long and short perio
in the estimate of the influence, add to it his interest theory, theory of monopol
In the main he must be considered as an eclectic, although later origina
Eclectic as to the way in which he attempted to combine what is best in t
whole classical theory, Ricardian theory, and led him what was acceptable
the marginal utility to a kind of synthesis which have proved to be the bas
for good deal of later thinking. On the other side he was eclectic, as he ve
much was influenced by Germans. He tried to combine the theoretical ar
historical approach, although he never was really quite in sympathy with tl
two great historians of the time in Great Britain. The men who represente
the historical school as you know were William Ashley, who died only a fe
months ago, and Cunningham, the first real important historian of Engli
economic life. He had not much sympathy with them, neither with their writin
nor with their conclusions. They both were protagonists of protection of wh
they called favorable trade as over against free trade. Whereas Marshall real
belonged to the old school, at that time Marshall had outlived the age of laisse
faire, and theory of laissez-faire. Here again as an eclectic he tried to combi
his more or less scarcely concealed orthodoxy with his very great desire f
social reform. His history had sort of feeling that after all it was more or le
superficial and real stress was laid upon his critical and original analysis. (
course in that sense Marshall had immense influence, but it was very large
limited, and he had comparatively little influence over the movements on tl
other parts of the world, whereas rest of the world were influenced much l

ter writers than Marshall. The other writer was a subtle thinker and that
s Edgeworth.

Edgeworth was a man who started out early in life with that remarkable
ork, with that mathematical cycles. He devoted most of the time to profound
alysis of statistical method and of quantitative approach to problems. He
fered from Marshall because above all he was a philosopher. He was the
ost impractical of all men as an individual and also as an economist, and
state would ever think of taking Edgeworth's practical advice on any
onomic question. Yet, notwithstanding all that he was very good in dealing
th economic problems, and above all he was a courteous gentleman. I had
ite a controversy with him many years ago. He is able to refuse your request
a nice way and also makes you feel that you are inferior to him. Edgeworth
erefore worked rather on the side lines of economic theory, while Marshall
orked on the main line, main thing.

There were other great things, great social reform. It started with Toynbee,
o in his book dealt with industrial revolution and that they were primarily
pretty much everything that had to deal with the labor problem and the
ial problem, and in 80's and beginning of 90's their concept was regarded
ost with horror by most of the economists of the day, and yet they lived
see these views accepted. The critics on the other hand were perhaps a little
s successful as a permanent force. Of course, at first largely under the
luence of Germans Leslie and Ingram represented sociological side of
onomic interest, but they were scarcely completed. You understand what
ders of classical school were driving at. A rigorous critic was Cannan, still
h us and whose critical study on distribution in England is a great
quisition. Smart came in from mathematical school but a business man. He
ame economist and became convert of German school and brought the
ctical affairs to a new analysis.

England of course never had a wealth of economists at no time, but always
de up in quality what she lacked in quantity. Same thing is true since 1900.
theory Pigou, who is perhaps a cross between Marshall and Edgeworth.
is a remarkable man of ability in mathematics, not much interested in
ctical affair yet he is very much impressed by the modern social problems
d the needs for change. His contributions are familiar to you all.—His work,
'ealth and Welfare", and others. And again not gone to the bottom of some
thods of great problems when dealt with particular problems. Perhaps chief
lictment we can make is that he is too sudden. He presents all the niceties
each side of the question and leaves you perhaps in doubt as to what his
nclusions are. In that way he has exerted less influence in other countries
an his talent would let him.

In history the movement was brought about by great thinker, Ibsen, really
mirable historian and then to a less extent by Carter. They turned their
ention rather to practical problems. It is not a wonder that man like Kane

should be devoting all his energies to that field. Of course the war cut a wi
sway in English thought, and at the first onset of army of 1,000, half a doz
fine thinkers were killed. There is today yet a wide gap in economic write
Only in new comers that we may expect to see England occupy the sa
position she so long occupied.

In Germany the situation was different in the end of the 19th century.
was a period of great men, 4 or 5 great men who exerted immense influen
People who were interested in the application of the newer critical ideas
practical problems. Sociologist and especially authorities on public and priv
finance and agriculture. But everything in Germany at that part of the cent
centered around the historian Schmoller on the one hand and Bucher on
other hand. Younger Germans worked out the historical problems. Soc
reform critic was represented by Adolf Held, who left his good work on soc
history of England, and then Brentano, still alive, a very old man, represent
the attempt made to bring into German life the idea of Anglo-Saxon liber
And Brentano and Held between them were responsible for the whole soc
labor problems, first in Germany then the rest of the world. Since the beginn
of the century there are three men of real first class importance that dese
careful consideration.

First is Sombart, great analyzer of modern capitalism. His great book
modern capitalism are known throughout the world, but he is not an import
theorist, as he himself sometimes thinks. Sociologist economist who wa
genius—genius at times when not spending his life in insane asylum. After
there is a narrow line between insanity and genius, they both are abnorm
This man was Weber, whose contributions cover almost every side, religi
all the other phases of sociological questions and has produced a great influe
all over the world. Third, is the chief representative theorist, an Austrian w
lived in Germany. This was Professor Schumpeter, who was very m
influenced by the work of Clark and others.

That brings us about the movement in this country, which perhaps m
interesting of them all. First and foremost is Professor J.B. Clark, whose b
is in the same class as Ricardo and Jevons and the rest. He for the first ti
independently worked out in a much greater clarity the doctrine of spec
productivity and broadening the rent concept, taking all the share of
distribution. This had great influence on the thinking men all over the wo
He has much more influence because of his fundamental distinction betw
static and dynamic theories. He worked the static theory out leaving
dynamic to his successors.

During the past 25 years there have developed three or four different sch
and currents in this country and every where else. First you have psycholog
movement represented by Professor Fetter of Princeton, who made fami
the psychic income in the newer conception of capital, annual yield or serv
and who applied his doctrine not simply to all durable goods but also to

*l*ue of human service. As over against him you could put the ideas of that *r*markable thinker Mr. Veblen, in his economics of enterprise, who lays so *m*uch more stress upon the institutional framework of society, and who has *to* be criticized, criticized for the fact that only he subordinates industry to *fi*nance.—the whole finance control of the modern industry. He emphasizes *th*e fact that under our modern capitalist system the object according to him *go*es rather to profits than surplus. This is little extreme but, little powerful *an*alysis, which throws light upon dark recess of economic life. In the third *pl*ace, the idea represented by Davenport, a first class thinker of Cornell, who *oft*en lectures to us, who is responsible for two things: He makes us familiar *wi*th opportunity cost as over against other costs of Ricardo and others. And *...* the conviction that psychology is utterly useless in economics, and that *an*other thing has no use is the doctrine of social value, and social value *ac*cording to Davenport is protagonist of individual, rather in his theory *pe*rhaps he goes too far in his opposition to those ideas.

Finally the most widespread is the one that was started by our own Mitchell, *wh*o represents the quantitative approach to the economic science, which at *th*e present time perhaps is the [most] popular of all, although before very long *wh*en we come to anal[yze] more closely that the field within which this new *qu*antitative [econo]mics may be expected really stand will require a new *ex*plana[tion] of the whole field of economic science. But within *co*mparat[ively] narrow field is perhaps most productive and popular. We are *ve*ry fortunate in this country now to have a movement in this line of first *cla*ss thinkers among young men. [Ends of first two-thirds of lines in this *pa*ragraph are missing.]

It is quite evident that economics centers in this country because it a center *of* economic life. This has been always been true. Our problems have become *so* enormous, so complicated that it is very fortunate that men of first class *ab*ility are devoting themselves for this work. All that we can say is that *thr*oughout the world today the problems are getting to be about the same, *an*d probably next generation will see everywhere, in Italy, Scandinavia, and *oth*er parts of the world an activity in economic thought and liberality, open-*mi*ndedness which never existed before. We are no longer concerned about *th*e inductive and deductive schools. We are willing to recognize them however, *an*d according to whatever method and by whom they are accomplished. And, *ch*ances are that next quarter of the century will be far more favorable for *th*e elucidation of economic problems than has ever been done in any part *of* the organization. The only thing I hope that I have in the first place impressed *up*on you that all theories are relative and they are bound up with particular *in*stitutions of the time and place. Second, that all scientists in social problems *mu*st recognize the importance of the predecessors, and it is a very foolish idea *to* think that we can afford to neglect the past thinkers because in some respects *the*ir analysis does not carry our views. The advancement of the science of

economics by physiocrats, by Adam Smith and rest, will more and more]
important and their views will remain like polar stars in economic life. In futu
the details have to be filled out and dark recesses have to be filled out. If ч
can learn from this course sympathy and appreciation and tolerance then n
object will be complete.

Research in the History of Economic Thought and Methodology

Edited by **Warren J. Samuels,** *Department of Economics, Michigan State University*

REVIEW: "Methodology and the history of economic thought, two distinct but interrelated economic fields, are currently enjoying a boom , and the volumes under review afford convincing evidence of the intellectual interest and high quality of contemporary work in these areas."

- Kyklos

Volume 7, 1990, 294 pp. $73.25
ISBN 0-89232-040-3

J A I P R E S S

Volume 8, 1990, 288 pp. $73.25
ISBN 1-55938-233-3

CONTENTS: Editorial Board. Acknowledgments. Frank Knight Before Cornell: Some Light on the Dark Years, *Donald Dewey.* The End of Scarcity and the Art of Living: The Similar Visions of Knight and Keynes, *William S. Kern.* The Institutionalism of John R. Commons: Theoretical Foundations of a Volitional Economics, *Yngve Ramstad.* SYMPOSIUM ON THE FRENCH REVOLUTION AND THE HISTORY OF ECONOMIC THOUGHT. A New History of the French Revolution, *Anne C. Meyering.* Fraternity, Free Association, and Socio-Economic Analysis, *Mark Perlman.* From Utopian Capitalism to the Dismal Science: The Effect of the French Revolution on Classical Economics, *William M. Dugger, DePaul University.* Reflections on the Age of Sophisters, Economists, and Calculators, *Y.S. Brenner.* Burke, The French Revolution and Public Choice Theory, *E. Ray Canterbery and Edgar Fresen.* Karl Marx and the French Revolution, *John E. Elliott.* REVIEW ESSAYS. Campen's Benefit, Cost, and Beyond: Review Essay, *A. Allan Schmid.* Has There Been Advances in our Understanding of "Scientific Advances" in Economics?: Deutsch Et Al's Advances in the Social Sciences 1900-1908: What, Who, Where, How?: Review Essay, *William J. Barber.* Raising *Petitio* to a *Principii*: A Review Article, *Murray Wolfson.* JKG's *Economics in Perspective:* Review Essay — Countervailing Perspective. New Books Received.

Archival Supplement 2, 1991, 255 pp. $73.25
ISBN 1-55938-245-7

CONTENTS: Introduction. Frank A. Fetter's PRESENT STATE OF ECONOMIC THEORY IN THE UNITED STATES OF AMERICA, 1927. Introduction, *Warren J. Samuels.* Present State of Economic Theory in the United States of America, 1927, *Frank A. Fetter, (deceased).* Frank H. Night's THE CASE FOR COMMUNISM, 1932. Introduction, *Warren J. Samuels.* The Case for Communism, From the Standpoint of an Ex-Liberal, 1932, *Frank H. Knight, (deceased).* Jacob Viner's THE SEARCH FOR AN IDEAL COMMONWEALTH, 1914. Introduction, *Douglas A. Irwin.* The Search for an Ideal Commonwealth, 1914, *Jacob Viner, (deceased).* John Maynard Keynes on the 1914 Financial Criss: A Note with Documents, *D.E. Moggridge.* Professor A.P. Lerner on "ISRAEL AND THE ECONOMIC DEVELOPMENT OF PALESTIONE": TWENTY YEARS LATER, *Arie Arnon.* Lewis K. Zerby's YOU, YOURSELF, AND YOUR SOCIETY. Introduction, *Warren J. Samuels.* YOU, YOURSELF AND YOUR SOCIETY, *Lewis K. Zerby. (deceased).*

Volume 9, 1992, 300 pp. $73.25
ISBN 1-55938-428-X

Volume 10, 1992, 270 pp. $73.25
ISBN 1-55938-501-1

Edited by **Warren J. Samuels,** and **Jeff Biddle,**
Department of Economics, Michigan State University

Problem of Context for Friedman's Methodology, *J. Daniel Hammond.* **Realism, Closed Systems and Friedman,** *Tony Lawson.* **Friedman and Realism, Uskali Maki. REVIEW ESSAYS. Multiple Reviews of Hutchison's** *Before Adam Smith, Robert F. Hebert, S. Todd Lowry, Michael Perelman, and Margaret Schabas.* **Asimakopulos's** *Investment, Employment, and Income Distribution, Nina Shapiro.* **Hilliard's** *J.M. Keynes in Retrospect, D.E. Moggeridge.* **Hollis's** *The Cunning of Reason, Geoffrey M. Hodgson.* **Klamer, McCloseky, and Solow's** *The Consequences of Economic Rhetoric, Jerry Evensky.* **Loasby's** *The Mind and Method of the Economist, Evelyn L. Forget.* **New Books Received.**

Volume 11, In preparation, Spring 1993
ISBN 1-55938-502-2   Approx. $73.25

Edited by **Warren J. Samuels,** and **Jeff Biddle,**
Department of Economics, Michigan State University

CONTENTS: Editorial Board. Acknowledgments. **Why Did Malthus Oppose Birth Control?,** *Geoffrey Gilbert.* **Rational Expectations, Rational Belief, and Keynes' General Theory,** *Wiliam Darity, Jr., and Bobbie L. Horn.* **Economic Theory in Industrial Policy: Lessons from U.S.v. AT&T,** *Timothy J. Brennan.* **The Political Balance of Trade ...?,** *Salim Rashid.* **The Ethical Content of Economic Categories: The Concept of Ethics,** *Bernd Biervert and Josef Wieland.* **Attention and the Construction of Economic Reality,** *Lawrence A. Berger.* REVIEW ESSAYS. **Klamer and Colander's The Making of an Economist: Multiple Review,** *Vincent J. Tarascio, Frank Thimpson, Richard D. Whitley, A.W. Coats.* **Stivers's Reformed Faith and Economics: Multiple Reviews,** *Ralph E. Ancil, Jim Horner, Steven G. Medema, John P. Tiemstra.* **Neusner's The Economics of the Mishnah: Multiple Review,** *S. Todd Lowry, Barry Gordon, Harry J. Holzer.* **Dugger's Radical Institutionalism,** *Malcolm Rutherford.* **Roy's Philosophy of Economics,** *Jochen Runde.* **Morriss's Power: A Philosophical Analysis,** *Randall Bartlett.* **Leiss's C.B. MacPherson: Dilemmas of Liberalism and Socialism,** *Andrew Altman.* **Glass and Johnson's Economics, Progression, Stagnation or Degeneration,** *John B. Davis.* **Waligorski's The Political Theory of Conservative Economists,** *H. Scott Gordon.* **West's Adam Smith and Modern Economics: From Market Behaviour to Public Choice,** *Jerry Evensky.* **Books Received.**

Also Available:

Volumes 1-6 (1983-1989)
 = Archival Supplement 1 $73.25 each